"Dr. Piotrowski has written a wonderful book introducing readers to the topic of biblical interpretation. I truly cannot wait to get it into the hands of my seminary students! It will be extremely helpful, especially as I and others train pastors-to-be in sermon preparation. This work is truly a gift to the church."

John D. Currid, Chancellor's Professor of Old Testament at Reformed Theological Seminary

"The Bible may be the divinely inspired Word of God, but it is misread and misinterpreted more than any other book. In response, Nicholas Piotrowski has written an exceptionally helpful guide to foster interpretations of the Bible that are 'legitimate and ethical.' This accessible, informative study is essential reading for anyone who wants to handle Scripture in a way that is both christocentric and God honoring."

T. Desmond Alexander, senior lecturer in biblical studies at Union Theological College, Belfast

"Accessible, engaging, easy to digest. These are not typically the words used to describe a book about the weighty topic of biblical hermeneutics. Yet Nicholas Piotrowski has given us just this kind of useful introduction to studying the Bible accurately and ethically. He guides readers toward the importance of reading Scripture with their antennas attuned to its multiple contexts (literary, historical, and christological). Filled with insightful illustrations and examples, *In All the Scriptures* is a great entrée for all who want to understand the Bible better."

Jeannine Brown, professor of New Testament and director of online programs at Bethel Seminary, St. Paul, Minnesota

"Books on hermeneutics can be dense and technical—important, but seemingly impenetrable to the person just becoming acquainted with the field. In place of this, Nicholas Piotrowski has given us just what we need: an accessible, practical, and even devotional understanding of what goes on when we read the Bible. This new introduction to hermeneutics addresses the challenge of reading the Bible well with awareness of context—not just the Bible's context but also our own—preparing us for the challenge of reading the Bible well in our modern world. Highly recommended!"

William Fullilove, associate professor of Old Testament and dean of students, Reformed Theological Seminary, New York City

D1554766

NICHOLAS G. PIOTROWSKI
FOREWORD BY GRAEME GOLDSWORTHY

IN

ALL + THE

SCRIPTURES

THE THREE CONTEXTS OF
BIBLICAL HERMENEUTICS

IVP
Academic
An imprint of InterVarsity Press
Downers Grove, Illinois

InterVarsity Press
P.O. Box 1400, Downers Grove, IL 60515-1426
ivpress.com
email@ivpress.com

InterVarsity Press® is the book-publishing division of InterVarsity Christian Fellowship/USA®, a movement of students and faculty active on campus at hundreds of universities, colleges, and schools of nursing in the United States of America, and a member movement of the International Fellowship of Evangelical Students. For information about local and regional activities, visit intervarsity.org.

The publisher cannot verify the accuracy or functionality of website URLs used in this book beyond the date of publication.

Cover design and image composite: David Fassett
Interior design: Jeanna Wiggins
Images: blue sky: © John O'Neill / EyeEm / Getty Images
  gold foil texture: © Katsumi Murouchi / Moment / Getty Images
  blue and red abstract painting: © oxygen / Moment / Getty Images
  fish-eye lens landscape: © Xinzherng / Moment / Getty Images

ISBN 978-1-5140-0218-6 (print)
ISBN 978-1-5140-0219-3 (digital)

Printed in the United States of America ♾

InterVarsity Press is committed to ecological stewardship and to the conservation of natural resources in all our operations. This book was printed using sustainably sourced paper.

Library of Congress Cataloging-in-Publication Data
Names: Piotrowski, Nicholas G., author.
Title: In all the scriptures : the three contexts of biblical hermeneutics
  / Nicholas G. Piotrowski.
Description: Downers Grove, IL : InterVarsity Press, 2021. | Includes
  bibliographical references and index.
Identifiers: LCCN 2021034703 (print) | LCCN 2021034704 (ebook) | ISBN
  9781514002186 (paperback) | ISBN 9781514002193 (ebook)
Subjects: LCSH: Bible--Hermeneutics.
Classification: LCC BS476 .P564 2021 (print) | LCC BS476 (ebook) | DDC
  220.601--dc23
LC record available at https://lccn.loc.gov/2021034703
LC ebook record available at https://lccn.loc.gov/2021034704

| P | 25 | 24 | 23 | 22 | 21 | 20 | 19 | 18 | 17 | 16 | 15 | 14 | 13 | 12 | 11 | 10 | 9 | 8 | 7 | 6 | 5 | 4 | 3 | 2 | 1 |
| Y | 42 | 41 | 40 | 39 | 38 | 37 | 36 | 35 | 34 | 33 | 32 | 31 | 30 | 29 | 28 | 27 | 26 | 25 | 24 | 23 | 22 | 21 |

To my students and colleagues at

Indianapolis Theological Seminary,

for the glory of God and the good of the church

CONTENTS

FOREWORD

Graeme Goldsworthy

MUCH OF THE LITERATURE ABOUT hermeneutics that has been produced over the last fifty years or so has focused on how the philosophical position of the interpreter determines both the questions being asked about interpretation and the proposed answers. Most hermeneuts would agree that presupposition-less investigation simply does not exist. To suppose that it does is to adopt a self-defeating presupposition.

When our two youngest children saved up to buy the early computers capable of a few games but little more, I was prompted to think about the advantages of word processors. It was a new world with a new language to adapt to. I learned a new anagram GIGO (garbage in, garbage out) as a principle that applied to computer programs. Of course, the reverse also applied: good stuff in, good stuff out.

As I began to read about various ways of interpreting the Bible, I realized that everyone should recognize that they approach the biblical text with certain already formed ideas about its nature and importance. I count myself blessed to have come to faith and been nurtured within the predominantly evangelical and Reformed ethos of the Anglican Diocese of Sydney (Australia). The prevailing theological climate led me to form the conviction that the Bible is the inspired Word of God and is our final authority in all matters of faith and morals. As I matured and especially as I entered a long process of theological studies, I realized more and more that the literature on biblical interpretation, now referred to as *hermeneutics*, expressed a wide range of presuppositions about the nature of the Bible and its authority. The history of interpretation, going right back to the early second century, demonstrated how the philosophical presuppositions that the reader brought to the task of interpreting the Bible determined the outcome. Whether it was the Greek philosophies of Plato and Aristotle or the humanism of the so-called Enlightenment of the eighteenth century, the philosophical presuppositions of the interpreter determined the outcome: it was indeed a matter of GIGO.

In the light of these few personal notes, it gives me great pleasure to respond to the invitation to provide a foreword to Nicholas Piotrowski's contribution to the now quite dauntingly extensive literature on general and biblical hermeneutics. So, why another book on hermeneutics, and why should we be pleased? I taught a course on hermeneutics for eighteen years (1995-2012) to fourth-year BD students at Moore College in Sydney. In that time I had to survey the literature as it already existed, and as it emerged in an increasing volume. I found there were two main emphases in the literature: that which expressed the hermeneutics of suspicion or skepticism about biblical authority, and that which emanated from a hermeneutic of faith and confidence in God's Word.

Many of the earlier works (1940s and 1950s) on hermeneutics by conservative writers concentrated on the practicalities of dealing with the linguistics of the text within the historical contexts of the biblical narrative. In time there was a more conscious blending of evangelical presuppositions with the emergence of biblical theology, Reformed apologetics, and the consequent "big picture" approach to the Bible.

The need for specialization in seminaries has regrettably tended toward a fragmentation of disciplines. In some cases, the Old Testament and New Testament departments rarely talk to each other. It is as if we have two Bibles. How many theological curricula include even a basic course in Biblical Theology as a requirement for all students? I suspect not many. How much does the integrating dynamic of good biblical theology inform the theological hermeneutics of the average seminarian? And, as a consequence of the neglect of such integration, do we not see good expository preaching in the local churches a rarity rather than the general rule?

These convictions and concerns that I have developed over seventy years as a Christian mean that I am more than pleased to commend this present work. This is not just another book on hermeneutics but rather a wake-up call to meet the challenges of the present. It addresses us in a rapidly changing post-Christian world, in a way that covers all the bases for Bible-believing Christians. I commend it for the clarity of its well-ordered content. I commend it for its firm convictions about the inspiration and authority of Scripture. I commend it for the application of evangelical and Reformed presuppositions to the comprehensive range of matters involved in reading ancient texts. I commend it for addressing some of the false trails pursued by both early and more recent interpreters. I commend it for the clear trinitarian and christological dimensions that inform our understanding of the unity and the distinctions between Old and New Testaments, between type and antitype, between prophecy and fulfillment, between the first readers and ourselves, and between the objective gospel of Jesus of Nazareth and the present inner working of the Spirit to connect us with that gospel. If Christ is the only Savior, then he must save our hermeneutics from unbelief and the apostasy of unbiblical philosophical foundations. If he truly is the truth, then he, as he is clothed in his gospel, must teach the truth about the interpretation of his Word. If he truly is the Creator-Word come in the flesh, he must interpret to us the ultimate meaning of everything in this universe, including the Bible.

One of the features that I would expect of a sound evangelical and Reformed text on hermeneutics is the integration of the several theological disciplines that are so often left without clear connection in the theological curricula. The demonstration of the symbiotic relationship of exegesis to biblical, historical, systematic, and pastoral theology, is a feature of this book for which we should be thankful. I would have been greatly enriched to have had such a text when I began theological studies and especially when I was later called on to teach a course in hermeneutics.

ACKNOWLEDGMENTS

R OOSEVELT ONCE SAID, "Be sincere, be brief, and be seated." But what to do when in one's sincerity there are *so many* people to thank? At the risk, therefore, of under-acknowledging the many people to whom I am thankful, I will get to the point. My highest gratitude is to the living Lord, Jesus Christ. Because he is alive, he speaks. And because he speaks, sinners have something to listen closely to and something in which to hope. As the Great High Prophet, he speaks continually through his Spirit-inspired word, and so the very impetus even to care about hermeneutics begins with that truth and the joyful expectation that we will hear the voice of the Good Shepherd calling to us from the Scriptures. I also owe profound gratitude to my wife, Cheryl, and my two boys, Silas and Andreas. The former is a rock of support (and not a little help with grammar!); the latter will be thrilled to see there are indeed pictures in this book.

The mentors from whom I have learned hermeneutics are legion; the reader will see their names throughout this work. Particularly, I want to recognize Dennis Ireland, John Currid, Bill Barcley and Nick Perrin. While I have never met Graeme Goldsworthy, his writings have been very influential for me, and I am deeply thankful for his kind foreword. Specifically for this project, I am very much indebted to the following brothers for reading all or part of this book and providing trenchant feedback: Kris Holroyd, Theron St. John, Noah Debaun, Dane Ortlund,

Don Sherman, Evan McNeff, Andy Watkins, Christian Butner, Lucas Johnson and Jonathan Zavodney. Thank you all!

This work began in concept when I was a teacher at the Washington Christian Academy, took definitive shape as I served at Crossroads Bible College, and came to fruition as I today lead Indianapolis Theological Seminary. I am thankful, therefore, to the students, administration and leadership at each of those institutions for their support of me and my publishing pursuits. Many additional people along the way also provided logistical support, prayer and encouragement. Again, each of these brothers and sisters deserves cornucopian recognition, but to stay in good with ol' FDR, I'll merely list them here: Bruce Winter, Randy Worland, Dr. Charles Ware, Jeff Holwerda, Josiah Jones, Chris Sarver, Brice Giesbrecht, the library staff at Clear Creek Baptist Bible College, the elders and pastoral staff at Castleview Church, the Northside Baptist Church Wednesday night Bible study group, Rob and Debbie Wingerter as well as Ron and Allison Wingerter at Mahseh Center, Rick and Carla Shadiow, Justin Ware, Susan Albers, Kristine Gilbertson, Lauren Ruark, Josh Wagner and the ITS board.

Of course, I also thank IVP Academic for the privilege to publish with them, and especially Dan Reid and Anna Moseley Gissing for their patience and grace toward me. And finally, I thank you, my reader.

Soli Deo gloria.

INTRODUCTION

Why Hermeneutics (Again)?

THIS IS A BOOK ABOUT CONTEXTS. It is about what we find in the Bible, and where we find ourselves in the world.

Like many, I currently do not work in the field in which I majored in college. I studied biology—ecology to be specific. Ecology is the study of ecosystems, where the focus is not primarily on just the flora or the fauna or the weather or the climate. Rather, the focus is on *all* these things and more—insofar as they exist together in the same environment and, so, inevitably influence each other.

Take a coastal wetland for example. Specifically, take a particular species of fish living in that wetland. A lot can be learned about the fish when it is extracted from its environment and taken to the lab. That creates a control so that nothing interferes with a careful scientific method. Its age, weight, length, general health, recent meals, and so forth can be studied without distraction. If enough fish are gathered, one can also know something of the entire fish population. But at the same time studying *only* the fish also *inhibits* our knowledge of the fish and can even mislead us to think we have thoroughly understood the fish when, in fact, we have not. What about studying the fish's *context* as well? Does the fish not live in an environment that affects the fish? And does the fish not equally affect that environment? If we study the fish's weight and find that many are smaller than expected we still do not know *why* that is. It is one thing to have data, it is another to *interpret* the data. It could be that the fish are small because the scientist only caught juveniles. Well, where are the adult fish? It could be that all the fish are small because overpopulation has caused a food shortage. Well, how did that happen? Or there could be other reasons that food is scarce. So, what are those reasons? Is there pollution? A hard winter? An easy winter? A competitor fish? I could go on, but suffice it to say for now that factors *outside* the fish are playing a key role in affecting the population, and therefore affecting what the scientist sees in an individual fish. Then, to understand those factors one needs to consider weather patterns, recent events in the watershed, changes in temperature both in the long and short term, seawater brought in by tides, currents that flow from thousands of miles always, fresh water from streams and rainfall, severity of recent winters, snowmelt from mountains hundreds of miles away, changes in vegetation, permanent and migrant birds, predators, preys, microbes, runoff from farms, highly populated neighborhoods nearby or popular tourist destinations, pH, algae (I went to college when "red tide" was a particular problem in Maryland). I will stop there. It is dizzying just to think about, let alone try to understand, the seemingly unending matrix of how all these things relate to and affect each other, and then to place the role of the fish into that intricate ecosystem. But difficult or not, to understand the fish one would have to know so much *outside* of the fish. These are all things the ecologist must consider all at the same time.

While that scientific field is still very fascinating to me, I am not an ecologist. I am a professor of New Testament and hermeneutics. How does one trained in ecology come to teach on interpreting biblical texts? Well, it is not so great a leap actually. *Texts exist in contexts too.* No text, utterance, or expression ever exists in the abstract, but surrounding every form of communication there are several factors that influence the communiqué. And inversely, the communicator seeks to influence those same factors. The use of language to communicate meaning is shaped by the speaker's/author's context as well as a listener's/reader's context. The context influences what is said/written and the context directs the listener/reader how to make sense of the speech/writing.

Consider this sentence: "I just couldn't pass." It has at least four different meanings depending on who said it, where they said it, to whom they said it, and the reason they said it. Is this a young college student at home talking to his father and explaining why he dropped a class, in the hopes of convincing him nonetheless to keep paying more tuition? Is this a motorist in a car explaining to the passengers why they are still stuck behind a slow-moving truck, and that it is not her fault they are late for the wedding? Is this a basketball player in the locker room explaining to his coach why he turned the ball over, in a subtle attempt to blame his teammates for not getting open? Is this my wife at home explaining to me why she bought an auction item, because I am not convinced we need another set of scrapbook supplies? Each of these different contexts—complete with varying speakers, locations, audiences, and recent events prompting the comment—make "I just couldn't pass" actually mean entirely different things.

To be sure, this is a simplistic example, and one does not need to read a book on hermeneutics to navigate its potential interpretive diversity. We already have an intuitive sense that language depends on contexts in this way.[1] But the simplicity of the example serves the point. If attention to context with such a simple statement opens up several interpretive options, and we already tacitly know the need for attention to context, then how much more attention to context is necessary when we read texts

---

[1] While a bit technical and much of the book assumes a knowledge of Greek, the introduction and chap. 3 of Margaret G. Sim's *A Relevant Way to Read: A New Approach to Exegesis and Communication* (Eugene, OR: Pickwick, 2016) nonetheless explains well how authors and writers assume audiences have knowledge of all sorts of contexts, and how audiences instinctively draw on those contexts for interpretation. See also Jeannine K. Brown, *Scripture as Communication: Introducing Biblical Hermeneutics* (Grand Rapids, MI: Baker Academic, 2007), 35-38.

thousands of years old, written in lands thousands of miles away, by people we have never met, in response to historical events we did not experience? I would submit to you that America's favorite verse, John 3:16, has a meaning shaped by complicated literary, historical, and theological realities beyond the T-shirt or poster where we commonly see it today.

But what are such literary, historical, and theological realities to which the astute Bible reader must attend? The rest of this book is an attempt to teach—as simply as I can—some first principles in such an inquiry that can sharpen your Bible-reading acumen. In other words, this is a book about contexts. And that means it is a book on hermeneutics.

What Are Hermeneutics?

Hermeneutics are *the theoretical study of the science and art of how to legitimately and ethically interpret texts.* I say it is a *science* because, as we will see, there is a series of methodological steps to take in arriving at a text's meaning. But it is also an *art* insofar as an interpreter needs some imaginative capacities. An interpreter needs intuition. An interpreter needs to see the big picture to make sense of the parts, as well as creativity to assemble the parts into the big picture. Now, to be sure, I do not advocate a *fervid* imagination, *unbound* intuition or *wild* creativity. But the scientific part of hermeneutics and the artistic part must join hands in cooperation while at the same time keeping a watchful eye on each other. The science will make sure the art does not become unguided, and the art will make sure the science does not become mechanical or stale. So where imagination and creativity give way to speculation, a good interpreter can rein it in with scientific responsibility. All that goes to say that there is an element of hermeneutics that simply cannot be taught, but passed on by a kind of elbow knowledge (mentor to disciple) and much experience (we should not be afraid to try, struggle, and receive constructive criticism). So, while this book will focus on the scientific side—the part of the theory that can be delineated in heuristic terms—you should not close the book when you are done and think yourself a master. Much time, experience, trial and error, reading, and rereading *with others* will make you more the hermeneutical artist throughout your life.

Thus, as a science and an art, hermeneutics concerns how to *legiti-mately* interpret texts. I am sure you can think of an example in your life (maybe even recently) when you left a Bible study or sermon scratching your head and asking, "Is *that* what that passage is really about?" Sometimes it is easy for teachers and preachers to see things in the text that are not really there. Too much art! Well, we want to come away from our reading of Scripture with confidence that we have understood the main idea. If we have a hermeneutical practice that is theoretically well grounded then we will not only have confidence ourselves, but if we ever teach our interpretation to others they will be convinced *from the text*. They will not say, "She sounded smart!" or "Wow, he's clever." Rather they will say, "I am convinced because I can see *how the text should be read*, and this is a valid conclusion." That is what we want at the end of the day: to understand and communicate the truth of God's Word.

This leads me to the last point of our definition. Hermeneutics is about how to *ethically* interpret texts. As creatures who are insatiably social, we like to share our ideas with others. Whether we preach, teach, or just chat, we like to share what we see in the Scriptures. Therefore, if our hermeneutic leads us to erroneous conclusions, we will most likely pass that error on to others. And if we convince others of our error, then we are leading them astray as well (see Jas 3:1-2)! We will be functionally lying about God. Thus, "Bad interpretation is bad."[2] Additionally, we need to remember that we are dealing with other people's words. When we interpret Micah, for example, we need to bear in mind that we are handling Micah's intellectual property. How do you feel when someone repeats what you said and puts a bogus spin on it? I am sure you are, like everyone else, quick to say, "That's not what I meant!" You do not like being misrepresented; you do not like interpreters treating you unethically. Words, sentences, and paragraphs are wonderful inventions given by God to those created in his image, and they are able to convey precise ideas. It is those precise ideas that the interpreter owes to the author to get right.[3]

---

[2]Dan McCartney and Charles Clayton, *Let the Reader Understand: A Guide to Interpreting and Applying the Bible*, 2nd ed. (Phillipsburg, NJ: P&R, 2002), 27.
[3]Brown, *Scripture as Communication*, 127.

Thus, hermeneutics is the theoretical study of the science and art of how to legitimately and ethically interpret texts. What that theory should look like, then, is the primary burden of this book.

Why Study Hermeneutics?

I have taught a lot of classes at the high school, college, and seminary levels, as well as in churches. Hands down, hermeneutics is the most important one. And while students are not as enthusiastic about taking Hermeneutics at first—as they are with topics like New Testament or apologetics—by the end of the class they often tell me it was their favorite course and/or the most impactful course they have taken. This is because throughout the course it occurs to them, little by little, what effect careful attention to hermeneutics can play on their reading, interpretation, devotions, personal life, and ministry. I hope the same will happen to you as you move through the following pages. All the same, allow me to present a few reasons why studying hermeneutics is so important.

I will start with the negative side. If we *do not* study hermeneutics, we will create "God" in our own image. Everyone has a conception of what they think God is like. From our culture, upbringing, and experience, everyone has fashioned some notion of God in their mind (even atheists). It is inevitable. The question of God is too culturally pervasive for us not to have some inclination of what he or she or it is like (or what kind of god does *not* exist) before we ever read a single verse of the Bible, Torah, Qur'an, Veda, or anything else. If we do not pay attention to how we are reading and interpreting, then we will simply read these preconceived notions into the text. That is, what we already think about God will influence how we read, sometimes so much so that we *only* see what we already think about God! J. I. Packer, in his famous *Knowing God*, says the second commandment—the prohibition against idolatry—forbids not only graven images, but also false *mental* images. He says idolatry happens not only when we have false gods before our eyes, but also when we have false ideas of the true God in our minds. In those cases we are not thinking of God as he truly is. And what do we call a conception of

God that is untrue? We call it idolatry.[4] If we do not pay attention to how we are getting our knowledge about God—our hermeneutical approach to the Scriptures—we will then default to our preconceived notions of God, read them into the text, and then come away thinking we have understood God but really only reinforced our initial idolatry. More on this and how to counter it in chapters one and two.

Second, if we do not study hermeneutics, we will miss important things in the text. This is related to the first problem. If we think we are seeing things in a passage that are not truly there, then we will also miss what *is* there. When we misinterpret, we not only come away with wrong ideas, but we also squander an opportunity to gain a right understanding. We miss the voice of God in the Bible for the static of our confused hermeneutic. Moreover, there is an "historical gap" between us and the original authors, readers, and their contexts. Above, I mention that contexts shaped their writing (thousands of years ago) and our reading (thousands of years later). Well, how much should *our* context affect the reading of *their* texts? I would argue as little as possible. But in order to minimize the influence of our contemporary situation on reading ancient books, we need to know a bit of *their* historical context. We need to cross this historical gap and imaginatively situate ourselves in their world. If we cannot do that, then we will again miss important things in the text.

Third, if we do not study hermeneutics we will never have a consistent theology. Compare Romans 4 and James 2. It appears that Paul and James are saying exactly opposite things! Or compare Psalm 137 and Matthew 5:38-48. Again, are the psalmist and Jesus contradicting each other? Well, the issues are hermeneutical in all of these cases. Yet, if we do not know how a legitimate and ethical hermeneutic can steer us between these texts, then we will not know how to handle either within a consistent theological system. Instead, we will simply populate our minds with our favorite "life verses" that are easy for us to handle and basically ignore what the rest of the Bible contributes to developing our worldviews. Our theology will remain an inch deep and never fill out with the full counsel of God.

---

[4]J. I. Packer, *Knowing God*, 2nd ed. (Downers Grove, IL: InterVarsity Press, 1993), chap. 4.

Fourth and finally, if we do not study hermeneutics, our use of texts could be unethical. To be sure, some texts of Scripture are so clear that very little reading sophistication is necessary. And in some cases we could stumble upon the right meaning even if our hermeneutic is under-developed. But instinct and chance will only get us so far. The majority of our interpretations will miss the mark. Then, insofar as we want also to *apply* the Scriptures, if we do not arrive at a legitimate meaning of the text, we will apply wrong principles to life. In turn, we will teach others to apply wrong principles as well, and ministries of confusion are unwittingly propagated. I am sure you have heard of those who have bombed abortion clinics. I would argue that in each case lies an unethical hermeneutic. It is one thing to be pro-life; it is another to kill under that banner. Why do people take such terribly sinful (not to mention clearly contradictory) actions? While the motivations of people can rarely be reduced to one cause, I would argue that those persons were probably taught by someone else. They often have "chapter and verse" to justify their actions. Thus, someone in their past had an irresponsible and unethical hermeneutic and directed them along sinful paths.

If we *do* study hermeneutics, on the other hand, then we can run these four dangers in reverse. If we *do* study hermeneutics we will develop legitimate reading practices that result in knowing God better through the Scriptures as we repent of our mistaken assumptions about God, toppling the idols of our hearts. If we *do* study hermeneutics we will become more adept at making key observations in our study and overcome the gap between the biblical world and our own. If we *do* study hermeneutics we will increasingly move toward a consistent theology. And if we *do* study hermeneutics we will lead ourselves and others into ethical application. All of this, I would argue, glorifies our Creator and Savior, edifies the church, and results in a cogent worldview to fuel our lives and evangelism.

Everyone does have a hermeneutic. No one reads without some principles in place. The question is simply this: Is your hermeneutic legitimate and ethical? Taking the time to consider some hermeneutical theory will go a long way in helping you mend the defective parts of your reading practices and hone your interpretive skills with the confidence that you know what you are doing and why.

The Approach of This Book

On the first day of class I love asking my students what they think Ephesians 2:14 means: "For he himself is our peace, who has made us both one and has broken down in his flesh the dividing wall of hostility." As they make interpretive comments I list them on the board. Invariably the most common interpretations amount to this: Jesus made peace between us and the Father because he has removed our sin. In this interpretation "he himself" refers to Christ, and the "both" are God and sinners. Thus the "peace" is the creation of a relationship between God and us. The peace is needed because sin had created "the dividing wall of hostility" between God and us. This is a wonderful thought. The problem is that it is wrong on almost every level! Ephesians 2:14 does not mean that at all. The idea is true in and of itself: our sin has created hostility between God and us, and Jesus has made peace. Praise the Lord! But that comes from Romans 5:1, not Ephesians 2:14! We seem to have here a case of the right doctrine from the wrong text. My students have taken their already well-conceived theology and pasted it over Ephesians 2:14. Now you may ask, "What's the problem, then, if they still arrive at correct doctrine?" The problem is not what it affirms—Jesus made peace between God and sinners—but what it overlooks. If we simply import our prior theology into Ephesians 2 then we do not glean what Ephesians 2 is really about. And in that case, why read the Bible at all?

So, what *is* Ephesians 2:14 about? In this book I advocate a hermeneutical approach that explores three layers of context: literary context, historical context, and christological context. Allow me to illustrate.

The literary context. The Bible is not a collection of pithy one-liners. Rather it is a collection of *whole books*. To understand any part of a book, the scope of the entire discourse must be considered. Authors wrote down entire arguments, and there is a flow of thought running from the first verse to the last verse of any book. It is the interpreter's job to discern that flow of thought in the text, paying careful attention to what any given verse or passage contributes to the larger whole. Too often, our Bible reading amounts to dislodging our favorite verses or stories from that flow of thought. The downside to this is never to grasp the larger point of the whole book, which is the author's point in writing. I will detail more of what I mean by flow of thought and how to discern it in chapters three and seven.

For now, what happens to our interpretation when we zoom out a bit and read Ephesians 2:14 within its immediate literary context? Ephesians 2:11-22 reads:

> Therefore remember that at one time you Gentiles in the flesh, called "the uncircumcision" by what is called the circumcision, which is made in the flesh by hands—remember that you were at that time separated from Christ, alienated from the commonwealth of Israel and strangers to the covenants of promise, having no hope and without God in the world. But now in Christ Jesus you who once were far off have been brought near by the blood of Christ. For he himself is our peace, who has made us both one and has broken down in his flesh the dividing wall of hostility by abolishing the law of commandments expressed in ordinances, that he might create in himself one new man in place of the two, so making peace, and might reconcile us both to God in one body through the cross, thereby killing the hostility. And he came and preached peace to you who were far off and peace to those who were near. For through him we both have access in one Spirit to the Father. So then you are no longer strangers and aliens, but you are fellow citizens with the saints and members of the household of God, built on the foundation of the apostles and prophets, Christ Jesus himself being the cornerstone, in whom the whole structure, being joined together, grows into a holy temple in the Lord. In him you also are being built together into a dwelling place for God by the Spirit.

Do you notice in verses 11-12 the gulf that historically separated Israel and Gentiles? Then verse 13 delivers this beautiful line: "But now in Christ Jesus you who once were far off have been brought near by the blood of Christ." Thus, the "both" of verse 14 is Israel and Gentiles, and the "peace" is between these two groups. "He himself" is certainly Christ, but attention to verse 13 tells us *how* he created that peace: by his blood. So we do not just have some vague notions of Christ that can be gleaned from anywhere, but a particular emphasis on what he has done as indicated uniquely in Ephesians 2:14.

And still the passage goes on. Verse 15 emphasizes the unity of all believers, Israelite and Gentile. Then verse 16 indeed reminds us of our reconciliation with God (as in 2:1-10), but the main point now is that "both" have that peace with God and so also with each other. The reason for this is given in verse 18: there is only one Spirit whereby we "both" have access to God. Finally, verses 19-22 drive this home with phrases like "fellow citizens," "members of the household of God," and "the whole structure is joined together" as a crescendo to this glorious reconciliation to the one God, through the one Spirit, by the one Christ, forming one people. All this is crucial in the larger point of Ephesians 1–3 where Paul is reflecting on the glory of God's purposes in creating a single worshiping people out of all fallen humanity. This will pay out in Ephesians 4–6 as Paul applies such ideals to practical life issues.

The historical context. But what is that "dividing wall of hostility" in verse 14? Is it sin? Well, in addition to the literary context, the interpreter must also know something about the conceptual environment in which Paul and the Ephesians lived. If I said to you, "You need to step up to the plate," would you know what I mean? If you are an American, I am sure you would. I mean you need to take some responsibility and do your best. Maybe I will also say, "You need to hit it out of the park." Again, if you are an American you will understand that means you need to succeed in whatever this responsibility is. But if you are from most other parts of the world you are scratching your head right now. This is because I have used *baseball* metaphors. While baseball and its slang pervade American vernacular ("drop the ball," "toss you a softball," "three strikes and y'er out," "under the tag"), it has not infiltrated other English-speaking parts of the world. We must know baseball first (or be around others enough who do), then we can know the meaning of these terms. It is an issue of historical and cultural awareness.

Equally, Paul wrote to audiences he believed would understand him. So he used language as common to them as baseball is to (some of) us. He used the language of *the temple*. But we live in an entirely different day and age. Of course a lot of nuance can get lost in between. I take up these sorts of considerations in chapters four and seven.

For now, what happens to our understanding of Ephesians 2:14 when we attend to some historical context? A less known book (to us) called 1 Maccabees says, at 9:54 (RSV), "In the one hundred and fifty-third year, in the second month, Al'cimus gave orders to tear down the wall of the inner court of the sanctuary. He tore down the work of the prophets!" What is 1 Maccabees? It recounts some of the events about 160 years before the birth of Christ. Who is Al'cimus? Well, what matters here is that he is not particularly liked by this author. Look what he tried to do: "He tore down the work of the prophets!" The prophets are good, so tearing down their work is bad. What did he do to tear down their work? He "gave orders to tear down the wall of the inner court of the sanctuary." Why is that so bad? That is the wall in the temple precinct beyond which Gentiles could not pass. It created a permanent barrier between Gentiles and Jews, and also between Gentiles and God. The temple was understood as the place where God dwells, where God hears prayers, where God forgives sins, and where God receives worship. According to the author of 1 Maccabees, the Old Testament prophets say to keep that wall and that separation in place. But did they really?

It seems Paul disagrees! Whatever Al'cimus's motives were, or this author's opinion of it, matters not. Our attention to 1 Maccabees is just a foray into some of the vernacular of Paul's time. The issue in Ephesians 2:14 is that Paul says *Christ* "has broken down . . . the dividing wall!" Christ has opened up the access for Gentiles to come to God and so "you who once were far off [Gentiles] have been brought near [into the presence of God] by the blood of Christ" (v. 13)! Thus, the "law of commandments expressed in ordinances" (v. 15) which had kept Gentiles distant from Israel and from Israel's God (the "wall of separation") is now gone. Access to God requires them not. For "in Christ" (v. 13), "by the blood of Christ" (v. 13), "in his flesh" (v. 14), "in himself" (v. 15) all the requirements are met for "both," Israelite and Gentile, to "have access in one Spirit to the Father" (v. 18). Comparing Paul to 1 Maccabees, therefore, brings out some of the punch of Ephesians 2:14.

Still, are there not a lot of walls in the world? Why should we think Ephesians 2:14 speaks of a temple wall as in 1 Maccabees 9? Lo and behold, the literary context is still helpful. Verses 19-22 culminate exactly there, calling this new united-in-Christ-household-of-God "a holy temple in the Lord." Thus, the literary and historical contexts actually team up and help each other.

The christological context. Yet there is more. To call the united-in-Christ-household-of-God "a holy temple in the Lord" is a beautiful image. But what does it mean? What good does it do for Christians to think of their unity in Christ in terms of a temple? Again—as with the verse in question (Eph 2:14), and the author and first audience (Paul and the Ephesian Christians)—the *book* of Ephesians does not exist in the abstract. The entire book of Ephesians also has a particular context: the full canon of Scripture. The lifeblood of everything written before Ephesians, and recognized by Paul as Scripture, is flowing into Ephesians. Paul does not grab temple language out of thin air, but the temple (as well as the tabernacle before it) towers like a mountain over the entire Old Testament. What it means *there* is now pouring into Ephesians *here*. How such canonical themes weave in and out from book to book—and so develop, flow and climax in Christ—is the focus of chapters five, six, and seven of this book.

Let us now think of how this impacts our reading Ephesians 2. There are a lot of places we could look in the Old Testament for some insight into the temple's role in the canon, but I think the best place to look is at its inauguration in 1 Kings 8. There we are told that the ark of the covenant is present (8:1-9) and the glory cloud of the Lord fills the house (8:10-13). The significance of this is then recited in Solomon's prayer and blessing (8:14-61). We see there that the temple marks the fulfillment of God's promises (8:15-21, 24, 56), a manifestation of God's presence on earth (8:12-13, 27-30, 57), the place where God hears prayer (8:30, 32, 34, 36, 39, 43, 45, 49), the place where God judges and forgives sin (8:30-40, 46-50), the place where his people find strength and compassion (8:44-45, 50-52), the means by which the entire earth will know that he alone is the true and living God (8:23, 41-43, 60), and a motivation for holiness (8:40, 53, 61). My goodness! If the temple meant all that, just imagine how horrible it was when Nebuchadnezzar "burned the house of the LORD" in 2 Kings 25:9. What a loss!

Back to Ephesians 2:11-22. What is Paul doing calling Christians "a holy temple in the Lord"? Those are not small words! He is saying that the universal church of Christ is the locus today where God is doing all those things mentioned above. The creation of the church marks the fulfillment of God's promises. The church is where God manifests his presence on earth. The church is the place of prayer, and God hears those prayers. The church is the place where the judgment laid on Christ is applied for the forgiveness of sins. The church is the community that dispenses the encouragement and compassion of the Lord. The church is called to manifest the holiness of God. And the church—if it lives this way—will shine as a beacon of God's glory and grace into the darkness.

Now I would venture that most of us certainly do not view the church that way! Much less does the unity of the church weigh so heavily on our hearts. When we attend, however, to the literary, historical, and christological contexts of Ephesians 2:14 we see this magnificent vision! We could walk away thinking Ephesians 2:14 is just a Romans 5:1 reprisal, but in so doing we would have missed all this. So the Scriptures have taught, motivated, convicted, and challenged us in a way that is missed when we read too quickly or treat the Bible as a collection of pithy one-liners snatched out of their contexts and dropped into unrelated application. Paul did not write Ephesians 2:14 to stand alone. He wrote *all* of Ephesians. And he wrote it in a particular historical setting, with a specific Christ-exalting agenda. We do well to read it as such.

Admittedly, I set my students up. I give them just one verse and ask them about that one verse. The project is ready-made for failure. But I do this project with them because such single-verse, what-does-your-first-instinct-tell-you kind of reading is common in our time. Moreover, when we are prone to reading our otherwise good theological maxims *into* texts, we get a flat theology and truncated worldview that cannot deal with the complications of our world today. Careful hermeneutics, therefore, gives us a round and expansive theology, one that can fully form a worldview sufficient to navigate ever changing cultural tides—not just a collection of common theological quips and favorite verses spread too thin over all of life.

A Modest Goal

As mentioned above, hermeneutics is the theoretical study of the science and art of how to legitimately and ethically interpret texts. *Exegesis* is, then, the hands-on appropriation of such theory. This book is intentionally light on exegesis. The primary focus is on the theoretical underwriting of the exegetical process—hermeneutics. "Whereas *exegesis and interpretation* denote the *actual process* of interpreting texts, *hermeneutics* also includes the second-order discipline of asking critically *what exactly we are doing when we read, understand, or apply* texts" (emphasis original).[5] Obviously there is a tight relationship between these disciplines. They are like dance partners, requiring an intuitive give and take. But in this book, I should be clear: we are focusing primarily on just one of the dancers—the *lead* dancer, hermeneutics. While hermeneutics alone will be merely esoteric musing without truly digging into texts, nonetheless exegesis is unguided and (as I will argue in the first chapter) the slave of contemporary philosophical trends when the hermeneutical rationale is evacuated. Thus, comments on exegesis, as well as exegetical examples, will dot the pages along the way, but they serve only an illustrative purpose. The student should not close this book after reading it and believe they have explored all there is in the interpretive process. All this goes to say, this is a *starter* book. This book provides the hermeneutical pathways that the student will want to explore in a life-long journey of honing one's exegetical skills.

---

[5] Anthony C. Thiselton, *Hermeneutics: An Introduction* (Grand Rapids, MI: Eerdmans, 2009), 4.

This book also does not say much about homiletics, the rhetorical art of public teaching. It merely starts the learning process of how to *understand* biblical texts, not necessarily how to *communicate* them. This is important to remember lest readers think there is a straight line between what is read and what is said. Homiletics is an equally challenging field and teachers will want to think deeply (and seek guidance from others and gain a lot of experience) about the distance from the study to the pulpit.[6]

Finally, I will not have too much to say on application. To be sure, application to our hearts and lives is necessary, the final goal of all of this. But it is just that, the *final* goal. Good application comes when historical and systematic theology are stacked on the sure building blocks of exegesis and biblical studies.[7] And all that, of course, is laid on a solid foundation of hermeneutics. So, first things first. In this book I want to give as much focus to just hermeneutics as possible, as a first step on the intellectual journey toward sound application. Chapter eight, therefore, will have a brief word on some application pathways, but of course only after we have rounded the hermeneutical bases.

In sum, this book has a modest goal: the theoretical-philosophical foundation to reading the Bible. But to be sure, it is an important goal to pursue. Hermeneutics must ground exegesis. And exegesis must direct homiletics. And, finally, homiletics have for nearly 2,000 years guided the church (and will continue to do so) into its ethical behavior in the world, including its worship and witness. Thus if our hermeneutics are bad, then the entire Christian ministry is off-kilter from its foundation. It is a singular target, but one we cannot afford to miss.

My Audience

This book is intended for anyone who wants to read their Bible better and come away with more *legitimate* and *ethical* interpretations. It is particularly

---

[6]A bit of a modern classic on this is John R. W. Stott, *Between Two Worlds: The Challenge of Preaching Today* (Grand Rapids, MI: Eerdmans, 1982). Recently I have also found helpful Zack Eswine, *Preaching to a Post-Everything World: Crafting Biblical Sermons That Connect with Our Culture* (Grand Rapids, MI: Baker, 2008).

[7]See particularly Andrew David Naselli, *How to Understand and Apply the New Testament: Twelve Steps from Exegesis to Theology* (Phillipsburg, NJ: P&R, 2017), 5-8.

urgent that ministers of the word—pastors, missionaries, counselors, etc.—think about their hermeneutic as a regular habit of life. My hope, therefore, is that those early in their theological training will pick up this book. I hope it is useful to those in undergraduate Bible and religion programs, as well as for those preparing for seminary. It is written, therefore, at that level. I do also hope that pastors would read this work and even walk their church leaders through it. May it help them either remember some forgotten principles or challenge them to think in some new ways. Finally, any motivated layperson should benefit as well.[8]

A Warning, a Challenge, and an Invitation

I often tell my students that the goal of a theological education is never to make one haughty. The last thing I want is my students to sit in the pew on Sunday mornings, arms crossed and brow furrowed as they think to themselves, *Sheesh, this guy needs to take a hermeneutics course!* While knowledge can puff up, it need not and should not. It should result in humility, knowing that there is nothing we have that is not given to us. Praise the Lord. Instead, studying hermeneutics should help us to go deeper in our study and come away with a bigger vision of God and smaller view of ourselves.

Also, a theological education gives you the chance to think about how you will carry out your ministry. When we do not take time to reflect on what is best and what is wise, then we simply copy the methods of others, learned through osmosis. Hermeneutics is, then, the first step for ministers-in-training to ask, "What am I doing, and why?" How Word-centered will your ministry be? How carefully will you attend to the Word? My prayer is that this book will help you think about such matters early and often, and in the right way.

---

[8]I say "motivated" laypersons because, as it is likely already evident, this method requires study—and that means time, commitment, and hard work. I would be quick to point out, all the same, that there are other ways to read as well: contemplative reading; prayerful reading; devotional reading; what some call "spiritual reading." For these I can recommend Eugene H. Peterson, *Eat This Book: A Conversation in the Art of Spiritual Reading* (Grand Rapids, MI: Eerdmans, 2006); John Piper, *Reading the Bible Supernaturally: Seeing and Savoring the Glory of God in Scripture* (Wheaton, IL: Crossway, 2017).

Finally, as you study the Scriptures the Holy Spirit will convict you, exhort you, teach you, and comfort you as he conforms you more and more into the image of Christ. As he inspired the biblical authors to write, he will also illumine your mind to understand, especially when you read prayerfully and carefully—which is exactly the aim of hermeneutics.

For Further Study

Doriani, Daniel M. *Getting the Message: A Plan for Interpreting and Applying the Bible.* Phillipsburg, NJ: P&R, 1996. I could point to several quality books on the how-to of exegesis. This book is exceptionally helpful for English Bible readers. Doriani's method is clear and achievable, and he provides a lot of insightful examples.

Helm, David. *Expositional Preaching: How We Speak God's Word Today.* 9Marks Building Healthy Churches Series. Wheaton, IL: Crossway, 2014. This work provides a very helpful summary of the path from Bible interpretation, through theology, to practical ministry. The chapter on exegesis is particularly useful.

For Advanced Study

Brown, Jeannine K. *Scripture as Communication: Introducing Biblical Hermeneutics.* Grand Rapids, MI: Baker Academic, 2007. This is a very helpful book that brings a lot of sophisticated philosophical considerations to a more accessible level.

DeRouchie, Jason S. *How to Understand and Apply the Old Testament: Twelve Steps from Exegesis to Theology.* Phillipsburg, NJ: P&R, 2017.

McCartney, Dan, and Charles Clayton. *Let the Reader Understand: A Guide to Interpreting and Applying the Bible.* 2nd ed. Phillipsburg, NJ: P&R, 2002. This work is very strong on the redemptive-historical considerations in the hermeneutical task (what I call in the rest of this book "the christological context").

Naselli, Andrew David. *How to Understand and Apply the New Testament: Twelve Steps from Exegesis to Theology.* Phillipsburg, NJ: P&R, 2017. I recommend this book and DeRouchie's because they appreciate the building process from one theological discipline to another as mentioned above, all the while driving the interpreter back to exegesis. I put these books under "For Advanced Study" because DeRouchie and Naselli work much out of the original biblical languages; otherwise the books are very accessible.

1

THE TEXT AS
A MIRROR

A Selective History of Hermeneutics

R EADING THE BIBLE IS LIKE looking into water. If you have
ever stood on the bank of a pond and looked down, you surely noticed two things. For one, you could dimly see into the water and vaguely
make out the plants and fish. But also, you saw yourself and the luminous
sky above. That combination of the contents of the pond together with the
reflection of you and your world delivers this poignant message: *you are
a part of this ecosystem now.* Your presence impacts it. And that affects
what you see. It is hard to see past your reflection. But it is possible.

In this chapter I will lay out a concise history of biblical hermeneutics
with particular attention to the way interpreters have tried to move from
the meaning in the text to its relevance and application in their times.
William Yarchin comments that "much of the history of biblical interpretation concerns the question of referentiality in the Bible: to what extent

are the texts of Scripture to be read for what they *plainly* state, and to what extent *as figures* of something other than their plain reference?" (emphasis original).[1]

It is at that point that various hermeneutical approaches have been employed to navigate *how* such figures work, and whether that "something other than their plain reference" is still in line with the plain reference or something truly *other*. In the end, we will see that there are surer paths to legitimate and ethical interpretation, and the others are distractions. Some provide a clear scope for peering into the pond; others predominantly see the sky above.

If you are not a history buff, please do not be tempted to skip this chapter. I will conclude this historical survey with a very relevant application: an understanding of something called the "hermeneutical spiral." So hang in there. History will tell us a lot about today. As Gerald Bray puts it, "The Bible has shaped the life of the church in a way that nothing else has done, and Christians today are the product of the history of its interpretation."[2]

Alexandria and Antioch (Second–Fifth Centuries)

It might seem logical to start with Jesus or even before Jesus. But I want to save Jesus and his world for the next chapter. Let us begin with the first generation of readers that had a full Bible, after the New Testament had been completed and compiled.[3]

Jesus' apostles, who penned the New Testament, seem to have had quite a consistent hermeneutic.[4] And the church recognized that the apostles' authority now resided in their writings (e.g., 2 Pet 1:12-21).[5] But

---

[1]William Yarchin, *History of Biblical Interpretation: A Reader* (Grand Rapids, MI: Baker Academic, 2004), xii.

[2]Gerald Bray, *Biblical Interpretation: Past and Present* (Downers Grove, IL: InterVarsity Press, 1996), 8.

[3]On the canonization of the sixty-six books of the Bible see Herman N. Ridderbos, *Redemptive History and the New Testament Scriptures*, rev. Richard B. Gaffin, Jr., trans. H. De Jonge, 2nd rev. ed. (Phillipsburg, NJ: P&R, 1988); Michael J. Kruger, *Canon Revisited: Establishing the Origins and Authority of the New Testament Books* (Wheaton, IL: Crossway, 2012).

[4]To be sure, this is not an undisputed point. I will lay out my argument for this in the next chapter.

[5]Again, this is a reduction. Some also alleged that the living Spirit gave utterances from the resurrected Lord, and others relied on the authority of local bishops. But even with these

by the time they passed from history the church had spread over wonderfully vast distances. By the end of the first century there were Christian communities across North Africa, Asia Minor, and Greece, stretching as far west as Rome and even eastward beyond Roman territory. As would be expected, over such a large area there were different convictions about how to approach interpretation. Sometimes these different convictions were motivated by the varying theological concerns and pressures felt from the surrounding cultures.

Apologists like Justin Martyr (ca. 100–165) were too engaged in speaking up in the face of persecution to give much attention to hermeneutics.[6] We see, therefore, in the earliest Fathers a mixed methodology.[7] Much was simply literal, but it also had a "Christocentric bias" to it because that is what they saw in the New Testament.[8] The result was two approaches to move beyond literal interpretation to transcendent meanings: allegory and typology. In simplest terms, allegory attempts to dig under the straightforward and historical sense of texts to find hidden, mystical meanings. Typology, on the other hand, starts from the historical sense and perceives the way persons, events, and institutions in the Old Testament prefigure the person and work of Christ.

It is not uncommon to see the Fathers blend allegory and typology in an unsystematic way, though Irenaeus of Lyon (ca. 135–200) and Tertullian (ca. 160–220) did recognize the difference and speak against allegory.[9] Irenaeus wrote, "By transferring passages, and dressing them up anew, and making one thing out of another, they succeed in deluding many."[10] Instead, "If anyone, therefore, reads the Scriptures with attention,

---

additional forms of revelation and leadership, the Scriptures were never eclipsed as the foundation of the church.

[6]Unless otherwise noted, all dates in this chapter are taken from Michael Graves, ed., *Biblical Interpretation in the Early Church*, Ad Fontes Early Christian Sources (Minneapolis: Fortress, 2017) or Donald K. McKim, ed., *Dictionary of Major Biblical Interpreters* (Downers Grove, IL: IVP Academic, 2007).

[7]Iain Provan, *The Reformation and the Right Reading of Scripture* (Waco, TX: Baylor University Press, 2017), 151-71.

[8]Bray, *Biblical Interpretation*, 97.

[9]Stephen Westerholm and Martin Westerholm, *Reading Sacred Scripture: Voices from the History of Biblical Interpretation* (Grand Rapids, MI: Eerdmans, 2016), 54-63.

[10]Irenaeus, *Against Heresies* 1.8.1 (*ANF* 1:326).

he will find in them an account of Christ, and a foreshadowing of the new calling. . . . He was pointed out by means of types and parables."[11] The coming of the Son provides, therefore, "the explanation of all things" where anything that was hidden is now "brought to light by the cross of Christ."[12] And Melito of Sardis (d. ca. 180) calls Isaac "a type of Him who should suffer"[13] and in the exodus and Passover "a preliminary sketch is made of what is to be."[14] But the underdevelopment of hermeneutics in this first generation is evident in the way one interpreter can lean toward one approach and then switch to the other.[15]

For example, in a book called *The Epistle of Barnabas* (likely written as early as AD 100–130) the author asks in 6:10, "What, therefore, does 'into the good land, a land flowing with milk and honey' mean?"[16] He answers his own question: entering into the good land is a reference to the Christian understanding of regeneration or being born again (6:11-16), and the milk and honey—the food of infants—has to do with our need to be "nourished by faith" (6:17). This would be an example of allegory; there is nothing specifically in the text to point this way. But the author goes on with what appears to be a rather sophisticated—and quite intriguing—theological understanding of the relationship between Adam's role in the creation, Israel's call, redemption in Christ, and the final blessed state of humanity. This feels like typology, Adam and Israel prefiguring later realities in Christ.

It was not long before these two approaches were distinguished, however, and the two main schools of thought that finally emerged were associated with Alexandria and Antioch.

---

[11]Irenaeus, *Against Heresies* 4.26.1 (*ANF* 1:496).

[12]Irenaeus, *Against Heresies* 4.26.1 (*ANF* 1:496).

[13]Melito of Sardis, *The Catena on Genesis* (*ANF* 8:759).

[14]Melito of Sardis, *On Pascha* 36 (Alistair Stewart-Sykes, trans., *On Pascha: With the Fragments of Melito and Other Material Related to the Quartodecimans*, Popular Patristics Series [Crestwood, NY: St. Vladimir's Seminary Press, 2001], 46).

[15]This has contributed to some conclusions that there really is no difference between allegory and typology. I make the case in this chapter and throughout this work, that there are very many differences. Early examples of their conflation are no evidence to the contrary, but only an underdevelopment of both. See, e.g., Leonhard Goppelt, *Typos: The Typological Interpretation of the Old Testament and the New*, trans. Donald H. Madvig (Grand Rapids, MI: Eerdmans, 1982), 1-20.

[16]Translations from Michael W. Holmes, ed., *The Apostolic Fathers: Greek Texts and English Translations*, 3rd ed. (Grand Rapids, MI: Baker Academic, 2007).

Figure 1.1. Alexandria and Antioch were about five hundred miles apart by boat.

Alexandria, located at the mouth of the Nile, had been a center of learning and philosophy for centuries before the New Testament was written. Thus, by the time the church grew in Alexandria, it was already primed to have an influence beyond its borders. Additionally, Alexandria's tradition of Greek philosophy was very influential on church leaders. Interpreters of the Alexandrian school felt both an appreciation for the Greek philosophy that gave the city its renown, and also the need to make an apologetic to the world that Christianity was not a philosophically regressive system. They wanted to show the world that Christianity not only spoke intelligently into the philosophical climate, but even eclipsed the best of Greek philosophy.[17]

The Alexandrians reached for a hermeneutic to accomplish this task, therefore, and *allegory* was ready made for it. Thus, accounts like the calling of Abraham, the events of the exodus, or the temple cult were less important to the Alexandrians than an immediately applicable philosophical interpretation that could speak directly into the Greco-Roman world around them. Their appreciation for Greek philosophy had turned into the *application* of Greek philosophy.

---

[17]Vern S. Poythress, *Reading the Word of God in the Presence of God: A Handbook for Biblical Interpretation* (Wheaton, IL: Crossway, 2016), 119-21.

Clement of Alexandria (ca. 150–215) and Origen (ca. 185–253) are the conduits of this interpretive tradition into the wider Christian movement. Clement wrote, "I seek after God, not the works of God. Whom shall I take as a helper in my inquiry? . . . How, then, is God to be searched out, O Plato?"[18] While Origen was deeply concerned with historical matters, the literal historical meaning was only a starting point to move into the important matters of interpretation: getting to the allegorical meaning (developed in his *On First Principles*). For example, Origen believed in the historicity of the flood, but moved quickly to allegorical speculations on the meaning of the dimensions of the ark.[19] At other times, however, Origen simply rejected the historical claims of the text in favor of an entirely allegorical interpretation.[20] It suited his goal of combating heretics and reaching the Hellenized world, but it also fit his philosophical Platonism: if the objects and events of this world all have a deeper spiritual meaning, then so too the Bible. It is "everywhere sprinkled with riddles and dark sayings."[21]

To be sure, however, Origen believed that the passages that could be taken historically and literally made up the greater proportion than those that *had* to be taken allegorically. All the same, it was his Greek philosophical construct that swayed his hermeneutical tendencies.[22]

---

[18]Clement of Alexandria, *Exhortation to the Heathen* 6.1 (*ANF* 2:191).

[19]Jean Daniélou, *From Shadows to Reality*, trans. Dom Wulstan Hibberd, Studies in the Biblical Theology of the Fathers (Westminster, MD: Newman, 1960), 103-12.

[20]Ironically, it may be because Origen read the Bible *so* literally in a plain sense, that he had to resort all the way to allegory when things like "circumcise your heart" were nonsensical to him (Westerholm and Westerholm, *Reading Sacred Scripture*, 80-90).

[21]Origen, *On First Principles* 4.2, trans. G. W. Butterworth (London: SPCK, 1936; repr., Notre Dame: Ave Maria, 1966, 1973), 360-61.

[22]This is not to deny, however, that Origen thought Christianly. Of course he did. Only the contemporary philosophy influenced his otherwise Christian understanding of things. In fact, McCartney and Clayton make the interesting conjecture, "Since Origen's presuppositions about the Bible and God's word were more central to him than his Neoplatonic philosophy, it is arguable that Origen would have moved closer to a biblical worldview had he lived longer. In fact, in his later works (such as his commentary on Matthew and *Against Celsus*), he is not nearly as fanciful in his allegorizing as in his earlier works" (Dan McCartney and Charles Clayton, *Let the Reader Understand: A Guide to Interpreting and Applying the Bible*, 2nd ed. [Phillipsburg, NJ: P&R, 2002], 86). For a far more thorough and sympathetic explanation of the Fathers' allegorical methods, see Hans Boersma, *Scripture as Real Presence: Sacramental Exegesis in the Early Church* (Grand Rapids, MI: Baker Academic, 2017).

We see in this how easy it is that the pressing philosophical concerns of the day can float the interpretive boat. Either intentionally (because the exegete has the desire to speak into such a philosophical environment) or accidentally (because the exegete may not know to what extent they are influenced by their philosophical environment) interpretations are easily shaped by the cultural context of the reader. This is to be expected in a lot of ways, and I will return to this culture-reader-text dynamic below. For now, I point this out to show how the goal and result of exegesis can become lines for retrieving preset philosophical ideals.[23] I call this *eisegesis of the reigning Zeitgeist into the ancient biblical text.*

Eisegesis is the opposite of exegesis. Exegesis, as discussed in the introduction, is the process of drawing the meaning *out* of the biblical text. *Eisegesis* is when we read foreign ideas *into* the biblical text. A *Zeitgeist* is the collection of ideas and feelings that predominate a culture in any given era. It literally translates as "the spirit of the age." Many interpretations down the ages are the result of the reigning Zeitgeist—that collection of pervasive and dominant philosophical ideals of any culture— being read *into* biblical texts. In such cases we miss what is really in the text, and in turn simply pull out of the text what we ourselves read into it—the Zeitgeist—often enough not even knowing we are doing that.

The biblical interpreters of Antioch, however, approached things differently. They placed a lot more value on the historical locatedness of biblical texts, and found the meaning inherently bound to the actual events they describe. In turn, they reprimanded the allegorists for "depriv[ing] biblical history of its reality."[24] The creation account matters because it attests to God's involvement in history. The exodus matters because it happened. Abraham's life matters because God called him in space and time. History matters to the Old Testament writers, so the interpreter can find meaning there. Therefore, allegory is not necessary. In the end, the Scriptures are not a storehouse of hidden philosophical treasures, nor do they need to be rescued from their earthiness to suit

---

[23]See Daniélou, *Shadows to Reality*, esp. 58.
[24]McCartney and Clayton, *Let the Reader Understand*, 88.

Greek philosophy. They are God's revelation of himself in history and through history.

Yet the Antiochenes also knew that there had to be some kind of contemporary relevance. The Bible does not just list the brute facts of history. Diodore of Tarsus (ca. 330–394), therefore, allowed for "the higher interpretation," which he called *theoria*, as long as it worked in line with the historical meaning.[25] So the various genres of the Old Testament, while embedded in history and concerned with their own historical moment, look back and look forward to these "higher" meanings. "This fundamental distinction between *theoria* and allegory allows Diodore to perceive typologies created within the biblical narrative itself."[26] The simplest example of this would be the Passover lamb: it was sacrificed in Egypt for sure, but its "higher interpretation" (*theoria*) points to Christ as the final lamb who takes away the sins of the world.

Theodore of Mopsuestia (ca. 350–428) detected such typology when the Old Testament uses "hyperbole." His close attention to the historical sense of any text is what made him particularly aware when the authors used "hyperbole," which he called overstatements regarding some figure or event that could only make sense in relation to the coming Christ.[27] In Psalm 16:10, for example, David says the Lord will not let him see decay which is actually a reference to the coming Messiah, not David himself (as Peter says in Acts 2:24-32). So Christopher Hall summarizes:

> Theodore understands hyperbolic language, then, as purposeful exaggeration by a biblical writer in light of God's future greater acts. In a strict interpretation, David's body experienced decay. His words in Psalm 16 appear to run aground. Theodore teaches, however, that "they are found to be true in so far as they were said concerning Christ the Lord."[28]

---

[25]Anthony C. Thiselton, *Hermeneutics: An Introduction* (Grand Rapids, MI: Eerdmans, 2009), 109-10.

[26]Christopher A. Hall, *Reading Scripture with the Church Fathers* (Downers Grove, IL: InterVarsity Press, 1998), 161.

[27]Hall, *Reading Scripture*, 167-69.

[28]Hall, *Reading Scripture*, 168; closing quote from Theodore himself from his *Commentary on Zechariah*.

Thus, the Antiochenes saw themselves as working with the historical sense of the text that *itself* points to the christological horizon of meaning.

Theodoret of Cyrus (393–458) did not eschew allegory with the same force, but his preference for typology is clear. When writing on the suffering and victory expressed in Psalm 30, he writes of the historical experience of Hezekiah *and* Jesus:

> Isaiah brought Hezekiah the sentence of death in the evening, and towards morning brought him in turn the good news of life. And it happened likewise in the case of the salvation of everyone: the sacred apostles and the believers along with them lamented the Passion of the Lord, but towards morning the women came and brought the joy of the Resurrection.[29]

Thus, Theodoret has grounded the meaning of the psalm with a true historical referent (Hezekiah), and also illustrated how that history serves as a pattern for Christ's experience. As Hezekiah was as good as dead and revived the next day, Christ truly died and was brought back to life in three days. The primary mark of this kind of interpretation that distinguishes it from allegory is the anchoring of the meaning in real history that then provides the reflection on an intrinsic pattern across the Scriptures, especially in the person and work of Christ. Allegory, on the other hand, has no need for history and often enough runs *around* Christ.[30]

Before leaving the Fathers, a word should be said about Jerome (ca. 347–419) and Augustine of Hippo (354–430).

Both seem to embody something of the uneasy but also inseparable relationship between allegory and typology. Jerome had been a translator and proponent of Origen's writings, but eventually distanced himself and rejected his allegorical methods. Yet, in his later years Jerome would still turn to allegory in certain circumstances.[31] Augustine, similarly, distrusted allegory but nonetheless resorted to it from time to time. He is

---

[29]Theodoret of Cyrus, "Commentary on Psalm 30," in *A Commentary on the Psalms: Psalms 1–72*, trans. Robert C. Hill, vol. 101 of *The Fathers of the Church: A New Translation* (Washington DC: Catholic University of America Press, 2000), 189.

[30]Jean Daniélou, *The Lord of History: Reflections on the Inner Meaning of History*, trans. Nigel Abercrombie (London: Longmans, 1958), 140-41.

[31]Bray, *Biblical Interpretation*, 91-92, 103.

also remembered for many interpretive "rules" that the Antiochenes would have (largely) applauded.[32] Among them are important considerations of historical and literary contexts as well as an appreciation for the progressive nature of Scripture—the idea that the Bible slowly unfolds God's revelation, and so the later parts need to be understood in light of the earlier and vice versa. But he liked allegory ever since he met Ambrose of Milan; it was able to be used to combat the Manicheans and yet fit within his Neoplatonism.[33] That is to say, as we have seen above, it fit within his preconceived philosophical system and proved useful with other philosophical agendas. All this goes to show how influential a Zeitgeist can be even when hermeneutical principles are well conceived. It seems to be a constant breeze in the interpretive sails.

Two Paths Diverge (Sixth–Sixteenth Centuries)

The Middle Ages can be generally viewed in terms of the legacies of the Alexandrians and Antiochenes.[34] While the school of Antioch is not without its medieval alumni, it was the Alexandrian hermeneutic that had a larger influence on the Middle Ages.[35]

Gregory the Great (ca. 540–604) warned against the excesses of allegory, but nonetheless employed it quite readily himself, giving further development to Origen's multiple senses.

For his part, he believed that the primary goal of Bible teaching is ethical instruction. He was eager to see moral commands in any text, and allegory provided the means to such ends. He taught, for example, that when Jesus asks the blind man in Luke 18:41, "What do you want me to do for you?," this is instruction to us to always pray. For even though the Lord knows all, he is provoking the beggar to ask him anyway; thus

---

[32]Augustine, *On Christian Doctrine* 1-3 (*NPNF1* 2:522-73).

[33]Yarchin, *History of Biblical Interpretation*, 61-62.

[34]This book is written primarily in dialogue with the Western tradition. My hope, nonetheless, is that it will prove helpful for the worldwide church. For insights into historical and contemporary hermeneutical traditions in a global context, see William A. Dyrness and Veli-Matti Kärkkäinen, eds., *Global Dictionary of Theology* (Downers Grove, IL: InterVarsity Press, 2008).

[35]For more of the medieval diversity than what can be accomplished here, see Bray, *Biblical Interpretation*, 129-57.

"he counsels us [also] to be untiring in our prayers."[36] It is not enough for Gregory that Jesus' question be merely a historical detail of the narrative. It must also have ethical practicality. Another example would be the color and type of thread used for the tabernacle: it represents service in the church mixed with worldly employment. Why should colors and materials represent that? Well, Gregory had to do *something* ethically symbolic with it. As

Figure 1.2. Jerome (ca. 347–419) and Gregory the Great (ca. 540–604) by Juan de Sevilla Romero

Hall puts it, "Gregory has transmuted an Old Testament text into a trenchant devotional comment on ecclesiastical life."[37] Thus, allegory was able to get Gregory what he was looking for.

The Venerable Bede (673–735) is another early influence. He believed that reading the Bible should provide spiritual nourishment. Insofar as some texts do not provide such (or it is hard to see how), interpreters need to "know how to draw out the allegorical meaning."[38] These, like most others, recognized the importance of a historical interpretation, but often only to move beyond it to a sense more mystical and analogical. What they wanted, they found.

Thomas Aquinas (ca. 1224–1274), however, contended that the historical and spiritual meanings cannot be separated. He and his followers

---

[36]Gregory the Great, *Forty Gospel Homilies* 13, trans. David Hurst (Kalamazoo, MI: Cistercian, 1990), 97.

[37]Hall, *Church Fathers*, 130.

[38]Bede, *Expositionis allegoricae in Samuelem prophetam libri quatuor*; quoted in Bray, *Biblical Interpretation*, 146.

Figure 1.3. Thomas Aquinas (ca. 1224–1274) at the Church of Santa Maria Novella in Florence, Italy

propelled a new rise in literal reading. Built, then, upon that literal and historical sense, Aquinas gave attention to the sweep and scope of God's acts of salvation "ordained by God and extending from the creation to the apocalypse, with its center in Jesus Christ."[39] And to be sure, there were others in the Middle Ages who were not so prone toward allegory: Hugh of St. Victor (1096–1141); Bonaventure (ca. 1217–1274); Nicolas of Lyra (ca. 1270–1349); John Wycliffe (ca. 1320–1384). But the majority of the (Western) Church took this path, and even those who disagreed with it in principle nonetheless still employed it when needed.

In turn, one could say that medieval hermeneutics reached a crisis point when Jacques Lefèvre d'Étaples (ca. 1455–1536) observed how unclear exegetes were when they did refer to the literal sense. It is one thing to give the literal sense priority; it is another to elucidate what that means exactly. Moreover, Lefèvre insisted that there are actually *two* literal senses, especially in regard to Old Testament books: the evident historical

---

[39]K. Froehlich, "Thomas Aquinas," in *Dictionary of Major Biblical Interpreters,* ed. Donald K. McKim (Downers Grove, IL: InterVarsity Press, 2007), 982-83.

sense, but equally the prophetic sense (which he also called "literal") that points forward to the coming of Christ.[40] With Lefèvre's influence on Luther, Luther's influence on Calvin, and Calvin's influence on everyone, a decisive turn back to typology is here occurring.

Sola Scriptura Is a Hermeneutical Claim (Sixteenth–Seventeenth Centuries)

The Protestant Reformation was a time of questioning long-standing customs. The Renaissance motto *ad fontes*—"to the sources"—carried into the Reformation period and propelled scholars to return to studying the Scriptures in their original languages. When they compared their renewed findings to several points of medieval dogma, they found the latter out of step with the former.[41] Thus began a debate over where the locus of Christ's authority resides. Do church traditions hold equal (or more?) authority to the Scriptures? Or are the Scriptures the unrivaled highest authority for the church? The Reformers, of course, believed the latter. This, then, constituted the formal cause of the Reformation: *sola Scriptura*.

There are many implications to this rallying cry, *sola Scriptura*. For one, it means the Bible is the only authority for doctrine and piety. All other opinions must be tried against the Scriptures, never vice versa.[42] Second, Scripture is its own interpreter. There is no earthly power that authoritatively prescribes the meaning of Scripture, but Scripture interprets itself. When there is a dispute over the meaning of a given passage, then the rest of the Bible is brought to bear. This comes from Irenaeus and Augustine (*Scriptura sui ipsius interpres*). Third, and this develops

---

[40] Alister E. McGrath, *Reformation Thought: An Introduction*, 3rd ed. (Oxford: Blackwell, 1999), 158.

[41] To be clear, the Reformers did not disparage all of medieval theology, but considered only 1200–1500 an "era of decay." They still valued many earlier theologians insofar as they saw them working well from the text of Scripture (McGrath, *Reformation Thought*, 155-56). As Bray puts it, the Reformers did not reject the hermeneutic they inherited, but sought "to purify and systematize it" (*Biblical Interpretation*, 9).

[42] The Reformers made a distinction between the "magisterial" use of tradition and the "ministerial" use of tradition. Tradition is "ministerial" insofar as it teaches us and we can stand on the shoulders of others. But once tradition takes on a ruling and determining function—"magisterial"—that is the moment it mutes the Bible's ability to correct any poor traditions. To the Reformers the "*sola scriptura* principle thus involved the claim that the authority of the church was grounded in its fidelity to Scripture" (McGrath, *Reformation Thought*, 154).

out of the second, the Bible itself teaches us how to read it.[43] Later passages reference and interpret earlier passages. Thus, the later passages are applying a hermeneutic. Interpreters can look at that and glean how, in a sense, the Bible is asking to be read. As A. S. Wood puts it,

> *Sola Scriptura* insists that the Bible itself must teach us how to interpret the Bible. The first hermeneutical circle is to be drawn from the design of the Word. The sphere from which the methodology of hermeneutics is to be derived is that of Scripture itself. The true principles of biblical interpretation are themselves quarried from biblical sources. To break this circuit is to deprive interpretation of its essential dynamic and authority.[44]

Fourth, now developing out of the third, the whole Bible is about Christ. "What gave Luther's doctrine [of *sola Scriptura*] its unique reformational character was its radical Christocentric basis. . . . The great weakness of allegorical exegesis was precisely that it obscures the Christological witness."[45] Again, this is a conviction that emerges when the authority of the Bible is recognized, and therefore the Bible is carefully studied.[46] This means that the scope of the whole (and any part thereof) does not address the concerns of contemporary culture as a first priority; but its concerns are with Christ first and foremost. To put it another way, the Zeitgeist comes under the judging gaze of Christ. It does not set the agenda for reading or theologizing. It is this rejection of allegory and promotion of christological readings that resulted in several material causes of the Reformation, the other traditional *solas*.[47]

John Calvin (1509–1564) especially avoided allegory and spoke against it.[48] Instead he saw typological correspondences pointing to Christ, averring

---

[43]David I. Starling, *Hermeneutics as Apprenticeship: How the Bible Shapes Our Interpretive Habits and Practices* (Grand Rapids, MI: Baker Academic, 2016), 9-20.

[44]A. S. Wood, *Luther's Principles of Biblical Interpretation* (London: Tyndale, 1960), 12.

[45]Timothy George, *Theology of the Reformers* (Nashville: Broadman & Holman, 1988), 83.

[46]McGrath, *Reformation Thought*, 158-60.

[47]The doctrine of the clarity of Scripture also arises, in part, out of these hermeneutical convictions: allegory was simply far too esoteric, left only for the "experts."

[48]David S. Dockery, "New Testament Interpretation: A Historical Survey," in *Interpreting the New Testament: Essays on Methods and Issues,* ed. David Alan Black and Davis S. Dockery (Nashville: Broadman & Holman, 2001), 26-27.

that "the clarity of sacred Scripture is grounded in Christ alone."[49] For example, Calvin saw that the crying of the mothers in Jeremiah 31:15 is immediately followed with "the most delightful consolations" in the next two verses.[50] Israel's mothers should *not* weep for their children because they will come back to her. Then in Matthew 2:18 the crying is again mentioned, but not

Johannes Calvin.

Figure 1.4. Of all the Reformers, John Calvin (1509–1564) had the largest hermeneutical influence on the church.

the consolation, as again "Rachel's children" are taken from her. To Calvin, the reader is to see the repetition of Jeremiah's situation in the days of Christ and so equally expect the restoration that Jeremiah foresees: "as Jeremiah promises a restoration . . . so Matthew reminds his readers that . . . [Christ will appear] shortly afterwards as the Redeemer."[51] Thus, the historical circumstance in Jeremiah has elucidated a typological pattern of Christ's life.

Yet, while Martin Luther (1483–1546) affirmed these tenets, he still did allegorize at times. You can take the monk out of the monastery, but you cannot take the monk out of the man. This just highlights again how thoroughly pervasive Zeitgeists continue to bedevil people, even when they want to shed them on theoretical grounds. I think the reason is

---

[49]Hans-Joachim Kraus, "Calvin's Exegetical Principles," *Interpretation* 31 (1977): 18. Calvin was also particularly concerned with the biblical authors' historical circumstances and literary contexts (Kraus, "Calvin's Exegetical Principles," 12-18).

[50]John Calvin, *Commentary on a Harmony of the Evangelists, Matthew, Mark, and Luke*, trans. William Pringle, 3 vols. (Edinburgh: Calvin Translation Society, 1845–1846; repr., Grand Rapids, MI: Baker, 1981), 1:148.

[51]Calvin, *Harmony of the Evangelists*, 1:148-49.

because the cultures people live in exert an enormous hermeneutical influence, more than they themselves realize.

The "Modern" World Sure Is Out of Date (Eighteenth–Nineteenth Centuries)

The period known as the Enlightenment was marked by confidence in autonomous human cognitive abilities. There was a real "We can do it! We can improve the world!" mentality *if only we put our minds to it*. Right thinking and more assured methods of discovery would result in clearer paths of truth. The only hindrance to such progress was, of course, ignorance. Overcoming our ignorance—discovering more and more about our world through these new more certain methods—was, then, the goal.

What were these new methods of discovery and learning? The first was *rationalism*, where the dictates of human reason became the arbiter for what can be considered true. Now to be clear, I do not mean to suggest that the 1700s marked the birth of reason, nor that it was the first time thinkers gave attention to that which is "reasonable." Rather, that century saw the elevation in confidence in the abilities of reason to secure answers to our major questions. For centuries in the West, theology had been the "queen of the sciences." Therefore listening to the revelation of Scripture and the authority of the church were paramount. But René Descartes's famous "*I think* therefore I am" encapsulates the ethos of this new era. Increasingly less common was the idea that "*God is* therefore I am," making his revelation less necessary. In turn, theological distinctives, like the doctrine of the Trinity, were more commonly questioned.

David Hume (1711–1776) is commonly associated with the next major school of thought: *empiricism*.

Empiricism is the idea that only that which can be discerned through the human senses can give us certainty of truth. Only that which can been seen, heard, touched, smelled or tasted is sure data upon which to base our knowledge. To Hume, this created a gap between the knowability of this world and the claims theologians make about God. For God—and matters with which the Bible is mostly concerned—cannot be

Figure 1.5. David Hume (1711–1776) with St. Giles's Cathedral in the background, Edinburgh, Scotland

seen, heard, touched, smelled or tasted. So how could we ever *know* these things to be true without experiencing God through the senses? As with rationalism, the promulgation and popularity of empiricism cast a shadow of suspicion over the veracity of much of the Bible's teachings, especially miracles (like revelation, the teaching that God has spoken truth to humanity now codified in a book).

This leads to *naturalism*. While Hume never said miracles or the metaphysical claims of the Bible are impossible (just unknowable), his writings gave legs to the idea that all that truly exists—or is worth knowing—is the natural world. Given that the natural world operates on observable and predictable chains of cause and effect, miracles (like God speaking to humans through the process of inspiration) became less philosophically palatable than ever. And without that belief, there is little left for Christianity to stand on, other than its long-standing cultural presence. Now God is not only unknowable, but probably does not even exist.

The point here is not to trace the denigration of biblical doctrines like the Trinity, miracles, or revelation/inspiration, but the way the ascendency of these Enlightenment epistemologies also called for new hermeneutical approaches. Epistemology is the study of how we know—how we learn, synthesize knowledge, remember, and so forth. And hermeneutics is a branch of epistemology. Thus, these moves toward rationalism, empiricism, and naturalism are new epistemological commitments that have shaped Western hermeneutics ever since. Empiricism and naturalism especially challenged the belief in miracles, and since the Bible is *full* of miracle stories, other explanations had to be sought for where these stories came from. Surely the authors did not record historical events—because miracles are dismissed as impossible—but drafted tales that could inspire faith. The new driving hermeneutical questions, therefore, were less "What is in the text?" and more "How can we reconstruct the true history behind the text?" This gave rise to new understandings of Israel's history, the historical Jesus, and the origins of the church as scholars brought their empiricist and naturalistic assumptions to bear on the hermeneutical task.

It became popular to read the Old Testament not as a record of Israel's past but as "historicized prose fiction."[52] These are fictitious stories retrojected upon a people to give them identity and legitimacy. This happened primarily during the exile when (some of) Israel's sacred texts were assembled into what we now call the Old Testament. The miracles, therefore—and most of the historical narratives in fact—were myths made up to help the Jewish people understand why their city was recently destroyed and how to maintain hope for the future. So did Noah build an ark and survive a worldwide flood? Of course not. This is a story adapted from their Babylonian captors and given a Hebrew spin. Did Joseph go down to Egypt where God preserved him and helped him? No. This is a story to give hope when the Jews were also in captivity far from home. Did Joshua conquer the land? Surely not. These are stories to give Israel a claim on that real estate. All of this starts, as mentioned, with the assumption that the miracles recorded in these stories could not have happened. This new understanding of history and textual origins has become the alternate explanation to believing in such miracles.

---

[52]Robert Alter, *The Art of Biblical Narrative*, upd. rev. ed. (New York: Basic Books, 1981), 25-54.

In the New Testament, take Jesus' feeding of the 5,000 for example. Did Jesus really multiply two fish and five loaves for so many people? Not in this closed universe. It is more likely that Jesus' teachings motivated the boy with the fish and bread to share what he had. Others (far fewer than 5,000) saw his generosity and quickly followed suit. On and on the sharing went until all had enough to eat. So sure, in a sense Jesus fed a multitude. But not by a miracle. As time went on, eager followers hyperbolized the story into a miracle, until it was eventually written down by the Gospel writers, and so we have it today. But naturally this was not done by a miracle, because miracles are, well, so unnatural.

These are examples of the historical critical method, sometimes called "higher criticism." The meaning is not in the text but somewhere (hidden) behind the text, though the clues of which are still *somewhere* in the text. Thus, again we observe that a priori philosophical commitments have sent interpreters on inevitable trajectories. In other words, higher criticism is the product of the new Zeitgeist. The epistemological commitments from outside the Bible have become determinative in evaluating "what the Bible really means." New Testament theologian George Eldon Ladd would later comment, "The rejection of the biblical portrait of Jesus in favor of a hypothetical historical Jesus, and the effort to trace the stages between the two, is not the result of open-minded inductive study of our sources, but the philosophical presuppositions about the nature of history."[53]

Their reconstructions of "what really happened" spread further doubt over the biblical narratives. When this cold breeze of skepticism blew through the church, the once-faithful found it hard to believe the claims of Christianity any longer. The ancient ideals of the Bible simply no longer comported with the new Zeitgeist.

Enter Friedrich D. E. Schleiermacher (1768–1834). Schleiermacher lines up with the Antiochenes and Reformers insofar as he insisted in the historical "rootedness" of texts.[54] But he was also very much ahead of his

---

[53]George Eldon Ladd, *A Theology of the New Testament*, ed. Donald A. Hagner, rev. ed. (Grand Rapids, MI: Eerdmans, 1993), 177.
[54]Thiselton, *Hermeneutics*, 20-24.

time insofar as he understood the subjective side of interpretation as well. The Bible is very old and so there is a distance between its original authors and modern readers. Schleiermacher thought much about how to overcome that distance and concluded that maybe it is not altogether possible. The reader seeks to understand the text within his or her own presupposed philosophical system. Thus, to Schleiermacher the final step in the hermeneutical process is the "theological study that tries to understand the text and integrate it into the overall worldview of the interpreter."[55] And with that, he found a way to make Christianity compelling again. The teachings of the Bible no longer fit

Figure 1.6. Friedrich D. E. Schleiermacher (1768–1834) is considered the father of theological liberalism.

modernism's new philosophical arena, but that is okay. Christianity is not based on such propositional claims, for the essence of religion is *feeling dependent on God*, not doctrine or confession or belief in historical events. Schleiermacher was, in all, a Romantic. This new emphasis allowed people to continue in their Christianity while not necessarily believing in the miraculous or "irrational" claims of the Bible. This ultimately locates meaning in the modern reader or audience, not in the historical author or text. With Schleiermacher, therefore, we see another new breed of allegory. The new philosophical climate presented new challenges, which in turn motivated a new hermeneutic that could provide answers toward preserving Christian traditions. And these answers came in the attire of Schleiermacher's Romanticism. He is known today as the father of theological liberalism.

---

[55]McCartney and Clayton, *Let the Reader Understand*, 101.

Ours Is a *Post*modern World
(Twentieth–Twenty-First Centuries)

So what do we call our own era after the modern Enlightenment? *Post*modernism of course.[56] There are a lot of ways to understand postmodernism; as with the rest of this survey, I will discuss it in terms of its implications for hermeneutics. Postmodernism is basically a reaction to modern epistemological sensibilities. The Enlightenment confidence in the human potential to improve the world has not delivered, and in turn left the West a little disillusioned with the quest for truth. This has resulted in a decline in appreciating the objective value of truth claims and replaced such with an emphasis on individuals (or individual groups) to contribute their own interpretations of life, the universe, and everything.

Below we will explore, therefore, relativism and reader-response hermeneutics. But to understand them, and the postmodern spirit, we need first to consider *existentialism*. As mentioned above, the Enlightenment was a time of skepticism vis-à-vis the truth claims of the Bible. The biblical worldview simply did not comport with the modern Zeitgeist. Over time skepticism gave way to wide-scale rejection of those claims, including (as might have been expected) the very existence of God. What, then, is humanity if we are not created in the image of God? We are but the result of the unthinking, uncaring, impersonal, unintentional forces and physical laws that govern the universe. Thus, we are not the intended locus through which God will redeem the cosmos, but the accidental byproduct of a godless cosmos. Such an overarching view of humanity will inevitably create feelings of smallness, loneliness, meaninglessness, and despair. And indeed it has. But when we reflect upon ourselves, namely our passions and desires and loves and pursuits and values, we feel compelled to push back against such meaninglessness. Therefore, if we are not created with any identity or meaning (other than

---

[56]Some, however, find it more helpful to speak of *hyper*modernism because it is not as though the modern era is over as much as we are seeing the trajectories of the Enlightenment come to their full consequences (so far at least). Still others call it *liquid* modernity to emphasize the elasticity of life, thought, ethics, etc. that have resulted from Enlightenment ideals now pressed into our rapidly expanding (and in some ways contracting) technopolis.

the identity of temporarily collected molecules and the meaning of consumption) we must create *our own* identity and meaning. And that is where we are today. The West is a culture pulsing with the urgency to self-create our own identity and meaning. The universe has made—accidentally and very unexpectedly—a creature that refuses to accept its trivial place in the cold vastness of spacetime. We must create ourselves, therefore, through the expression of those passions and desires and loves and pursuits and values. In short, we must *choose*. We must choose who and what we want to be and then act upon such choices. We will not allow the unintentional forces of the universe to determine who and what we are. We must choose. And we must choose to do otherwise. To

do *other* than expected. To choose to do the expected, the norm, the traditional, would resign us to serving as just one more cog in the fatalistic cosmic machine. Friedrich Nietzsche (1844–1900) charged us to "build [our] cities on the slopes of Vesuvius."

Vesuvius was one of the most devastating volcanoes to ever erupt. Why would we build cities there? *Because the universe is telling us we can't.* So we will! And that is a metaphor for all forces at work to confine and pro-

Figure 1.7. Friedrich Nietzsche (1844–1900) was a forerunner of existentialism.

hibit our free choice-making. Schools, traditions, politics, parents, religions, laws, and so on all have the power to herd us into predetermined pens. Thus, to rebel is to exercise existential freedom.

And with that we come to our definition of *existentialism*. To choose is to be free to create the much-needed identity and meaning in our quest to overcome the pressing meaninglessness of our postmodern world. To restrict such free choice is, therefore, the height of violence. To stop someone from "discovering themselves" is to wipe away their only chance at identity creation and meaning-making.

This philosophical climate has impacted hermeneutics in at least two ways. First, one of the most influential New Testament scholars of the twentieth century is Rudolf Bultmann (1884–1976).

Bultmann cared deeply about the historical rootedness of the biblical text (thinking like a "higher critic," briefly described above), but also argued that the biblical worldview is simply no longer believable in our scientifically advanced world. He said, "We cannot use electric lights and radios and, in the event of illness, avail ourselves of modern medical and clinical means and at the same time believe in the spirit and wonder world of the New Testament."[57] The New Testament envisions a three-tiered universe: heaven, earth, hell. And these three tiers are permeable; persons and communications run between them. Revelation, angels, and even God himself come down from heaven. Satan and legions of demons come up from hell. Even Paul and John are "taken up" into heaven and sent back down (2 Cor 12:2-4; Rev 4:1-2). But can the modern man believe any of this? No. We have advanced so far in our knowledge of *this* world that it is now impossible to believe it is really connected to *those* worlds. Thus, the New Testament cosmology can only be described as *myth*. Bultmann, therefore, proposed a method of "demythologization" for understanding and applying the New Testament today. It is an approach to recognizing such "unbelievable" elements and reinterpreting them in terms of postmodern sensibilities—to take the mythological elements out. For example, the incarnation—the belief that the second person of the eternal Trinity has visited the world in the man Jesus Christ—is reinterpreted to reflect the future hope that anyone can become more (truly) human through decision-making. Or the biblical doctrine of justification by faith alone can no longer be believed as God's declaration from heaven that exonerates sinners on earth. Rather, it discourages the pallid human attempts at security through anything in this world, be they riches or reputation or revenge, and so on, and teaches a

---

[57]Rudolf Bultmann, *New Testament and Mythology, and Other Basic Writings*, ed. and trans. Schubert M. Ogden (Philadelphia: Fortress, 1984), 4.

humble trust in one's own fearless authenticity. Thus, Bultmann has "[re-stated] the existential truth contained in the myth."[58]

Second, this is another example of a Zeitgeist haunting the halls of our hermeneutics. Bultmann seems not to have *de*mythologized the New Testament as much as he has *re*mythologized it to fit his philosophical precommitments. Bultmann has been influential in many other ways than described here. But he serves the purposes of this brief historical survey in providing another example of the way the philosophical waters in which the interpreter swims have rushed over his hermeneutical gills with decisive results. Existentialism in, existentialism out.

With that, we turn to *relativism*. It is not hard to see how the existentialism described above gathers fuel from individualism and in turn further strengthens individualistic penchants. To "choose to do otherwise" necessitates that each person makes their own choices. In fact, there is a sense that any external influence is suspected of inhibiting that authentically personal choice in light of any matter. Therefore, the discovery of the good, the true, and the beautiful is *relative* to each person.[59] No one can tell another how to define and discover the good, true, and beautiful. That would stall the process of *self*-creation. Thus truth, ethics and the vision of the good life depend on—are *relative* to—each individual.

All this gets us to the final point regarding postmodernism: *reader-response* hermeneutics. As might be expected, with the new search for truth in individual choices, many have recently argued that meaning

---

[58]McCartney and Clayton, *Let the Reader Understand*, 108.

[59]To be sure, this kind of relativism is more commonly visible in various degrees of "groupthink." Entire communities share essential commitments and philosophical first principles which really give postmodernism (or liquid modernity) its defining marks. Various communities with differing truth claims are increasingly living right next door to each other (in my small neighborhood alone there are Hindus, secularists, hedonists, nihilists, Christians, Sufis, agnostics and surely others I have not met yet). Insofar as each community has its own epistemologies and cultural liturgies, they have their own methods for discerning what is good, true, and beautiful. How can any one group assert it is right and the others wrong? Postmodernism is often defined, therefore, as "an incredulity toward metanarratives." Each community has its own explanatory story to describe all things, and no one has the authority to place their story-truth claims onto others, creating an overarching story (metanarrative) to interpret and judge all other stories. When it comes to reading the Bible, it makes it very difficult to agree on the meaning of a text when so many competing a priori philosophical commitments vie to drive the interpretive agenda. In short, "Who knows? We're all right. (But more likely, we're all wrong.)"

does not reside in the text (or in the author who—like the ultimate Author of the universe—is now dead) but in the *experience* of reading the text. That is, meaning resides in one's private interpretation of the text as they bring their existential precommitments to bear. The text is there as a servant to the reader's agendas, and meaning is thus found in the response of the reader. Hence the name. Thus, these recent developments make it increasingly hard to establish priorities among conflicting interpretations. *Of course the text or the author cannot have control; that would inhibit the reader's freedom for self-creation and self-determination.* All this is custom built to serve any Zeitgeist where the text can fit any reader's philosophical penchant—oftentimes without knowing it.

One particular philosophical penchant today is the habit of *deconstructionism*. Deconstructionism is complex, but we can define it here simply as an attempt to read (and/or rewrite) narratives (in texts or anywhere narratives are told) in a way that moves the center of attention away from traditional (and sometimes obvious) interpretations and give voice to the characters and ideas at the margins. There are social, political, and economic forces at work in all this that now make it hermeneutically in vogue as well. Take for example the recent TED talk by Malcom Gladwell about David and Goliath.[60] Gladwell tells the story with particular emphasis on minor details, like some of the things Goliath says that might suggest he had poor eyesight. Also, Goliath's size is of course a major detail, but Gladwell brings in the "heretofore overlooked" point that his height likely meant he had a serious disease and was surely very clumsy. That he "needs" an armor-bearer suggests the same. Equally, David is small but his sling would have had the accuracy and deadliness of today's handguns. The location of the story too, and the kinds of rocks that were likely there, adds to the devastation of David's sling. Thus, whereas the central themes of the story draw readers to the conclusion in 1 Samuel 17:45-47, that the God of Israel goes to battle for his people and especially his Messiah (cf. 1 Sam 16:13), Gladwell has

---

[60] Also in his book Malcom Gladwell, *David and Goliath: Underdogs, Misfits, and the Art of Battling Giants* (New York: Back Bay Books, 2015).

given attention instead to the peripheral details and hidden truths. So what has typically been understood as God's fighting for David is now reread to say Goliath was greatly outmatched, and David the odds-on favorite to win from the word go. And so everything we thought we knew about the story is exactly opposite!

What is the point? Ours is a culture that is increasingly making efforts to push reigning social, political, and economic powers out of the center of influence to open up paths for the historically marginalized to rush in. And that is, in itself, good. But here is another clear example where the Zeitgeist has put pressure on interpreters to adopt a hermeneutic (deconstructionism) that can do the same with biblical texts. The previously ignored details of the text have now been *empowered* and the center of the text has been de-centered. Our postcolonial world cheers this, and so it pops up in our hermeneutics too.

This is more prevalent than maybe we realize. Of course, many would not follow the philosophical path that got us to this place in our survey; it began above, after all, with the nonexistence of God. Nonetheless, any fish in any river is carried—sometimes unwittingly, but inevitably—by the current. And that current is affected by events far, far upstream and quite broadly across the watershed. The fish needs a high degree of self-awareness and strength to swim against the flow. So too, today's Western Zeitgeist is characterized by existentialism, relativism, and deconstructionism. We are the fish; those are the waters. We need, therefore, a high degree of self-awareness and strength so as not to be swept away with the current.

Biblical Theology: A Return to Antioch (Nineteenth–Twentieth Centuries)

There have, of course, been reactions to these trends. The canonical approach and theological interpretation of Scripture are two more recent schools.[61] I will conclude our survey, though, by looking at a very Antiochene discipline called "biblical theology." This is an approach that

---

[61]See Brevard S. Childs, *Biblical Theology of the Old and New Testaments: Theological Reflections on the Christian Bible* (Philadelphia: Fortress, 1993); Daniel J. Treier, *Introducing Theological Interpretation of Scripture: Recovering a Christian Practice* (Grand Rapids, MI: Baker Academic, 2008).

understands the Bible as the record of the "history of salvation," or "redemptive history," a witness to God's actions in *history* for the *salvation and redemption* of humanity. Here interpreters look for unity across the biblical narrative—including recurring patterns and the presence of typology—as well as the diversity of all the parts.[62] The result is an appreciation of the direction the Bible as a whole is going (a progress through the pages of the Bible) toward a grand conclusion. The pinnacle of the narrative patterns and types in the Bible is, of course, the person and work of Jesus Christ—the unifying point to all the diversity. "This [leads] to the conviction that the Bible contain[es] both history and a word concerning the ultimate meaning of history."[63]

A particularly good example of this is found by reading Matthew 3:13–4:11 in concert with the second book of Moses. Jesus goes through the water (Mt 3:16) and is declared God's "Son" (Mt 3:17). Immediately the Spirit leads Jesus into the wilderness (4:1) where he remains for forty days and forty nights (4:2). He is there tempted with food (4:3-4), then with "testing" God (4:5-7), and finally with idolatry (4:8-10). Very interestingly, the book of Exodus reads the same way. There, Israel is called God's "son" (Ex 4:22-23), goes through the water (14:21-22), and is then led into the wilderness by God himself (Ex 13:17) where they are tempted in the exact same order: food, "testing God," and idolatry (Ex 14–32). Thus, Jesus' baptism and wilderness temptations look just like Israel's exodus. There is, therefore, a typological correspondence in the shape of the stories to invoke the similarities, but also to present Jesus as transcending the old. That is the work of biblical theology: to describe the similarities and the developments in the movement of the Scriptures— from start to finish—in christological terms. God has providentially moved both history and the writing of the Old Testament to highlight individual patterns, and a large sweeping arc toward fulfillment in the

---

[62]To be clear, there are other definitions of "biblical theology" than the one I provide here (see Edward W. Klink III and Darian R. Lockett, *Understanding Biblical Theology: A Comparison of Theory and Practice* [Grand Rapids, MI: Zondervan, 2012]). This is the one I mean throughout this book. When the student sees that term elsewhere, however, they will want to consider how that particular author is using it.

[63]Ladd, *New Testament*, 7.

New Testament. The benefit of such observations is to elucidate how God has been at work in history, and through revelation, to demonstrate his plan of redemption that meets its full purposes in the person and work of Christ.[64] History is therefore important because it is the stage of God's glorious acts of redemption. And the writing of redemptive history is important because Christ gives meaning to life, the universe, and everything.

The rest of this book operates within this tradition. It goes back to Antioch. It was certainly appreciated by Augustine and practiced by Aquinas. It gained wider attention with the Reformers. And now "biblical theology" has given it its most recent shape.

The Hermeneutical Spiral

The payoff from this historical survey is that we can draw two conclusions about the process of interpretation: (1) We see in texts what we expect to see. Our predispositions, presuppositions, biases, goals, and expectations heavily influence how we handle texts, and can actually determine what we see and what we do not see. They can cause us to see things that are not really in the text (we import them from our own worldview) and conversely miss things that are in the text (our worldview has no place for them, cannot process them, and so we are just blind to them). So strong are our philosophical precommitments and therefore reading proclivities. And (2) such predispositions, presuppositions, biases, goals, and expectations are invariably shaped by the cultures that made us and we currently inhabit.[65] A jellyfish does not know it is floating in saltwater, nor that freshwater is such a thing, but its membrane is so thin it simply takes in the saltwater *as a way of life*. The larger culture and subcultures that we inhabit do the same to us. Add to this how foreign the genres of Scripture are to us, and the vast historical distance between

---

[64]In chaps. 5 and 6, I will stress the point that christology involves Jesus' person and *all* his work, and that includes the creation and leading of the church. Therefore, christology leads inexorably to ecclesiology, what Augustine called *totus Christus*, an appreciation that brings a lot of hermeneutical clarity to the New Testament.

[65]See e.g., Brown, *Scripture as Communication*, 121-24.

the original authors and us, and the conditions are rife for being swept along by the Zeitgeist into unintended eisegesis. Yes, hermeneutics are hard! But the task is not hopeless.

Having these dispositions and presuppositions is *not* bad. We just need to be aware of them. We need to be smarter than the jellyfish, in other words. We need to be aware of what historical and cultural trends are influencing our way of thinking, as well as our proclivities and motives for reading.[66] To think we can eliminate such influences is both naïve and undesirable.

It is naïve because it is simply not possible (as I hope our historical survey has shown).[67]

The goal is not to jettison prior knowledge and commitments, therefore, but to be aware of them and how they could influence our reading. Then, because we are aware of them, we can hold them lightly and reflect on how they could be shaping our interpretations in unbiblical ways. To think for a moment these influences are not real, or we could somehow suspend them, is the moment we

Figure 1.8. It is not possible (nor desirable) to read as a purely objective observer, as though your mind were a receptacle to be filled.

are controlled by them in ways we are not aware.[68] Then we become subject to "the tyranny of hidden presuppositions."[69] They control us in ways we do not know.

---

[66]As Calvin has famously said, "Nearly all the wisdom we possess, that is to say, true and sound wisdom, consists of two parts: the knowledge of God *and of ourselves*" (*The Institutes of the Christian Religion* 1.1.1, ed. John T. McNeill, trans. Ford Lewis Battles, 2 vols. [Philadelphia: Westminster, 1960], 1:35, emphasis added).

[67]Christopher Bryan, *Listening to the Bible: The Art of Faithful Biblical Interpretation* (Oxford: Oxford University Press, 2014), 11-22, 48-55.

[68]Bryan, *Listening*, 48-56.

[69]Hans-Georg Gadamer, *Truth and Method*, trans. rev. Joel Weinsheimer and Donald G. Marshall, 2nd rev. ed. (London/New York: Bloomsbury Academic, 2004), 244-64.

Equally, it is undesirable to wipe the slate of our minds clean before reading. Knowledge is nothing if it is not cumulative. We learn from those who have gone before us and build upon the convictions we ourselves already have. Thus, "certain aspects of our preliminary understanding need to be corrected while other aspects seem to be proving their value."[70]

This is called the *hermeneutical spiral.* It is a *spiral* because the desire is that, through an awareness of ourselves and good reading practices, the distance between *our* worldview and *the Bible's* worldview can be shortened. We start with our own presuppositions and preconceptions and bring them to the Bible. If we are cognizant of them and how they affect us, then we can also see how the Bible is challenging them. If we are teachable, then the Bible will also change them, sending a corrective influence back to our minds. I call this "presuppositional repair." Then the next time we read the Bible we come with newly modified presuppositions. And the Bible can fix those too.

Figure 1.9. The hermeneutical spiral is an experience of reading the Bible where our presuppositions are tested and refined a little more each time we read.

On and on goes the process throughout our Bible-reading lives as we increasingly put on the mind of Christ. As Grant Osborne states,

> A spiral is a better metaphor because it is not a closed circle but rather an
> open-ended movement from the horizon of the text to the horizon of the

---

[70]Thiselton, *Hermeneutics*, 13.

reader. I am not going round and round a closed circle that can never detect the true meaning but am spiraling nearer and nearer to the text's intended meaning as I refine my hypotheses and allow the text to continue to challenge and correct those alternative interpretations, then to guide my delineation of its significance for my situation today.[71]

The key, then, is to strengthen the streams of influence running in the right direction, *from* the Bible *to* our minds, so that as we return to the Scriptures again and again our worldview will be more aligned with the Bible's own worldview. Cognizant of ourselves, we can then allow the Bible to challenge us as we bring every thought captive to the obedience of Christ.

Conclusion

So, is it possible to see past the reflection in the water? This is not a question easily answered, nor will it soon go away. But if the Bible is the place where the risen Christ is seen, then it is imperative that we read in such a way that does not distort his image. Our approach to Scripture will greatly influence whether the text reveals Christ or serves as a mirror of ourselves. Lest we import elements of our contemporary Zeitgeist, big or small, we need an interpretive method that draws the meaning out of the text to evaluate and challenge the Zeitgeist and correct our worldviews.

Consider what we have seen in this historical survey. The foregoing philosophies *de jure* have influenced the interpretation of Scripture in every age. The philosophies created the presuppositions and motives for reading the Bible, and the Bible has often given back to readers what they were looking for.[72] In some instances, a hermeneutic was actually devised to accomplish exactly that, and in turn justify the underwriting philosophy. In other cases, it just happened accidentally. So is it even possible to read the Bible (or anything!) without a philosophical predisposition that colors, or even predetermines, what readers see? Maybe not.

---

[71]Grant R. Osborne, *The Hermeneutical Spiral: A Comprehensive Introduction to Biblical Interpretation*, rev. ed. (Downers Grove, IL: IVP Academic, 2006), 22.

[72]In Bray's words, it is common for modern scholars to "[bring] their own fairly well-defined agendas to the biblical text, seeking to read out of it the ideas which in fact they are importing into it" (*Biblical Interpretation*, 7).

The question then becomes, What are the right presuppositions, motives, and expectations? If we cannot read without such a priori categories, are there at least a priori categories we should have? Does the Bible itself call us to a certain posture as we read? Does it provide a framework that orients readers? In other words, is there a set of presuppositions and expectations for reading the Bible that the Bible itself establishes? If reading without presuppositions is impossible, can we at least have the right presuppositions? The next chapter will ask just that. What instructions does the Bible itself give us for reading? With that, we turn to the hermeneutics of Jesus and his apostles.

For Further Study

Bray, Gerald. *Biblical Interpretation: Past & Present*. Downers Grove, IL: InterVarsity Press, 1996.

George, Timothy. *Reading Scripture with the Reformers*. Downers Grove, IL: IVP Academic, 2011.

Hall, Christopher A. *Reading Scripture with the Church Fathers*. Downers Grove, IL: InterVarsity Press, 1998.

Sire, James W. *The Universe Next Door: A Basic Worldview Catalog*. 6th ed. Downers Grove, IL: IVP Academic, 2020. This book masterfully illustrates the progression— or as he puts it, digression—from one philosophical system to the next in the West since the late Middle Ages. A very helpful resource for understanding, "How did we get here?"

For Advanced Study

Goldsworthy, Graeme. *Gospel-Centered Hermeneutics: Foundations and Principles of Evangelical Biblical Interpretation*. Downers Grove, IL: IVP Academic, 2006. Goldsworthy also understands the history of biblical interpretation in terms of the role of presuppositions and the increasing influence of culturally reigning philosophies on hermeneutics.

Osborne, Grant R. *The Hermeneutical Spiral: A Comprehensive Introduction to Biblical Interpretation*. Rev. ed. Downers Grove, IL: IVP Academic, 2006. A bit of a modern classic, this is a very thorough introduction to hermeneutics. As the title indicates it takes on our presuppositions' roles in reading and application.

Provan, Iain. *The Reformation and the Right Reading of Scripture*. Waco, TX: Baylor University Press, 2017. Provan takes great pains to explain the long lead-up to the Reformation, and why Luther and Calvin should be our hermeneutics teachers today.

Vanhoozer, Kevin J. *Is There a Meaning in This Text?: The Bible, The Reader, and the Morality of Literary Knowledge*. Grand Rapids, MI: Zondervan, 1998. In light of contemporary philosophical skepticism of the accessibility of meaning (or its very existence), Vanhoozer provides something of a touchstone for evangelicals. A must-read for anyone who has ever felt the sort of hermeneutical nihilism described above.

Yarchin, William. *History of Biblical Interpretation: A Reader*. Grand Rapids, MI: Baker Academic, 2004. This is a concise collection of primary sources on hermeneutical issues throughout church history.

2

WHAT DID JESUS DO?

The Hermeneutics of Jesus and the Apostles

I N STUDYING ECOLOGY, I was always fascinated by the way some newborn animals are ready to survive on their own straightaway. Others, however, stay with their parents (or a single parent) for a significant period of time until they learn enough to head out on their own. It seems it is the species that have the longer life expectancies—mammals— that require this special parenting time. It is as though the longer the lifespan, the longer the training time is necessary for thriving. While the commitment on the part of the parent is very high, the payoff in the long run for the species results in higher levels of life-success.

Again, the natural world provides a helpful comparison for our study of hermeneutics. If you want to know how to study the Bible, what "parent" would you look to? And would looking to that parent result in more fruitful lifelong hermeneutical thriving? We should look, of course, to the inspired authors of Scripture. We should look to the way biblical authors themselves read and interpreted biblical texts written before them. Thus, to Jesus and the apostles (the New Testament authors) we look for guidance. We should learn from them how to handle the Bible, and, yes, it will result in a more fruitful approach for our own study and interpretive habits. As David Starling puts it so well:

> Interpretation of the Scriptures is like a craft or a trade that must be learned if we are to draw the right connections, make the right intuitive leaps, and bring to bear on the task the right dispositions, affections, and virtues. Among the various exemplars from which we might learn the habits and practices that are necessary for wise and faithful interpretation, Scripture itself is supreme and uniquely authoritative.[1]

Good discipleship seems to demand such a conclusion.

The question of the moment is, therefore, how did Jesus and the authors of the New Testament read and interpret the Old Testament? In this chapter I will argue three things: (1) Jesus and the apostles paid attention to literary, historical, and redemptive-historical contexts when interpreting and applying the OT; (2) Jesus and the apostles regularly saw typological patterns in the Old Testament that they understood to climax in the person and work of Christ; (3) We should learn our hermeneutic from Jesus and the apostles, equally giving careful attention to the literary, historical, and redemptive-historical contexts of any passage, as well as employing typological principles to the Bible as a whole. Followers of Jesus Christ should, well, follow Jesus Christ—in doctrine, ethics, values, and so on, *and in hermeneutics.* Jesus and his handpicked apostles who penned the New Testament under the inspiration of the Holy Spirit are now our parents from whom we will learn principles and skills for hermeneutical thriving. Let us spend some time with them.

Literary Contexts

To begin, it seems clear that when Jesus and the apostles read the Old Testament, they did not think in terms of isolated, individual verses.

---

[1]David I. Starling, *Hermeneutics as Apprenticeship: How the Bible Shapes Our Interpretive Habits and Practices* (Grand Rapids, MI: Baker Academic, 2016), 17.

Rather, they read entire contexts. While they may quote just one verse at a time, they are actually indexing the larger context of the Old Testament passage from which the single verse comes.[2] That is, they did not treat the Old Testament as a collection of pithy one-liners, but as *whole texts* with theological implications larger than just a single verse. Let us see this in several examples.

First, in Matthew 4:1-11 we read of Jesus' famous "wilderness temptation." It is commonly recognized that when Jesus is thrice tempted by the devil, each time he responds with a quotation of Scripture (vv. 4, 7, and 10). But it is equally instructive to observe that all of these scriptural quotations come from *contexts in Deuteronomy* (8:3, 6:16, and 6:13 respectively). Thus, Jesus stays in the same literary neighborhood.

Table 2.1. Jesus demonstrates a literary contextual awareness when he returns to the same passage in quick succession.

Recurring Contextual Use of Deuteronomy 6–8 in Matthew 4			
Matt 4:4	But [Jesus] answered, "It is written, 'Man shall not live by bread alone, but by every word that comes from the mouth of God.'"	Deut 8:3	And he humbled you and let you hunger and fed you with manna, which you did not know, nor did your fathers know, that he might make you know that man does not live by bread alone, but man lives by every word that comes from the mouth of the LORD.
Matt 4:7	Jesus said to him, "Again it is written, 'You shall not put the Lord your God to the test.'"	Deut 6:16	You shall not put the LORD your God to the test, as you tested him at Massah.
Matt 4:10	Then Jesus said to him, "Be gone, Satan! For it is written, 'You shall worship the Lord your God and him only shall you serve.'"	Deut 6:13	It is the LORD your God you shall fear. Him you shall serve and by his name you shall swear.

Jesus' Old Testament quotes even come from a specific context in Deuteronomy where Moses is explaining to Israel how they should have responded when they were tempted. In short, Jesus is not just grabbing any ol' lines from the Old Testament that will suit his purposes in generic

---

[2]C. H. Dodd's *According to the Scriptures: The Sub-Structure of New Testament Theology* (London: Nisbet & Co., 1952), esp. chaps. 2–3, is the most famous work on this point, but many more such studies have been produced, particularly over the last three decades.

ways. Rather, he goes to the *one whole context* that most pertains to his situation and draws meaning *from that entire context* even though he only utters three sentences of it.

Matthew also returns to the narrative and theology of Isaiah 7–9 at the beginning and end of his prologue in 1:23 and 4:15-16. This suggests that Matthew thought in terms of the theology of the entirety of Isaiah 7–9 (or more). In Matthew 19:4-5, the evangelist quotes Genesis 1:27 and 2:24. Direct quotes and allusions to Zechariah 9–14 are all over Jesus' last week (Mt 21–27).[3] Several verses of Psalm 22 are throughout the crucifixion and resurrection narratives (Mt 27–28).[4] That Jesus and Matthew use multiple verses from the same contexts is highly suggestive that they had those larger literary passages in view beyond just isolated verses.

While we do not *always* see such clusters of Old Testament texts together in the New Testament, we do see enough to suggest concern for literary context even when this sort of grouping is lacking. One way is to see how an entire Old Testament context *coheres* with the New Testament context in which a verse appears. The Gospel of Mark has a nice example. In the first three verses Mark quotes Exodus 23:20, Isaiah 40:3 and Malachi 3:1. Here, then, is a string of Old Testament texts that *do not* come from the same literary context. Yet, each of these verses has in its own context issues of (1) the exodus event, (2) atonement, and (3) the temple. It is clear that Mark has these contextual themes in mind by the way he employs (1) exodus imagery throughout his book (e.g., 6:30-44 among others), (2) highlights Jesus' mission of atonement (10:45 is commonly called Mark's theme verse), and (3) the whole narrative climaxes in and around the temple (chaps. 11–16).[5] Clearly Mark has drawn from the entire context of these verses, not simply plucked them out and mashed them together for whatever other reason.

---

[3]H. Daniel Zacharias shows this well in *Matthew's Presentation of the Son of David*, TTCBS (London: Bloomsbury, 2017), 104-51.

[4]Zacharias, *Matthew's Presentation*, 171-86.

[5]Rikki E. Watts, *Isaiah's New Exodus in Mark*, BSL (Grand Rapids, MI: Baker Academic, 2000; repr. from WUNT 2/88; Tübingen: Mohr Siebeck, 1997); Nicholas G. Piotrowski, "'Whatever You Ask' for the Missionary Purposes of the Eschatological Temple: Quotation and Typology in Mark 11–12," *SBJT* 21 (2017): 97-121.

The Gospel of Luke and its follow-up volume, Acts, also show this tendency. Old Testament quotations pervade, yet key turning points consistently invoke verses from the same larger context: Isaiah 40–66.[6] Such strategic placement of material from the same Old Testament context makes the sum of Luke and Acts read like a fulfillment of *all* of Isaiah 40–66.

John has a very clever way of revealing this. His first sentence starts, "In the beginning." The reader cannot help but think of Genesis 1:1. Well it seems John has the entire creation story in mind throughout the Gospel. Issues of light and darkness, true "life," Jesus as the new "man," the work of the Spirit, and so forth dot the narrative.[7] The same is true with the use of Psalm 69 (2:17; 15:25; 19:28-29).

Paul demonstrates this tendency too. Again, just a couple examples will have to suffice. In Galatians 2:16 Paul states that justification is by faith in the gospel and not by works of the law. To prove this in 3:6, Paul reaches for Abraham as an example and quotes Genesis 15:6. Then in 3:8 he says that Abraham had this gospel preached to him in Genesis 12:3. Finally he cites Genesis 12:7 in Galatians 3:16.

Table 2.2. Paul demonstrates a literary contextual awareness when he returns to the same passage in quick succession.

Recurring Contextual Use of Genesis 12–15 in Galatians 3			
Gal 3:6	Abraham "believed God, and it was counted to him as righteousness."	Gen 15:6	And he believed the Lord, and he counted it to him as righteousness.
Gal 3:8	And the Scripture…preached the gospel beforehand to Abraham, saying, "In you shall all the nations be blessed."	Gen 12:3	I will bless those who bless you, and him who dishonors you I will curse, and in you all the families of the earth shall be blessed.
Gal 3:16	Now the promises were made to Abraham and to his offspring. It does not say, "And to offsprings," referring to many, but referring to one, "And to your offspring," who is Christ.	Gen 12:7	To your offspring I will give this land.

---

[6]David W. Pao, *Acts and the Isaianic New Exodus*, BSL (Grand Rapids, MI: Baker Academic, 2002; repr. from WUNT 2/130; Tübingen: Mohr Siebeck, 2000).
[7]Jeannine K. Brown, "Creation's Renewal in the Gospel of John," *CBQ* 72.2 (2010): 275-90.

Thus, Paul sees the entire episode from Genesis 12 (the time God gave the gospel to Abraham) through Genesis 15 (the time when Abraham believed) to serve the larger point he is making in Galatians. He also traverses back and forth through Genesis 15–17 in Romans 4. In Romans 11:3-4 he cites different parts of 1 Kings 19 three times. He did not just grab isolated verses that seem to work for him; he indexed whole contexts to make his arguments.

The author of Hebrews does this as well. Notice how many lines from Psalm 95 are quoted in Hebrews 3:7-11. And many terms and images from all over Exodus 25–26 are invoked in Hebrews 9:2-5. Peter quotes or alludes to no less than six different verses from Isaiah 53 in 1 Peter 2:22-25. James also links parts of Abraham's story over a large context (Gen 15:6 and 22:9 in Jas 2:21-23). And of course, it is well-known the way Revelation employs all kinds of material from across Exodus, Ezekiel, and Daniel.

To be clear, I believe Jesus and the apostles are doing a lot of interesting things with Old Testament contexts, many of which we will explore in chapter six. But we can at least conclude at this point that they did not pluck verses or ideas out of their literary contexts or misappropriate verses in noncontextual ways.[8] Rather, they read whole contexts. They found ideas and theological concepts that flow through several verses, major contexts, and sometimes even entire books. It is rare to find an Old Testament quote or allusion that has nothing to do with its original textual home.

Let us return to that temptation narrative in Matthew again. I say above that Jesus not only draws quotes from the same Old Testament

---

[8]Of course, there is debate about this. Richard N. Longenecker's *Biblical Exegesis in the Apostolic Period*, 2nd ed. (Grand Rapids, MI: Eerdmans, 1999) argues that the apostles did not give weight to the contextual meaning of Old Testament quotations, nor did they have a particularly distinct hermeneutic vis-à-vis other Jewish groups of their day. But Longenecker seems to be pressing the New Testament authors into the mold of what others did, rather than letting them speak for themselves. He does not leave space for them to be unique in any way. But Jesus himself was unique in every way, as was his life, death, and resurrection in the eyes of his followers. Longenecker is at least right that Jesus and the apostles did *not* use allegory. For more on the debate, see G. K. Beale, ed., *The Right Doctrine from the Wrong Text?: Essays on the Use of the Old Testament in the New* (Grand Rapids, MI: Baker, 1994).

contexts, but that the theology of that Old Testament context coheres with the context of Matthew, making a powerful point. But Jesus is not the only one to quote Scripture. The devil does it too in Matthew 4:6—he quotes Psalm 91:11-12. The great irony here is that the very next verse, Psalm 91:13, employs imagery of Satan's defeat![9] (More on this in chapter five.) Thus, the devil has picked a couple verses that seem to suit his purposes, but in so doing he has ignored their original literary context to the end of twisting their meaning. By attending to the literary context Jesus, on the other hand, provides a legitimate and ethical interpretation and application.

Finally, it seems that not only did New Testament authors draw from larger Old Testament contexts, but also expected readers to pay attention to the contexts *they have now written*. Staying with Jesus' temptation in Matthew (4:1-11), we have already considered how right before the episode Jesus goes through the waters of baptism and is declared God's "Son" (Mt 3:16-17). Additionally, right afterwards Jesus goes up onto a mountain to teach about the law (Mt 5:17-48). Where else is someone called God's "Son" before they go through water into the desert to be tempted, finally arriving at a mountain to hear God's law? Again, the answer is Israel. In Exodus 4:22 Israel is called God's "son," in Exodus 14–15 they pass through the Red Sea, in Exodus 16–17 they are tempted, and in Exodus 19–20 they arrive at Mount Sinai to receive the Ten Commandments. Clearly Matthew wants readers to make these connections. But to do so we cannot isolate the baptism narrative in Matthew 3 from the temptation narrative in Matthew 4, or from the Sermon on the Mount beginning in Matthew 5. They need to be taken together. Context must be considered.

The Bible is sometimes treated like a collection of pithy one-liners, memorized and applied without regard to the literary context of any verse. But Jesus and his apostles demonstrate that they did pay attention to contexts when we see them returning to the same context time and

---

[9]David B. Sloan, "Interpreting Scripture with Satan? The Devil's Use of Scripture in Luke's Temptation Narrative," *TynBul* 66 (2015): 231-50.

again, and the thematic coherence between an Old Testament verse's original literary home and its New Testament appropriation.

Historical Contexts

Next, it is important to observe how Jesus and the apostles also appreciated the historical rootedness of the Old Testament.

It is clear that Jesus believed Elijah was a real historical person and the events of his day are important to observe (Lk 4:25-27). The Queen of Sheba truly came to Solomon and that carries major theological freight (Lk 11:31). Jonah really went to Nineveh and that tells us something (Lk 11:32). Abraham, Isaac, and Jacob were real people (Lk 13:28). Noah survived an actual flood, whereas others in his day did not (Lk 17:26-27). Lot's misadventures in the city of Sodom were historical (Lk 17:28-29). It is, in fact, the historicity of these stories that gives power to the point Jesus is making when he invokes them. A good example of this is when Jesus compares his resurrection to Jonah's three days in the "belly of the great fish" (Mt 12:40). If Jesus thought Jonah's experience was ahistorical, then the power of the comparison to his resurrection is lost.

Of course, Stephen (Acts 7), Paul (Rom 4; 9; 1 Cor 10; Gal 3), the author of Hebrews (Heb 4; 11), James (Jas 2), Peter (1 Pet 3; 2 Pet 2), John (1 Jn 3) and Jude (Jude 5, 11, 14) all agree with Jesus on this. Salvation is real because it happens *in history*, thus it is no small observation that Jesus and the New Testament authors "presupposed the reality of history and the reality of the past given in the Old Testament."[10]

This carries over, of course, to the New Testament where Jesus' life (Mt–Jn)—including his miracles and resurrection—as well as the beginnings of the church (Acts) are presented as historical realities that matter for the very reason that they are historical. Then, all the letters of the New Testament are clearly written in response to these recent historical events. Moreover, it does not seem as though Paul just sat down to write letters to churches because he was feeling nostalgic and missed them. Rather, there

---

[10]Vern S. Poythress, *Reading the Word of God in the Presence of God: A Handbook for Biblical Interpretation* (Wheaton, IL: Crossway, 2016), 331.

was something happening in the world to which he felt the need to respond. Thus, all the New Testament books are also firmly rooted in history, and presuppose the necessity of historical mindedness.

Redemptive-Historical Contexts

Yet all these historical details are not just brute facts, and the literary cohesion of larger contexts is not just artistry. Rather, Jesus and the apostles also believed that history and the literary record of it have reached their climax in the coming of Christ. The historical narrative of the Old Testament as a whole and the very details therein are all preliminary for the coming of Christ. Throughout the Old Testament God has been setting the stage of history for Jesus to meaningfully step onto it. As Iain Provan puts it, Jesus and his apostles "pay attention to the apparent communicative intention of Scripture as a collection of texts from the past, taking full account of the nature of the language in which these intentions are embedded and revealed as components of Scripture's unfolding covenantal Story."[11]

It is simply impossible to exhaust the examples that demonstrate this. Look briefly at Matthew 12. There Jesus says he is greater than the temple (12:6), greater than Jonah (12:41), and greater than Solomon (12:42). None of this makes sense unless we know something about the Old Testament theology of the temple, Jonah, and Solomon. Moreover, it also tells us that truths about the Old Testament temple, Jonah, and Solomon pertain to Jesus *in a greater way*. It is as though God gave Israel a temple system, prophets, and kings so that when Jesus came into the world and said things like "something greater than . . . is here," we would see his life and ministry full of the meaning of those things. That is, the Old Testament provides a symbolic ecosystem into which Jesus can step and his words and actions be filled with interpretive power.[12]

---

[11]Iain Provan, *The Reformation and the Right Reading of Scripture* (Waco, TX: Baylor University Press, 2017), 107, 129, 150. He goes on, "They do not read it 'spiritually,' if that term is meant to distinguish a certain kind of reading as nonliteral. They certainly do not read it allegorically" (*Reformation*, 107).

[12]See e.g., Starling, *Hermeneutics as Apprenticeship*, 105-28.

The New Testament is saturated with Old Testament people, institutions, and events now consolidating and revolving around Jesus—too many to fit in an introductory book like this. But consider Jesus' wilderness temptation in Matthew and its contexts one more time. Above we observed how it mirrors Israel's experience coming out of Egypt. Matthew is clearly inviting the comparison: what was expected of Israel—God's "son"—is now realized in this new "Son of God." The mission of Israel in the Old Testament is now reaching its climax and coming into an era of fulfillment.[13] In fact, Matthew *loves* the word "fulfillment." It is all over his Gospel.

Yet, compare that to the temptation narrative in Luke 4:1-13. Notice in Luke that the order of the second and third temptations is reversed! Jesus is first tempted with food (Lk 4:3), just as in Matthew. But in the second temptation in Luke the devil shows Jesus the kingdoms of the world and calls Jesus to worship him (Lk 4:5-7), whereas in Matthew that is the last temptation. In Luke, the last temptation is to "test" the Lord (4:9-12) when the devil himself (mis)quotes the Scriptures, whereas in Matthew that is the second temptation. Why has Luke inverted the last two? The inversion really disturbs the Israel-Jesus comparison I just mentioned. Well, there is also a change in the *literary* context. In Matthew, Jesus is baptized right before his temptation. I said that furthers the Israel-Jesus comparison. But in Luke, Jesus is not baptized right before the temptation. Instead, immediately prior to the temptation in Luke is a genealogy (Lk 3:23-38). Again, literary context is indispensable for us. If we look at that genealogy we notice something interesting: it goes all the way back to Adam. Could it be that whereas Matthew tells the temptation story to invite theological comparison between Israel and Jesus, Luke tells the same story—with a slightly different nuance and different contextual surroundings —to invite a comparison with Adam? It is also interesting that Genesis 3:6 says, "When the woman saw that the tree was good for *food*, and that it was a delight to the *eyes*, and that the tree was

---

[13]Joel Kennedy, *The Recapitulation of Israel: Use of Israel's History in Matthew 1:1–4:11*, WUNT 2/257 (Tübingen: Mohr Siebeck, 2008).

to be desired to make one *wise*, she took of its fruit and ate." When we compare that to Luke's temptation narrative we see how his unique order reinforces the comparison to this first temptation in the garden. The first temptation of humanity comes in the form of (1) food, then (2) an appeal to the eyes, and finally (3) the desire for wisdom. By inverting the order of the temptation in Luke 4 this is drawn out: Jesus is tempted in Luke first with (1) *food*, then (2) *shown* the kingdoms of the world, and finally (3) the devil tries to appeal to Scripture, the source of *wisdom*. Israel had a certain mission that Jesus is now fulfilling; so says Matthew. And Adam also had a particular mission from God that Jesus is now fulfilling; so says Luke.[14] Thus, Matthew and Luke can tell the same story, yet their subtle literary differences evince their eye toward redemptive-historical contexts as they interface with different parts of the canon.

Luke 24: "He interpreted to them in all the Scriptures the things concerning himself." In addition to examples like these, New Testament authors also make *explicit* statements demonstrating their understanding that Jesus fulfills the Old Testament in its entirety. More than that, they claim the Old Testament cannot be understood without the retrospective interpretive light that the life and ministry of Jesus cast over the Old Testament. Jesus—and particularly his cross and resurrection—provide the hermeneutical key for the Old Testament. In the following passages we will see, therefore, that Jesus does not only fulfill individual Old Testament prophecies and expectations sprinkled here and there throughout the Old Testament, but he fulfills the Old Testament *as a whole*.

We will start with Luke 24. After Jesus' resurrection he appears to two of his followers on the road to Emmaus, though they do not recognize him. They explain to him that their hopes have been dashed because Jesus had been crucified (24:20-21), but also that there is amazement in the air because some claim to have seen him alive (24:22-23). Jesus responds in verses 25-26, "O foolish ones, and slow of heart to believe all that the

---

[14]Sloan ("Interpreting," 247-48) illustrates this further in the way Psalm 91 is used again in Luke 10:19 in transferring Jesus' authority to his disciples for "a reversal of the ascent of Satan that originated with Genesis 3."

prophets have spoken! Was it not necessary that the Christ should suffer these things and enter into his glory?" Jesus says, basically, "You should not lose hope nor doubt what you heard of the resurrection, for this is *all that the prophets have spoken.* The seers and prophets of Israel *all* spoke of the Messiah's coming suffering and glory. And because they spoke thus, the cross and resurrection were 'necessary.'" Had they read what we call the Old Testament well, they would see this was always God's plan. As Richard Hays comments, "The disciples on the way to Emmaus had already heard it reported that Jesus was alive, but *because they did not know how to locate this report within Israel's story*, it seemed a curious and meaningless claim."[15] Verse 27 goes on to say, "And beginning with Moses and all the Prophets, he interpreted to them in all the Scriptures the things concerning himself." Thus, in Jesus' mind *all* the Scriptures have to do with him.[16] Jesus understood that every author of the Old Testament wrote with a slant toward his ministry, and that this is demonstrable from the pages of the Old Testament itself. This is no retrospective reinterpretation of the Old Testament, therefore, but the Old Testament itself from beginning to end is climbing to the coming of Christ.

Luke 24:44-47 takes this a step further. Not only the cross and resurrection, but now "repentance for the forgiveness of sins should be proclaimed in his name to all nations." So the effects of that cross and resurrection—the creation of an international worshiping and witnessing community (which we call the universal church)—were also foreseen in the Old Testament. To that Jesus says in verse 46, "Thus it is written." But where was that written? The answer is, in no one location. Again, the sweep of the Old Testament as a whole, all the prophets taken together, testify to Jesus' sufferings, resurrection on the third day, and the creation and mission of the church.

---

[15]Richard B. Hays, *Reading Backwards: Figural Christology and the Fourfold Gospel Witness* (Waco, TX: Baylor University Press, 2014), 16; emphasis original.

[16]By "Moses" and "the Prophets" Luke means all the Old Testament Scriptures. "Moses" is another term for what we call the Pentateuch, the first five books of the Old Testament, and "the Prophets" are the rest of the Old Testament. Some in the first century spoke of a three-part division to these Jewish Scriptures, which Jesus also references in Luke 24:44, again seeing them all about him: "everything written about me in the Law of Moses and the Prophets and the Psalms must be fulfilled."

To be sure, the phrase "in all the Scriptures" in Luke 24:27 could be taken to mean not that all the Old Testament is about Jesus, but that many *passages* of the Old Testament are about Jesus, and these happened to be found "in all the parts" of the Scriptures. And "everything written about [Jesus]" in Luke 24:44 does not have to mean that everything written *is* about Jesus, but that Jesus found the various things about him and explained those limited number of passages to the disciples.

I would make two points against this reading, however. First, despite the various interpretive options for verses 27 and 44, the emphasis in Luke 24:25 is clear: that the issues of Jesus' cross and resurrection are what is to be believed from "*all that the prophets have spoken.*" Thus, the sum total of "all the prophets" is his cross and resurrection. Yes, the words of Luke 24:27 and 24:44, "in all the Scriptures," *can* be taken in varying directions. But Luke 24:25 reins them back in and gives us precision: the phrase "all that the prophets have spoken" summarizes all their content. If we could ask, "Is there a *cumulative* emphasis to the Old Testament?" Jesus answers, "Yes, my sufferings and then glorification—my cross and resurrection—is the sum total of 'all that the prophets have spoken.'" Thus, Jesus understood and taught his disciples that "the things concerning himself" are the subject matter "*in all the Scriptures*" (24:27).[17]

While there are passages and whole contexts from the Old Testament that each—in and of themselves—pertain directly to the coming Christ, it is equally important to recognize the Old Testament in toto does as well. When the verses, passages, and books are taken as a *collective whole*, the Old Testament as a complete work creates a singular mosaic of the coming Messiah.

Sometimes we can see those individual passages and contexts pointing to Christ, sometimes we have to zoom out to appreciate the collection of Old Testament details working together for the larger interpretation. More on this in chapter six.

---

[17]As Sloan aptly puts it, "In Luke's Gospel Jesus is both the greatest interpreter of Scripture and the greatest topic of Scripture" ("Interpreting," 231).

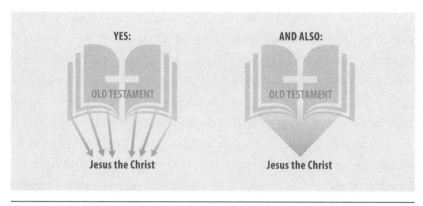

Figure 2.1. Individual verses in the OT point to Christ, as does the OT in its entirety.

Nearly every New Testament author: "Believing everything laid down by the Law and written in the Prophets." My second argument against that reading is the weight of other New Testament passages that explicitly state that the Old Testament is all about the coming Messiah— more to the point, that the Old Testament is not properly understood without an eye to the coming Messiah. Here are some examples from the preaching of Peter and Paul, followed by passages from nearly every New Testament author where this claim is made.

In Acts 3:18 Peter says that "what God foretold by the mouth of all the prophets, that his Christ would suffer, he thus fulfilled." Again, "all the prophets" speak of Christ. Peter goes on to say that "all the prophets who have spoken . . . also proclaimed these days" (3:24). What "days"? The context shows that Peter is talking about the days of Jesus' death (vv. 15, 18) and resurrection (vv. 15, 26). He even calls his audience "sons of the prophets and of the covenant" insofar as they are now participating in the movement of the gospel to all nations (vv. 25-26). Thus the events of Peter's day, kicking off the international mission of the church immediately following the death and resurrection of the Messiah, mark the fulfillment of "all the prophets."[18] Similarly, in Acts 10:43 Peter says, "To

---

[18]Right in the middle of this context, Acts 3:21 suggests that "establishing all that God spoke by the mouth of his holy prophets" (RSV) still awaits a future realization. I would argue, all the same, that that future realization has already begun in the international preaching of the gospel and *is the entire point* of Acts. So while the full realization of that is the constant mission of the

[Jesus] all the prophets bear witness." Again, he says this right after preaching Jesus' death and resurrection on the third day.

Paul demonstrates this point in Acts as well. He says in 13:27 that Jesus was not recognized *because* the Scriptures were not understood. Paul then goes on to say that Jesus' death and resurrection comprise the fulfillment of "what God promised to the fathers" (vv. 32-33). When Paul is on trial in Acts 24, he claims that he belongs to "the Way" (a term for Christians early on) which means "believing everything laid down by the Law and written in the Prophets" (v. 14). Finally, on trial again, Paul says in Acts 26 that in preaching Christ's cross and resurrection to Gentiles he is "saying nothing but what the prophets and Moses said would come to pass" (vv. 22-23).

This theme pervades Paul's letters as well. In Galatians 3:6-9, 16, 29 Paul says the promises made to Abraham were delivered in Christ and in those who believe in him. Verses 23-24 even connects the Old Testament law with a fulfillment beyond itself: justification through faith in Christ.[19] In 1 Corinthians 15:1-4 he says Christ's death and resurrection on the third day were both "in accordance with the Scriptures."[20] Second Corinthians 1:20 tells us "all the promises of God find their Yes in [Jesus]." In 2 Corinthians 3:14, to read the Old Testament *apart* from Christ is like having a veil over one's eyes. "But when one turns to the Lord [Jesus] the veil is removed" (v. 16). This theme comes up at key moments in Romans as well. In 1:2 Paul tells us that the gospel was "promised beforehand through the prophets in the holy Scriptures." The particular Scriptures Paul has in mind seems to be legion insofar as the rest of Romans quotes

---

church, the palpable excitement across the book of Acts is that that mission has now (finally) begun because the Spirit is now given *after Jesus' cross and resurrection*. See Dennis E. Johnson, *The Message of Acts in the History of Redemption* (Phillipsburg, NJ: P&R, 1997).

[19]Galatians 3:23-24 are notoriously difficult verses. I do not pretend to have explained them here, but I simply observe that all of Galatians 3 is about understanding the Old Testament in light of Christ—and vice versa—and the law is another element of the Old Testament that finds a telos in Christ.

[20]Again, just as we saw in Luke 24:46 there is no one verse that says that. This "in accordance with the Scriptures" must mean a sweeping theme of the Old Testament. A superb article on this is Stephen G. Dempster, "From Slight Peg to Cornerstone to Capstone: The Resurrection of Christ on 'The Third Day' According to the Scriptures," *WTJ* 76 (2014): 371-409.

or alludes to no less than twenty-four books of the Old Testament. In 3:21 we read that "the Law and the Prophets bear witness to" justification by faith alone in particular, and that God's own righteousness is only now proven "at the present time" with Christ's atoning work (vv. 25-26). And in 16:25-27 we read that the gospel was a "mystery that was kept secret for long ages" but now "disclosed" through his preaching "and through the prophetic writings" available at last "to all nations." It seems that to Paul, the public international proclamation of the gospel works together with the Old Testament to fulfill God's plan for the ages. The very fact that Paul was preaching Christ among the Gentiles at all indicated that the Old Testament is being fulfilled in that moment. Also in Romans 15:4, Paul says "whatever was written in former days was written for our instruction" right after applying a psalm to Jesus (v. 3).[21] Finally, in 2 Timothy 3:15 Paul tells his disciple that the Old Testament Scriptures "are able to make you wise for salvation through faith in Christ Jesus." Again, note that it is things about *Christ Jesus* that are to be believed from reading the Old Testament.

Hebrews demonstrates this when it compares the various and sundry ways God has revealed himself in the Old Testament (1:1) to the superior way *by his Son* "in these last days" (1:2). The rest of the book reads as though God was busy throughout the Old Testament (especially in the covenants, priests, and sacrifices) to prepare the world with types and shadows of what Jesus would someday be in a fuller and permanent way.

First Peter has one of the clearest statements on this. In 1 Peter 1:10-12 we are told that the prophets—led by the Spirit—were "predicting the sufferings of Christ and his subsequent glory" (i.e., the cross and resurrection, v. 11). They did not know the timing of the coming of the Messiah, nor any of the specific details that we now know with the New Testament (vv. 10-11), but they at least knew "they were serving not themselves" but those of us who would later see the salvation revealed in Christ (v. 12).

---

[21]What is particularly interesting in Romans 15:3-4 is that Paul is making a moral application to the church in the wider context, and even then he runs his application through Christ. That is, he does not just quote the Old Testament as moral instruction, but as moral instruction *understood through Christ*. More on this in chap. 8.

Interestingly, Peter says the prophets even knew they were paving the way for their writings to come into focus only once the Messiah arrived (see e.g., Deut 18:15; 30:6; Is 6:9; 29:18; Jer 30:2-3; Dan 12:4, 9-10).[22]

Finally, we come to John where we encounter again the words of Jesus himself. He says in John 5:39, "The Scriptures . . . bear witness about me." It seems Jesus' first disciples understood this somewhat right away. In John 1:45 Philip calls Jesus "him of whom Moses in the Law and also the prophets wrote."[23] And later Jesus also says, "[Moses] wrote of me" (5:46).

It is not hard to show how the New Testament is all about Jesus, but it turns out that the Old Testament is about Jesus too. *How* the Old Testament, whether in any given detail or in its entirety, points to Christ is more difficult to see at some times than others. We will have to give that a lot of attention in chapters five, six, and seven. For now, it is enough to see that nearly all the New Testament authors claim in one way or another that the Old Testament as a collective whole testifies to the coming of Christ. Some even say that the Old Testament is not understood properly until that forward-leaning toward Christ is grasped—and specifically the details of his cross and resurrection, and subsequent international preaching of the gospel.

Typology Is Biblical (Allegory Is Not)

Taking these points together—Jesus and the apostles' attention to literary, historical, and redemptive-historical contexts—it is clear that the New Testament authors thought typologically. Not only did they see the climax of revelation in Christ, but also particular recurring patterns in the Old Testament (namely people, events, and institutions) were models of Christ and his work. In fact, we even get the term from Paul's comment in Romans 5:14. There Adam is called "a type [Greek, *typos*] of the one who was to come [namely Christ]." And in 1 Corinthians 10:6 Paul tells

---

[22]Jason S. DeRouchie, *How to Understand and Apply the Old Testament: Twelve Steps from Exegesis to Theology* (Phillipsburg, NJ: P&R, 2017), 416-22.

[23]This can still make sense in light of the confusion in Luke 24. Here Philip is aware that Moses and the prophets speak of *some kind* of coming figure.

us that Israel's experiences in the wilderness are types for the church to learn and apply.[24]

We will have a lot more to say about typology in chapters five and six, but we can take this opportunity to nuance our definition. In the previous chapter I called it a practice that perceives the way people, events, and institutions in the Old Testament prefigure the person and work of Christ. We can add to this that typological readings work with literary and historical contexts. That is, no one of these contextual concerns can do without the other; they work together. And so typology arises out of careful consideration of literary and historical patterns. They are literary because (1) their images and themes correspond across Scripture, and (2) because elements of the type and their resonance with Christ are found *in* the literary details of texts.[25] They are not imported from the reader's imagination or the reigning Zeitgeist. They are historical because (1) the types actually existed in space and time, and (2) their interpretations are still influenced by cultural contexts of the Old Testament. They are not fables nor are they limited in their value to their correspondences with Christ. Thus, the first two contexts (literature and history) *create and ground* the third (christology) and give guidance to the right practice of typology.[26] Typology is not about just commenting on Christ, because any interpretive practice can do that, but about getting to Christ ethically and legitimately—and that will have to be in concert with all contextual matters, not one context bullying over the others.

We can say, therefore, that the Bible itself is typological history. And this is different from allegory. Typology arises out of texts and concerns

---

[24]Many translations render the word *typoi* in 1 Cor 10:6 as "examples," but I think that misses Paul's theological rationale. Israel's life was not just a test case in what not to do, but an actual pattern of theological truths that now apply to the church through Christ. While the word *tupos* can be translated as "example" (as in Phil 3:17 or 1 Thess 1:7), in this context it is far more than just an example. Redemptive-historically speaking (as Paul does in 1 Cor 10) types are more like *patterns* in God's actions. Thus *tupos* in Heb 8:5 is sometimes rendered as "pattern" and that is good. Translations of Rom 5:14 are often just "type." First Peter 3:21 uses the term *antitupos*, from which we get the word "antitype." More on all this in chaps. 5 and 6.

[25]Frances Young, "Typology," in *Crossing the Boundaries: Essays in Biblical Interpretation in Honour of Michael D. Goulder*, eds. Stanley E. Porter, Paul Joyce and David E. Orton, BIS 8 (Leiden: Brill, 1994), 34-45.

[26]In this way, both Young and Daniélou are correct in what they affirm, but Young is too narrow in what he denies.

itself with the issues the text itself foregrounds, looking for recurring patterns across the Scriptures, and can be articulated and defended by the text itself. Allegory connects to derivative ideas outside the text. Moreover, the Bible was not written *as* an allegory. Thus it is a *violation of genre*. What kind of misinterpretation would one produce if they read a history book like a novel, or vice versa? Or a horoscope like a weather report? Or a play like a transcript? The *Oxford Encyclopedia of Biblical Interpretation* says, "As for the Bible itself—in a way reminiscent of Homeric epic—allegory does not seem to be its first intention."[27] In the case of Gal 4:21-31, it is "unlikely that [Paul] was giving his readers such a model to follow," but using "a rhetorical device, not a theological hermeneutic."[28] Although he uses the word "allegory" in 4:24 it is clear that he does not mean by it what we have seen through church history. Likewise, parables are not allegories.[29] All one needs for interpreting parables is, again, in the literary, historical, and redemptive-historical contexts, not in mystical discoveries between the lines. The same is true of apocalyptic, prophetic, and poetic imagery; they are not allegory either. Yes, they use metaphors but that is not enough to classify them as allegory. They are instead distinct genres themselves with their own indicators in the text for their interpretation. Allegory, however, *reorganizes* a genre with ideas from outside the text. We will consider this in more depth in chapter seven.

The theological upshot of all of this is that typology depends on the conviction that God is sovereign over historical events and the inspiration of Scripture. God has orchestrated redemptive history so that its final shape is christological, and so led biblical writers to record said history in ways that connect people, events, and institutions backward and forward across the canon. "This figurative sense of Scripture is grounded in the structural unity of God's design: the same divine characteristics are revealed in successive strata of history."[30]

---

[27]Elliott, "Allegory and Allegorical Interpretation," 1:18.

[28]Elliott, "Allegory and Allegorical Interpretation," 1:19.

[29]"Parables serve to reconfigure our view of reality, whereas allegories simply reaffirm a standard view" (Elliott, "Allegory and Allegorical Interpretation," 1:19).

[30]Jean Daniélou, *The Lord of History: Reflections on the Inner Meaning of History*, trans. Nigel Abercrombie (London: Longmans, 1958), 140.

Thus, repeated patterns in the Bible are not coincidental or axiomatic, but divinely intentional.[31]

With that, a summative definition is in order. We can call typology *a hermeneutical conviction that God has sovereignly organized history and revelation such that Old Testament people, events, and institutions prefigure the person and work of Christ in concert with literary genre and history.*

Learning from Our Parents

In sum, I am arguing that Jesus and the apostles read in terms of big literary contexts, in a historically minded way, understanding that redemptive history builds to reach its crescendo in the person and work of Jesus Christ, *and that we should read the same way.* Few would disagree with the first two points, what I am calling literary context and historical context. But am I guilty of what I called in the previous chapter, "a hermeneutical spiral running too strongly in the wrong direction?" Am I allowing predispositions, presuppositions, biases, goals, and expectations to heavily influence my reading? Am I finding Christ in the Scriptures because I'm *trying* to find Christ in the Scriptures? Yes. Yes I am. The presupposition that all the Scriptures are about Christ *is* driving my hermeneutic. The question, you will remember, is not "Do presuppositions influence our reading?" but *"Which* presuppositions are the right ones to influence our reading?" Do our presuppositions violate the text of Scripture, or are our presuppositions the same as Scripture's presuppositions? Is there a set of presuppositions that the Bible is asking us to have and use, an angle at which the Bible wants us to approach it? Are there goals the Bible wants us to have as we open it? If so, the Bible itself will have to tell us. And it tells us to read everything in context: literary context, historical context, and christological context—for the person and work of Christ are the logic that binds and unites all of the great variety across redemptive history into a coherent whole. It is what holds the Bible together. Christ "is himself the grand theme of the 'story-line'

---

[31]Note Romans 5:14 again. Adam did not become a type once Jesus came along; he already was one.

of both Testaments, the focal-point giving coherence to the total 'picture' in all its complexities."[32]

But this is not a vicious circle. Although we have to come with initial presuppositions, awareness of them can help us alter them as the Bible guides us. Then, little by little, we can adopt appropriate presuppositions that do not frustrate our reading—fighting against the Bible's presuppositions—but actually *help* us read the Bible as the Bible reads the Bible. We can let the Bible have its way with us not just in doctrine and ethics but also in our hermeneutic.[33]

Sometimes it is argued that the apostles were inspired by the Spirit in a unique way, so we cannot reproduce their hermeneutic. But that is like saying, "Yes, the Bible teaches this, but we will do it differently anyway." Instead, we should affirm that the apostles indeed were inspired by the Spirit and the content of what they said can only come by revelation. So we do not claim that the *content* of our teaching is "all the truth" (Jn 16:13), just that we are trying to follow the apostles' example in methods of interpretation as best we can. There is no indication in the New Testament that the apostle's hermeneutic is off-limits. If it were, where else would we turn for a hermeneutic? It could only be our self-made philosophical systems, and we have seen in the previous chapter where that leads. Instead, we should be imitators of the apostles, "exemplars of canonical competence, skilled at seeing the broader symbolic, thematic and historical patterns that crisscross on Jesus Christ and unify the Scriptures."[34]

Conclusion

Lion cubs wrestling with each other is cute to watch on *National Geographic*. But something very deadly is actually going on. They are learning how to hunt! Thus merely *watching* one's parents is not enough. Practice

---

[32]Alec Motyer, *Look to the Rock: An Old Testament Background to Our Understanding of Christ* (Grand Rapids, MI: Kregel Academic, 1996), 22.

[33]For more on the good role of right presuppositions, see McCartney and Clayton, *Let the Reader Understand: A Guide to Interpreting and Applying the Bible*, 2nd ed. (Phillipsburg, NJ: P&R, 2002), 61-77.

[34]Kevin J. Vanhoozer and Daniel J. Treier, *Theology and the Mirror of Scripture: A Mere Evangelical Account*, SCDS (Downers Grove, IL: IVP Academic, 2015), 101.

is needed as well. As followers of the risen Christ, we should learn our hermeneutics from him. If the heart of Christian discipleship is faithfulness to the teachings of Jesus Christ (on issues like doctrine, ethics, missions, etc.), then why would we not learn our hermeneutic from him as well? Therefore, the hermeneutical approach of this book revolves around the literary, historical, and christological contexts of every passage of Scripture. Disciples of Jesus can do no less.

For Further Study

Hoffmeier, James K. and Dennis R. Magary, eds. *Do Historical Matters Matter to Faith?: A Critical Appraisal of Modern and Postmodern Approaches to Scripture.* Wheaton, IL: Crossway, 2012. A very helpful collection of essays that also touch on arenas closely adjacent to hermeneutics.

Motyer, Alec. *Look to the Rock: An Old Testament Background to Our Understanding of Christ.* Grand Rapids, MI: Kregel Academic, 1996. A deft introduction to "the master theme of the Bible."

Starling, David I. *Hermeneutics as Apprenticeship: How the Bible Shapes Our Interpretive Habits and Practices.* Grand Rapids, MI: Baker Academic, 2016. This work explores the way biblical authors interpreted those who had come before. Starling also considers literary and historical issues and the way New Testament authors understood Israel's story to climax in Christ. Postures and virtues for reading are also considered.

For Advanced Study

Beale, G. K., and D. A. Carson, eds., *Commentary on the New Testament Use of the Old Testament.* Grand Rapids, MI: Baker Academic, 2007. This commentary is devoted to exploring Old Testament contexts (among other things) when quotations of and allusions to single verses appear in the New Testament. It should be on every serious Bible interpreter's shelf.

France, R. T. *Jesus and the Old Testament.* Vancouver: Regent College Publishing, 1992. This book takes a look at even more issues surrounding Jesus' understanding of Scripture.

Wenham, John. *Christ and the Bible.* 3rd ed. Grand Rapids, MI: Baker, 1994. There are a host of other issues than just hermeneutics when considering the relationship between the Old Testament and New Testament, and particularly Christ and the apostles' view of the Old Testament. This work is a bit of a modern classic, covering many such issues succinctly and without too much technical jargon.

3

IN THE TEXT

The Literary Context

M Y STUDY OF ECOLOGY INCLUDED a course called Oceanography. It was about how the various dynamics of the ocean work together. From temperatures, to depths, to photosynthesis, we thought about how many contributing factors make the ocean what it is, and how different it is the world over. One of the most fascinating considerations is how currents flow through the oceans for literally *thousands* of miles. The very water molecules in which we waded off the eastern shore of Maryland had just days before been down in the tropics! And weeks later they would be in Europe!

That means the temperature, surf, nutrients, plankton, jellyfish, and so on were all affected by whatever happened thousands of miles away. If that "Gulf Stream," as it is called, were not there, or flowed in a different direction, life on North America's eastern continental shelf would be entirely different. In fact—not only in the water but on land as well—the climate and weather patterns on the East Coast would also be different.

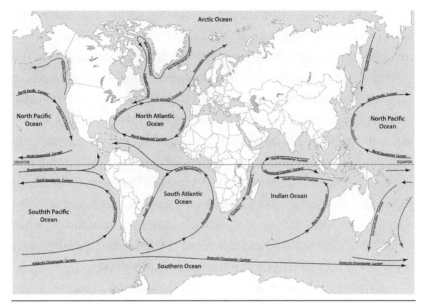

Figure 3.1. A global map of ocean currents shows how connected and interactive the entire planet is.

The same is also true for England, western Europe, and Scandinavia when the Gulf Stream flows past their coasts next. It is simply amazing that the sun warms a body of water in the Caribbean, affects plants and fish and winds and evaporation, and then that water flows north and affects entire continents and millions of people half a world away!

Now, when someone fishes off the cost of Portugal, or sets lobster traps in Nova Scotia, or surfs in North Carolina, they may not be thinking about Guyana, Belize, or Cuba. They are focused on their local fish, lobsters, and waves. Nevertheless, those fish, lobsters, and waves are vitally connected to what is happening at the equator. The Atlantic Ocean is a singular intraconnected system as waters flow all over it, bringing the influence of one part straight into the others.

Integrity, Coherency, and "Metatheology"

In a similar beautiful intraconnectivity, each book of the Bible works the same way. There are streams that originate in the first chapter of a book and flow into the rest of that book, taking with them all the nutrients of the first chapter and distributing them into the various other parts of the book. Then, what happens in those various parts of the book sends more nutrients further on. Themes and key words are established early in a book and continue to exert an interpretive influence throughout, bringing little climaxes and conclusions along the way. In turn, those various parts of any book reorganize and redeploy those themes and key words to further the book's larger theological agenda on the way to its final point. Often, however, we chop up biblical texts and read shorter passages (sometimes even just a single verse) and interpret those shorter passages *in the abstract*. We isolate those shorter passages and therefore miss the significance of those larger book-wide influences. But the books of the Bible were finalized and canonized as *whole* texts. Therefore, each book has its own coherency that depends on its own integrity.

Allow me to explain what I mean by these two words, "coherency" and "integrity." These will be important terms as we move on. *Coherency* is the attribute of a book when its various parts fit together, relate to and depend on each other. That is, each book has one overall message it is trying to communicate. Let us call that the book's "metatheology." It is the overall point of the book as a whole. Believe it or not, each book of the Bible, regardless of how big or small, can be summarized in just a few sentences.[1] Yes, there are smaller passages and individual stories within each book, and there is a potential danger in simplifying such interesting diversity, flattening the beautiful landscape of any book. We should certainly avoid that danger. Yet we need to understand that each book has an overall metatheology, and the smaller passages and individual stories therein contribute to shaping that metatheology. We, as readers, do well to see that larger picture any book is painting. If we do, we will better understand what the book is accomplishing and we will better understand those smaller passages and individual stories within the book. The way the smaller passages and individual stories come together to paint that bigger picture is what I am calling "coherency." It all fits together where smaller details contribute to the whole, and the whole binds all the details together.

---

[1] I will demonstrate this in chap. 5.

Confidence in our interpretations comes when we can make sense of *all the parts of the book* (yes, all!) in light of the rest of the book. That is coherency.[2]

It should be clear that this can only happen if we respect each book's integrity. By integrity I mean the *wholeness* of any book, and its ability to hold itself together and even interpret itself. Each book has what the author discerned is enough content and detail to make his point. If we isolate passages from the rest of their larger book-wide literary context, we violate that book's integrity. Furthermore, we do not need to import ideas from somewhere else. Sometimes in reading Paul, for example, our thoughts go to something we read in the Psalms. Or (worse) when reading the Prophets, we import ideas from our own world. But Paul does not need to be rescued like that. Paul put everything needed for interpretation in the text he wrote. It has the pieces necessary to interpret all the other pieces. And contemporary ideas could not be further from the prophets' and apostles' intents. To import foreign ideas is to violate a book's integrity.

To understand this, it might help to think of the way we speak of the integrity of a bridge. If a bridge's integrity is compromised, it is not able to do what it needs to do: hold up cars. But if its integrity is good, then that means it has all the parts it needs, none are weakened, and the bridge therefore does not need any additional support to hold up said cars. So too, texts stand on their own and get the job of communication done without the need for supplemental help. A text may *in itself* reference something external, in which case, attention to that external thing is still faithfulness to the text itself. We will see examples of that in chapters four and six. But nothing should be imposed that the text does not call for on its own terms. All of its parts cohere, as is. And it has the integrity it needs to communicate, as is.

---

[2]For more on contexts and coherence, see Jeannine K. Brown, *Scripture as Communication: Introducing Biblical Hermeneutics* (Grand Rapids, MI: Baker Academic, 2007), 103-108. The process for such discoveries is often called "discourse analysis," which is a study of "how smaller pieces fit into larger wholes . . . [and] ways in which one piece of a text supports or reinforces another . . . contribut[ing] to the overall force" (Vern S. Poythress, *Reading the Word of God in the Presence of God: A Handbook for Biblical Interpretation* [Wheaton, IL: Crossway, 2016], 203).

This is the starting point toward legitimate and ethical interpretation. What makes one interpretation better than another? I would argue that the interpretation that can account for all the details of a book—and how they relate to and depend on each other—is far more legitimate than the interpretation that rubs against, or even contradicts, another part of that same book or an interpretation that imports foreign ideas. An interpretation is ethical if it treats the book according to its integrity—treating the book as the book wants to be treated—as a whole unit of thought, again, without imposing ideas and readings from the outside. Each book holds itself together by its parts (integrity) so those parts work together in interpretation (coherency). The best interpretations, therefore, approach ethical legitimacy when they deal with smaller passages or individual stories within a book in ways that give due attention to the whole book's integrity and can articulate that passage or story's meaning *coherently* with the rest of the book's content.[3]

This chapter is called "In the Text." Clearly I mean in the *whole* text, in the whole book. In this sense we can talk about the "world in the text," for there is an entire universe of ideas that comprise the book and must be attended to. But I also mean *in* any passage, story, or unit of the book. It is those passages and stories and larger literary blocks that build up into the whole text. They are what give the whole book its structure. Just as the ocean is an intraconnected whole, that does not change the fact that each *local* ecosystem has its own unique characteristics. And those unique characteristics are often appreciated by attending to the smallest of details. In the same way, even as the whole book has its own integrity and coherency, the smaller passages need to be appreciated for all their beautiful intricacies.

To do this, and still not abstract these passages from their book-wide context, three steps are necessary. We need to (1) read the entire book in

---

[3] J. P. Louw comments, "The arrangement of the selected material becomes a vital factor as soon as a number of utterances are linked together. These have to be ordered and articulated because any sensible string in communication is selective. This is especially true in the case of written material. . . . The way or the manner . . . in which a notion is communicated, is the heart of its effectiveness" ("Discourse Analysis and the Greek New Testament," *BT* 24 [1973]: 101).

one sitting, (2) discern where discrete units of thought begin and end (as well as transitions), and (3) reflect on what contribution each unit makes to the larger book-wide metatheology in order to track the flow of thought between the smaller units and, by extension, through the whole book. As we shall see, all three of these tasks overlap with each other such that attending to any

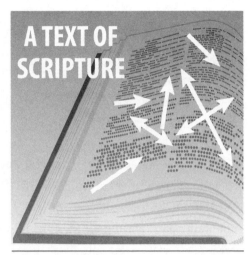

Figure 3.2. All the literary details of a text interact with and bear on each other to create a coherent "world within the text."

one often necessitates revisiting the other two, and vice versa.

This is sometimes called a "close reading," where big-picture and intricate details are attended to so as to appreciate the literary artistry of the text. Beyond the esthetics, though, in doing this kind of reading we are starting to set up "textual controls," limitations to our interpretations within the bounds of the literary details. Prioritizing the text this way helps keep us from wandering off into fanciful and allegorical interpretations, and more confidently in the realms of ethical legitimacy.

Reading the Whole Book

As mentioned above, we need to see the entire ocean if we are going to appreciate how the streams are flowing. Similarly, we need to understand the entire book—including its structure and flow of thought—if we are going to arrive at its metatheology and, in turn, appreciate its parts.

To do this there are a handful of important steps. First, *read the entire book in one sitting*. We commonly read a chapter or two, or even less sometimes, and then come back to the next chapter the following day, or something like that. While this practice is great for meditating on some details, it can cause us to miss the flow of thought of the entire book. For in any given book of the Bible there are themes and concepts and key words that the author plants in one part that will bloom in another. Think of these as the nutrients flowing from one part to another. Well, if there is too big a time gap between reading chapter one and, say, chapter ten, we will not see those connections. Thus, reading a book in one sitting will help us make the connections throughout the book (follow the streams and harvest the nutrients, if you will). Yes, I mean even the larger books like Luke or Romans or Job or the Psalms! If reading so much at once is a big time commitment, it will be worth the time committed to it.[4]

Additionally, *read slowly.* Too often we can read really fast like mountain bikers blazing through the forest. But in such a case, have we really read? Have we really dwelt in, observed, and experienced the forest? Slow down and think. Jot down some notes. Go back to the previous passage if you think you should reread something. In fact, often we only notice the streams flowing through a book somewhere in the middle or at the end. It is as though our metatheological knowledge lags behind a couple chapters as we read. But that is okay if we are reading it all at once and reading slowly. The conclusion of the book will tie things off in our minds. Then, of course, you can read the entire book again![5]

As you read in this way, note especially the connections between the beginning of the book and the end. Biblical authors love to frontload their works with the major themes they will develop and preempt the problems they will address. Then at the end, they like to tie matters off. These sorts of observations help identify the "frame" for understanding. A frame is a set of major ideas inside of which the details of the text operate.[6] Once we see that we will also better identify

---

[4]A very helpful chart of approximately how long it takes to read each book of the Bible aloud can be found in Andrew David Naselli, *How to Understand and Apply the New Testament: Twelve Steps from Exegesis to Theology* (Phillipsburg, NJ: P&R, 2017), 196.

[5]Richard B. Hays demonstrates this well with the Gospels (*Reading Backwards: Figural Christology and the Fourfold Gospel Witness* [Waco, TX: Baylor University Press, 2014]). By "reading backwards" Hays means two things. For one, the Gospels teach us how to read the Old Testament (a similar point of the previous chapter), but also that the end of the Gospels (namely the resurrection) creates retrospective lenses for rereading the book.

[6]More thoroughly, Kenneth Duncan Litwak comments, "A 'frame' consists of the cues or markers that one uses to indicate to his or her audience the context of an utterance or text and the hints

the major theologically formative moments of the book, those little climaxes and turning points along the way. I call these "loadbearing" verses and "hinges" in the text. Loadbearing verses (and loadbearing passages) are those moments in a book where it seems all else is driving, or that point around which the rest of the book is revolving. Hinges are where the flow of thought takes a new direction, usually after one such miniclimax or loadbearing passage.

Since we will revisit metatheologies in chapter five, just two examples will have to do for now that I hope will demonstrate the value of attending to a book in its entirety—respecting its integrity and looking for its coherency.

Let us begin in the beginning. Genesis is all about beginnings. Not only does creation begin, but Genesis also describes the beginning of God's *purposes* in the creation. It narrates the beginning of sin that disrupts those purposes, as well as (and herein lies the book's greatest focus) the beginning of God's plan to restore those purposes. Notice, in 1:28 it says God "blesses" the first man and woman and gives them this privilege and responsibility: "Be fruitful and multiply and fill the earth and subdue it and have dominion over the fish of the sea and over the birds of the heavens and over every living thing that moves on the earth." As you read through Genesis in one sitting you will clearly notice the repetition of the concept of "blessing," as well as its inverse, "cursing." Moreover, you will notice the refrains of fruitfulness and multiplication as well as concepts of "dominion" (kings, land possession, etc.).[7] Yet, there are all sorts of problems: some women cannot conceive and there are many resisting forces to anyone's kingly dominion (whether it is Adam, Noah, Abraham, or Joseph). All the while, the reader will remember Genesis 3:15, where one "offspring" (another commonly repeated phrase in Genesis) will reverse all these problems and restore that original creational purpose. That

---

the author or speaker gives the audience for interpreting the statement.... 'Framing in discourse' refers to how a narrative is introduced and shaped, and how this relates to what readers expect of the narrative" (*Echoes of Scripture in Luke-Acts: Telling the History of God's People Intertextually*, JSNTSup 282 [London: T&T Clark, 2005], 2-3).

[7]See Stephen G. Dempster, *Dominion and Dynasty: A Theology of the Hebrew Bible*, NSBT 15 (Downers Grove, IL: InterVarsity Press, 2003), 55-92.

concept of offspring, in fact, acts like a weave running through the book tying everything else together. Why do we care that Sarai cannot conceive? What is it to us whether Abraham might kill Isaac? Why are we interested in Joseph and his brothers? These are not just timeless stories of common human interest—as though our hearts naturally go out to a woman who cannot conceive, or we just know that murder is wrong, or we find in Joseph's story shades of our own families. Rather, these stories matter because they are part of the unfolding drama of God's design for restoring humanity to its original creational intent through one of Adam and Eve's offspring. If the offspring is not born (Sarai's story) or he is killed (Abraham's story), God's purposes of restoration will fail! And sin will remain a permanent destructive force against all Genesis 1:28 had envisioned.[8] Isaac is born, however (Sarai conceives!), and God provides a substitute (Abraham does not sacrifice him!). But if Isaac is not that ultimate offspring after all, then one of his grandchildren must be, and Joseph looks like a *great* candidate as the story unfolds. In that case, the nearly mortal attack on him and his deportation from the land of promise are more threats against God's purposes in creation and redemption. But in the end, there is an intriguing twist when *Judah*—alas not Joseph after all—is given the promise of dominion at the very end in 49:8-10! It is then to Judah and his line of offspring we look as the book closes. Judah and his tribe will bring the Genesis 3:15 salvation to humanity and restore us to our original Genesis 1:28 place in the cosmos![9] I call that the metatheology of Genesis.

In this quick survey of Genesis we have found a "frame."[10] We can now understand the individual stories of Genesis as part of this larger picture

---

[8]G. K. Beale insightfully highlights that Genesis 1:28 is humanity's original Great Commission with which humanity is tasked and the rest of Genesis (the rest of the Bible in fact) is looking to restore (*A New Testament Biblical Theology: The Unfolding of the Old Testament in the New* [Grand Rapids, MI: Baker Academic, 2011], 30-33, 63-85). Humanity's redemption from sin, therefore, entails the reclamation of God's cosmic purposes. See as well Dempster, *Dominion and Dynasty*, 47-49.

[9]See esp. T. Desmond Alexander, "From Adam to Judah: The Significance of the Family Tree in Genesis," *EvQ* 61 (1989): 5-19; Alexander, "Genealogies, Seed and Compositional Unity of Genesis," *TynBul* 44.2 (1993): 255-70.

[10]Technically, this is called a "literary frame." There are also "culturally stored frames" and "intertextual frames." The best general summary on frames can be found in Umberto Eco, *The Role of the Reader: Explorations in the Semiotics of Texts*, ASem (Bloomington: Indiana University Press, 1979), 17-27.

that Genesis 1:28, 3:15, and 49:8-10 decisively shape. This helps us, then, not to atomize the stories, reading them in abstraction from each other nor apart from the larger point of the whole book. Each story can be understood as part and parcel contributing to filling out the frame and, together with the frame, shaping the metatheology. Details of each story remain important, and there are a lot of smaller points Genesis makes along the way. But even those smaller points need to be nestled inside the larger purposes of the book.

Let us take the first book of the New Testament as well. In Matthew 1 there is a lot of focus on Jesus as the son of Abraham and the son of David (1:1, 17). This causes the reader to think of the sort of promises God has made to Abraham and David. Now much could be said here but suffice it for now to say that God's purposes through Abraham were to bless all peoples (Gen 12:3) and his promise to David was that he would rule God's people forever (2 Sam 7; in fact, all nations according to Psalm 2). It is significant to notice, therefore, that Matthew ends with these words from Jesus: "All authority in heaven and on earth has been given to me. Go therefore and make disciples of all nations, baptizing them in the name of the Father and of the Son and of the Holy Spirit, teaching them to observe all that I have commanded you. And behold, I am with you always, to the end of the age" (28:18-20).

When Jesus speaks of his "authority" over "all nations" the reader must remember those Abrahamic and Davidic themes evoked in chapter one in order to understand the point. The Gospel is telling us (if I may paraphrase): "In this Jesus of Nazareth, God has finally blessed the nations *by* giving them the Davidic king to rule and baptize and teach through his disciples the world over. My Gospel is the account of *how* God has brought that about." Everything in the Gospel of Matthew, therefore, gets colored by this larger emphasis. It is the umbrella under which everything else operates, the frame inside of which the rest of the picture is encased.

Within this larger framework, we could say Matthew 16:13-21 is a major hinge pericope. That is Peter's great confession where he says, "Thou art the Christ, the Son of the living God," and Jesus responds by saying, "I will build my church and the gates of Hades will not prevail against it." To this point everyone has been perplexed as to who Jesus is (7:28-29; 8:27, 34; 9:7; 11:3; 12:2, 23, 38; 13:54-56; 14:1-2, 26; 16:1). Now one person, Peter, has linked him to the house of David by calling him "the Christ."[11] Now that we know who Jesus is—he is *the Christ*—the narrative pivots to focus on *what this Christ will do*. Thus 16:21 reads, "From that time Jesus began to show his disciples that he must go to Jerusalem . . . and be killed, and on the third day be raised." This is the *first* announcement of his death and resurrection to which the rest of the narrative will now drive. Once he accomplishes that, only then can the blessing of the nations (promised to Abraham) under his lordship (promised to David) commence in 28:18-20. And in this way his church is built. Seeing such frames and hinges helps us coherently situate the rest of the narrative, since it matters that the parables of chapter thirteen, for example, are before this moment and the transfiguration is after, and so on.

For some books this is easier to do. But do not let the time-consuming, and sometimes difficult, work deter you. It is worth it. The size and number of moving parts in larger books are exactly why this must be done in one sitting. If we do this well, we can already start to draw provisional ideas about a book's metatheology and how the parts cohere. We can also make a provisional outline of the whole book which helps us identify those loadbearing and hinge moments.

Reading Discrete Passages

Only now—after committing to respecting a book's integrity and starting to look for its coherency—can we focus on smaller passages and individual stories. Working in *this* order will help guard us against reductionism as we dig into the intriguing details.

Within the larger scope of a book, there are discrete units that in and of themselves are complete thoughts. We call each such unit a "pericope" [pə-rĭk-ə-pē]. We can say that in one sense they are self-contained, with

---

[11]The term "Son of the living God" is also a Davidic moniker; we will explore that in chap. 5.

a definite beginning, middle, and end. That is, they present a new idea, problem, situation, or setting in the book. They develop that idea, problem, or situation. And they conclude the idea, solve the problem, finish the self-contained story (at least to a degree). While, again, each pericope makes a significant contribution to the development of the metatheology of the book, and each pericope should be understood finally as integrally part of the whole book, nonetheless each pericope has details that are worth mining—and there is value to studying the pericope in its own right.

The first step is to discover these pericopes.[12] As on the whole-book contextual level, we will have to treat each pericope as a unit, and that means finding where it starts and stops. And so we ask, What are the reasonable bounds of a pericope? As mentioned, each pericope needs a beginning, middle, and end. What new issue is the author trying to resolve? What is the new situation the characters are walking into? How has the emphasis shifted? These all mark turning points in the larger text as the flow of the book moves from one pericope to another. Then, the author develops the issue or tells the story with building tension; this is the middle. Finally, the pericope ends when there is a resolution to the initial problem(s), or the tension in the narrative is resolved (at least in part; the resolution to a pericope could be that the situation worsens).

For example, in Mark 4 Jesus is telling parables, and in verses 33-34 he seems to be done for the day; a new turn in the narrative then develops. In verses 35-36 Jesus wants to depart that area and so takes leave of the crowd. Then in verse 37 we see a new problem: "a great windstorm." So we can consider verses 35-37 the beginning of this pericope. In the middle, the disciples question why Jesus is of no help (v. 38). The fear that they might die heightens the tension. We might be tempted to think verse 39 is the conclusion when Jesus calms the storm. But verse 40 reveals that for Mark the real conclusion is not the stilling of the storm but the penetrating questions, "Why are you so afraid? Have you still no faith?" Finally, verse 41 provides a sort of reflective epilogue: the disciples

---

[12]Sometimes you will see the plural spelled *pericopae*.

ask themselves (and we the reader are to ask the same question!), "Who then is this, that even the wind and the sea obey him?" Thus, we have a beginning, middle, and end to this account, and so a clearly defined pericope, Mark 4:35-41. The problem is real, it gets worse, and in the end it is not only resolved but the whole episode teaches us truths about Jesus. We are not done with Mark 4; we will come back to it. That is enough for now, to illustrate a pericope.

Commonly though, many pericopes flow seamlessly into the next, intentionally blurring the lines between them. Ezekiel 34:1 presents the problem of the bad shepherds that is resolved when the Lord says in verse 15, "I myself will be the shepherd of my sheep," and later says in verse 23, "I will set up over them one shepherd, my servant David." Problem solved, right? Verse 24 even concludes with what appears to be a final seal: "I am the LORD; I have spoken." Sounds very much like the end of that unit of thought. But verses 25-31 is still talking about a future redemption and even concludes with more sheep imagery. So is the pericope really all of chapter thirty-four? Well, verses 25-31 could be part of the previous pericope, or they could stand on their own. The encouraging thing is that sometimes we really do not have to decide. Because we are so focused on the whole-book flow of thought, pericopes that fade into the next one should not faze us. We can just account for such in our outline.

Pericopes can also be very difficult to identify in poetic texts. Isaiah 40:1-11 is a pericope but does not have the regular pattern of problem and resolution (it is more like a self-contained table of contents for what comes next in Isaiah), so we need other ways of identifying them.

One such way to identify a pericope is by observing "textual markers." These are cues in the text where the author signals a new idea, a conclusion to a running idea, or a change in thought. Some of the most common in the Bible are "After this," "And it came to pass," "Hear the word of the Lord," "This is what the Lord showed me." The authors want you to track with them in their flow of thought, so look for the common sort of indicators where the text is signaling a new idea, conclusion to a running idea, or change in thought. When you find them you can more clearly identify the reasonable bounds of a pericope.

Specific literary devices can be more sophisticated textual markers. I will mention just two here. The first is called an "inclusio." An inclusio is a set of repeated terms or ideas at the very beginning and the very end of a pericope.[13] They serve as bookends as it were, encapsulating and shaping the ideas in between. For example, Romans 5:1-2 reads, "Therefore, since we have been justified by faith, we have *peace with God through our Lord Jesus Christ*. Through him we have also obtained access by faith into this grace in which we stand, and we *rejoice in* hope of the glory of *God*." And then Romans 5:11 reads, "More than that, we also *rejoice in God through our Lord Jesus Christ*, through whom we have now received *reconciliation*." In this example terms and concepts from verses 1-2 are repeated in verse 11. This marks off a clear pericope. The verses in between, therefore, are understood as part of Paul's reflections on these specific ideas.

Finding inclusios in narrative texts is especially important because it is so easy to get lost in the details. A good inclusio can orient our reading to see what a story is ultimately about. In 1 Samuel 3:1 we read, "Now the boy Samuel was ministering to the LORD in the presence of Eli. And *the word of the LORD* was rare in those days; there was *no frequent vision*." And the pericope ends in 3:21–4:1 with "And the LORD *appeared* again at Shiloh, for the LORD revealed himself to Samuel at Shiloh by *the word of the LORD*. And the word of Samuel came to all Israel." This is an exciting moment in Israel's history! There had been no widespread revelation for years, but now begins Samuel's ministry. There will be revelation again; the Lord will speak to his people again! This helps us understand the significant contribution 1 Samuel 3 uniquely makes to the development of the book as a whole, and also highlights some important themes running through 1 Samuel 3 we might otherwise overlook. It also helps us not to get distracted with secondary issues. Such secondary issues are, of course, relevant to the

---

[13]They can also serve to open and close larger literary units comprised of several pericopes, or even cap the beginning and end of an entire book.

story, but we interpret them all the better when we can recognize how even they serve the larger theme created by the inclusio.

The "chiasm" is the other literary device I will mention at this time; it is like a more sophisticated inclusio. It too begins and ends with repeated terms or ideas, but also adds an organized middle section with mirroring sides. The effect is to highlight the middle.[14] For example, Psalm 2 is organized in a chiasm. It looks like this:

¹Why do the nations rage

and the peoples plot in vain?

²The kings of the earth set themselves,

and the rulers take counsel together,   } A

against the LORD and against his Anointed, saying,

³"Let us burst their bonds apart

and cast away their cords from us."

⁴He who sits in the heavens laughs;

The Lord holds them in derision.

⁵Then he will speak to them in his wrath,   } B

and terrify them in his fury, saying,

⁶"As for me, I have set my King on Zion,

my holy hill."   } C

⁷I will tell of the decree:

The LORD said to me,

"You are my Son;

today I have begotten you.   } C′

⁸Ask of me, and I will make the nations your heritage,

and the ends of the earth your possession.

---

[14]It is called a chiasm because the Greek letter *chi* looks the same on each side while touching in the middle: χ.

⁹You shall break them with a rod of iron

and dash them in pieces like a potter's vessel."

$\left.\right\}$ B′

¹⁰Now therefore, O kings, be wise;

be warned, O rulers of the earth.

¹¹Serve the LORD with fear,

and rejoice with trembling.

A′

¹²Kiss the Son, lest he be angry,

and you perish in the way,

for his wrath is quickly kindled.

Blessed are all who take refuge in him.

Can you see how the psalm begins and ends focused on life on earth, and particularly how the nations of the earth relate to their Creator? That is an inclusio. But between the inclusio there is also a mirroring of ideas. You can see the mirroring thoughts in the lines I have indented and labeled with letters A, B, and C in verses 1-6. Then verses 7-12 are labeled C′, B′, and A′ to show how the second half of the psalm mirrors the first half. An outline of Psalm 2, therefore, looks like this:

A.   verses 1-3: the actions of the nations on earth

B.   verses 4-5: the response of the Lord in heaven

C.   verse 6: the Lord's decree as a solution to A

C′.   verses 7-8: the Messiah repeats the Lord's decree

B′.   verse 9: the response of the Messiah on earth

A′.   verses 10-12: the actions the nations on earth *should* take

Seeing how these verses parallel each other reveals structure, and therefore a clearer path to following the flow of thought.[15] The chiasm

---

[15]For more on common textual markers, see David A. Dorsey, *Literary Structure of the Old Testament: A Commentary on Genesis–Malachi* (Grand Rapids, MI: Baker Academic, 1999), 21-25.

takes verses 6-8 and really highlights them. They are (quite literally) the central thought.

In the previous section I emphasized the importance of the metatheology of whole books. In this section I demonstrated the way each individual pericope also has its own theology that is vital to observe. These periciopes are self-contained in one right. But they should never be abstracted entirely from their whole-book context. We move on now, therefore, to consider how individual pericopes and passages work together to distinctly shape a book in its entirety.

Reading "In and Out" for the Flow of Thought

Now that we have our pericopes, we still need to think about their literary contexts. When most talk about literary context, they mean what comes immediately before and immediately after the pericope in question. I too mean that. But I also mean—it is worth repeating—the context of the entire book. Yes, the immediate context can bear a lot of interpretive influence over a pericope, just as the most local weather system more immediately affects a coastline. And we will attend to this. But it cannot be forgotten—and I think it often is—that books of the Bible are each *singular* texts. Just as currents a long way off created that local weather system, so too local literary contexts are what they are because of larger book-wide trends. Following here, therefore, we will think about local contexts and their interplay with the whole-book context.

We start with the local context. Augustine insisted that if a reader is uncertain about an interpretation, "it remains to refer to the whole context, to the sections that precede and that follow the ambiguous passage, holding it in the middle between them, so that we may see which of the several meanings that present themselves the context will vote for and allow to fit in with itself."[16]

To see this, let us return to our Mark 4:35-41 example. Right before this episode of the stilling of the storm, Jesus had just told the parable of the mustard seed in 4:30-32. The kingdom of God is like a mustard seed;

---

[16]Augustine, *On Christian Doctrine* 3.2 (printed in William Yarchin, *History of Biblical Interpretation: A Reader* [Grand Rapids, MI: Baker Academic, 2004], 69).

though it is small now it will grow up to become "larger than all the garden plants" (v. 32), so large that all kinds of birds come to nest in it. And that is Jesus' last parable for the day. Yet this transition between pericopes in verses 33-34 is intriguing. We are told that Jesus *only* spoke parables to the crowd, but explained everything privately to his disciples. When, therefore, "on that day" (v. 35) Jesus "leaves the crowd" (v. 36) the text has created an expectation that Jesus will now explain the parable to his disciples. What ensues, however, is the storm and the great miracle of stilling it. Could this be a form of explaining the parable? In verse 38 the disciples think they are going to die in the storm. But when Jesus calms the storm (thereby saving them) he asks, "Why are you so afraid? Have you still no faith?" (v. 40). As readers we should ask ourselves, "Faith in what?" Should the disciples have assumed Jesus would calm the waves and winds of the storm? He never had before. He never promised that he would. Why should they have had faith in *that*? Judging by their reaction in verse 41—their fear goes up, not down—they clearly did not think Jesus could do that! The immediate context helps us out: if they are the mustard seed (one Galilean rabbi and twelve followers; it does not get much smaller than that) and Jesus says they will be the biggest, then they certainly cannot die that day. Indeed, it turns out this *is* a teaching moment in the wake of the parable. Their experience drives home the parable, even creates a level of faith in the parable they did not have before. So when Jesus calls for their faith, it is not that he will calm all the storms of their lives. Rather, he is calling them to have faith in the parable of the mustard seed. It *will* grow into the greatest of all plants, and his calming of the storm shows that Jesus can guarantee so much.

That is the pericope right before the miracle. What comes after? In Mark 5 Jesus enters Gentile territory for the first time. He is met by a demon-possessed man who lives among the tombs (5:2-3), and nearby there is a large swine herd (5:11). Thus, Jesus and his disciples are now entering the demonic, spiritually dead, and unholy parts of the world. Yet, Jesus not only heals the man (5:15), he sends the demons and the swine into the very sea that had nearly killed the mustard seed (5:13).

Then, the once-demon-possessed man starts to spread the news of the kingdom through ten Gentile cities (5:20)! *The mustard seed is already starting to grow!*

This example of Mark 4:30–5:20 shows how three individual pericopes —self-contained units in one sense—exert an interpretive influence back and forth over each other. Reading pericopes that are next to each other like this goes a long way in understanding each of them in their own right, but also starts to elucidate the larger flow of thought running throughout the book.[17] It is interesting how these dynamics—smallness yet greatness, victory out of defeat—reemerge elsewhere in Mark. At the cross, the kingdom could not have seemed smaller. All the disciples had scattered and Jesus was left to die alone. At the cross, the mustard seed is not the *greatest* of all plants, but ground to dust! But from smallness comes greatness, from defeat comes victory. On the third day Jesus is raised to life, after which he regathers his disciples (16:7), and the church has been growing ever since! Thus, Mark 4–5 is not a small collection of parables and stories and that is it. But they shape the warp and woof of the larger Markan narrative that redeploys such themes in sophisticated ways. The point is that we should catch these important emphases as we encounter them across the narrative so that they sink into our bones. In the end we will appreciate Mark's metatheology and understand its peri-copes therein with more clarity.[18]

Before we conclude, let us take an example where many of these concepts come together. Daniel's metatheology can be appreciated when we see how a huge chiasm relates entire pericopes to each other through much of the book. Have you ever noticed how many of Daniel's stories are so similar? Daniel in the lion's den in chapter six reads very similarly to his friends' experience in the fiery furnace in chapter three. The four beasts in chapter seven and the four empires in chapter two are both

---

[17]See helpfully, Richard L. Pratt, Jr., *He Gave Us Stories: The Bible Student's Guide to Interpreting Old Testament Narratives* (Phillipsburg, NJ: P&R, 1990), 205-29.

[18]Seeing these thematic connections helps us resist the temptation to allegorize the storm as God's wrath that Jesus "stills" on the cross. Yes, that sentiment is true. But it is not the point of Mark 4; we miss the point when we run off in such directions.

overcome by a heavenly figure. And right in the middle of all this both Nebuchadnezzar in chapter four and Belshazzar in chapter five are brought low after arrogant boasting. Finally, these chapters are encased by an emphasis on exile in chapters one and nine. An outline of the book, then, looks like this:

I. Chapters 1–9—God alone is sovereign; His people are afflicted by pseudo-sovereigns

    A. Ch. 1—Exile; People of God afflicted

      B. Ch. 2—Four empires brought low by God's king (type in history)

        C. Ch. 3—King sets himself up as god; People of God afflicted

          D. Ch. 4—Nebuchadnezzar brought low

          D′. Ch. 5—Belshazzar brought low

        C′. Ch. 6—King sets himself up as god; People of God afflicted

      B′. Ch. 7—Four empires brought low by God's king (eschatological)

      B′. Ch. 8—Four empires brought low

    A′. Ch. 9—Return from exile; Messiah afflicted

II. Chapters 10–12—Visions of the future

Observing this chiasm helps us immensely. First, it divides the book into two major sections. The chiasm ends with chapter nine, so we see in chapters ten and following something else is going on. It also draws us to the middle of the chiasm, Daniel 4:34-35. There, Nebuchadnezzar says,

> At the end of the days I, Nebuchadnezzar, lifted my eyes to heaven, and my reason returned to me, and I blessed the Most High, and praised and honored him who lives forever,
>
> > For his dominion is an everlasting dominion,
> > > and His kingdom endures from generation to generation;
> > > all the inhabitants of the earth are accounted as nothing,
> > and he does according to His will among the host of heaven
> > > and among the inhabitants of the earth;
> > and none can stay his hand
> > > or say to Him, "What have you done?

This, then, is the overall point of chapters one through nine. For a people in exile (the emphasis of chapters one and nine), this is *exactly* what they need to hear (on the lips of their pagan oppressor no less!). This helps orient our reading to understand how the other details of the rest of chapters one through nine relate to this metatheology, and in turn keeps us from allegorizing Daniel by pushing the details of his story into the mold of *our* Zeitgeist.[19]

These sorts of themes, running through pericopes and filling out a book's metatheology, are best seen by "reading in and out" as I call it. Starting with a pericope you are studying, read the chapter before and after it. Then, read your pericope again. Then, read two chapters ahead of it through two chapters after it. Then read your pericope again. Then read three chapters ahead through three chapters after. Thus, you will read narrow and increasingly widening contexts until you have read your entire book in this way. Again, this is time consuming, but it is worth it. You will understand that pericope's placement and its role in the whole book, and until you do that you have not understood that pericope. The entire rest of the book informs the meaning of the pericope and what the pericope contributes significantly to making the whole book what it is. Again, there are no standalone verses or pericopes. All is in context.[20]

As you read this way—read the entire book, study a pericope, read the narrow and increasingly wider contexts—you will start to read in line with the text's flow of thought. It is not enough to understand *what a text says*, but also *how a text says it*. Repeated words and phrases will jump off the page at you, especially if they run through a specific pericope you are studying in more depth. You will also identify those loadbearing

---

[19]Incidentally, this also helps us understand why Daniel is not in chronological order (a chronology of the chapters most likely goes like this: 1, 2, 3, 4, 7, 8, 5, 9, 6). Relaying a succession of events is not the goal, but a thematic organization of the events to highlight the center of the chiasm in the context of the chiasm's outer parts.

[20]More on the relationship between local contexts and larger whole-book contexts can be found in Jason S. DeRouchie, *How to Understand and Apply the Old Testament: Twelve Steps from Exegesis to Theology* (Phillipsburg, NJ: P&R, 2017), 99-103, 323-43; Naselli, *Understand and Apply*, 136-57, 188-90. I particularly like what Naselli calls "phrasing."

verses in pericopes and hinge verses in pericopes that will help you understand the flow of thought and make a more confident outline.[21]

Conclusion

Are you seeing already how interpretation is both a science and an art? There is a science to it, and I hope this chapter has given you some helpful methods. But there is also an artistry to it that cannot be taught, but you will grow in it with experience. All the same, let the takeaway from this chapter be this: we have to resist the tendency to atomize. It is very common to take a verse or a story or a portion of Paul, or whatever, and abstract it and isolate it from the rest of its original literary home. This chapter has emphasized practices in our study that can help mitigate against this tendency, while still appreciating the finer details. This is sometimes called a close reading, where big-picture and intricate details are attended to in appreciation of the literary artistry of the text. It is giving full weight to the entire "world in the text." Legitimate readings need interpretations of such details that are coherent, and thereby give indication of a book's metatheology. The integrity of each book demands so much. We will return to some of these considerations when we look at genres in chapter seven. For now, I hope you get the sense of how crucial reading in context—narrow and wide—is for interpretation.

Surfers intuitively understand this. Sometimes surf's up. Sometimes it's not. While the focus at any particular moment is on catching a specific wave, that wave—as well as those immediately before and after—are created by the whole-ocean contexts spanning near and far. That is why they check the tide, the weather, the wind, and the swells to know what the surf will be like on *their* beach. They may also read up on recent shark sightings. But the point is, as oceans are experienced one beach at a time, those beaches are created by the rest of the ocean. So too, we can only read one sentence at a time, but each sentence is its own wave being pushed by the mass of literary context behind it, and will in turn flow into the rest of the book.

---

[21] For more strategies for attending to whole-book contexts, see Brown, *Scripture as Communication*, 216-25.

Next, we will think about our second layer of context: the historical circumstances of authors and original audiences.

For Further Study

Collins, Jon, and Tim Mackie. "The Bible Project." www.thebibleproject.com. This is a very helpful resource for whole-book contexts. Their team produces very accessible videos that focus on each book's full structure and flow of thought. They also have a series of brief instructional videos called "How to Read the Bible" that revolves around different genres.

Fee, Gordon D. and Douglas Stuart. *How to Read the Bible Book by Book: A Guided Tour*. Grand Rapids, MI: Zondervan, 2002. As the title indicates, this work looks at whole books and helps readers with related interpretive methods.

For Advanced Study

Dorsey, David A. *Literary Structure of the Old Testament: A Commentary on Genesis–Malachi*. Grand Rapids, MI: Baker Academic, 1999. This is a helpful work for seeing how the literary structure of smaller units interacts with the larger structure of whole books. Dorsey provides examples for every Old Testament book.

Leithart, Peter J. *Deep Exegesis: The Mystery of Reading Scripture*. Waco, TX: Baylor University Press, 2009. Leithart deals with more than literary context in this work, but in so doing he demonstrates well how other steps in the hermeneutical process are only fruitful when first rooted in the details of the text. He also alleges this is how the New Testament authors read the Old Testament.

Sim, Margaret G. *A Relevant Way to Read: A New Approach to Exegesis and Communication*. Eugene, OR: Pickwick, 2016. This is a quite sophisticated work on the importance of context for communication.

4

AROUND THE TEXT

The Historical Context

I WILL NEVER FORGET WHEN I FIRST learned about how a tree circulates water through itself. It is truly remarkable! It goes like this. Every tree survives and grows through the process of photosynthesis—the use of light to generate food for itself. The light provides energy to split apart water and carbon dioxide molecules in the leaves. Carbon-based foods are created, and oxygen is the byproduct. Now, where does that water come from in the photosynthesis processes? You likely learned this in grade school: water enters the tree through its roots. But photosynthesis happens in the leaves. For some trees, that means water has to travel up the tree dozens or even hundreds of yards. Maple trees in my front yard are at least 30 feet tall. There are Redwoods in California upwards of *ten times* taller! And their roots can extend up to 100 feet from their trunk. That's 400 feet from where water enters the root system up to the leaves where it is used for photosynthesis! How does it get up there? Well, there are very tiny "capillaries" in the trunk, vertical conduits channeling the water upward. As water splits into its parts (hydrogen and oxygen) during photosynthesis, the oxygen is emitted from the leaf, creating a vacuum which is then filled by the next bit of water in line, in turn pulling all the rest of the water in the capillary up a little bit

further (and in turn pulling more water in through the roots). It is like a giant straw. In fact, these capillaries in trees even look like very thin straws, and when you cut a tree across its trunk you can see them.

What's more, you can also learn a lot about the history of the tree by looking at these dendronic straws. Keeping with the theme of this book, you can even

Figure 4.1. A tree trunk cross section shows historic growth rates.

learn a lot about the history of the *entire ecosystem* in which the tree lives by looking at these straws. When a tree has a lot of water and light (spring and summer) it develops a new layer of thick capillaries (the straws) just inside the bark to facilitate the photosynthesis in the leaves. Growth is so fast that the capillaries are bigger and more spread out. These are the lighter rings in a tree's cross section. When there is less water and/or light available for photosynthesis (the fall) the tree has less food to build new material and less need for such big capillaries. So, new capillaries are smaller and tighter together. These are the dark rings. Thus, from the light and dark rings we can see the age of the tree and which years had the best growth. And that tells us about not only rainfall those years but several other climate phenomena too. Moreover, just as the environment affected the tree's growth, that very tree has affected its surrounding environment.

That is enough science for now. There is an obvious corollary with texts. Texts are written in response to events happening in the world.

Either the author's life, or the people to whom they write, or larger historical trends provoke the production of texts.[1] Typically, an author is trying to answer a question, or solve a problem, or correct some misunderstanding, etc. It is crucial, therefore, to understand authors' and their audiences' historical contexts—what is going on among them, and in the larger world—in order to understand the text. Anthony Thiselton calls this the "rootedness" of texts.[2] Just as we cannot understand a tree without attention to what has happened in the environment before (seasonal changes and how many seasons the tree has lived through), we cannot really grasp the meaning of texts without attending to the historical circumstances that influenced their writing. At the same time, as we can think about a large tree's impact on its surroundings (innumerable birds, reptiles, mammals, and insects live in trees), so too we can appreciate the rhetorical effect a text would have had on its first audience when we have such historical dynamics in view. Finally, when the author and first audience share a common set of assumptions and understanding, then there is an economy of communication between them. That is, the author does not need to spell everything out in great detail because the author can safely assume that the audience already has some basic shared knowledge, allowing the audience to pick up on the text's subtleties.[3]

But we are far removed from biblical contexts. It is very hard to tell how much of that undercipher we are missing in our reading because we do not have that shared historical experience that the author and first audience had. All the more reason to study to get into that shared cultural space with the authors and first audiences as much as we can. We call this the world "around the text."

---

[1]There were also compositional and redactional factors involved in the final formation of the canonical texts (big fancy terms for any biblical scholars reading this). But I cannot bog down this chapter with such details. Good introductions, which I discuss below, cover such issues well enough.

[2]Anthony C. Thiselton, *Hermeneutics: An Introduction* (Grand Rapids, MI: Eerdmans, 2009), 20-24.

[3]John H. Walton, *Ancient Near Eastern Thought and the Old Testament* (Grand Rapids, MI: Baker Academic, 2006), 18-27.

If we do not attend to this layer of context, the result is not only to miss that message, but to press onto the Bible our own cultural assumptions.[4] In short, attention to historical contexts helps keep us from eisegesis.

Furthermore, attention to the historical rootedness of the Bible actually gets at the very heart of the biblical message itself. The Bible does not present itself as a collection of abstract ideas or timeless maxims. Rather, the power of the biblical story is that *God has acted in history*.[5] He did not float theology down from above, or content himself with ethereal lectures from on high. No, he acted in history. He *created* history to begin with. Time and space, therefore, are God's instruments for accomplishing his purposes. He

Figure 4.2. Literary details commonly draw on "the world around the text," the historical setting shared between the author and first readers.

called Abraham. He led the children of Israel out of Egypt. He raised up David. He sent the Babylonians. And, of course, he sent his son, Jesus Christ. God is a doer, and he does his works of redemption in history. When we do read what might be called theological reflection (the Psalms, the epistles, some prophets)—less action on God's part and more explanation—it is always in reaction to something God has done. That is, theological discourse gives the meaning of the prior historical acts of God. Thus, to ignore the historicity of biblical texts cuts against the grain of Christianity itself, and even ironically subverts our own reading. But attention to the historical rootedness of the Bible is

---

[4]I will also argue in chap. 8 that an awareness of a text's historical location will guide us when we believe a biblical character is exemplary for us or not.

[5]And it is such historical realities that give confidence in its veracity (John Wenham, *Christ and the Bible*, 3rd ed. [Grand Rapids, MI: Baker Books, 1994], 17-18, 91-92).

to work with the grain, to recognize and appropriate the very *nature* of what is communicated.

Let us start with an example to show the importance. In Jeremiah 29:11 we read, "For I know the plans I have for you, declares the Lord, plans for welfare and not for evil, to give you a future and a hope." Now, why would Jeremiah write this? (Why would Jeremiah write anything let alone this verse?) Well, the people were about to be hauled off into exile by the Babylonian army! They were about to lose their land and their temple. Now this would be bad enough for anyone. But the Creator God had made a covenant with them which included *land* and *temple*. To lose these things brought real questions as to whether or not the true God was still *their* God, and whether or not they were still his people. Had God abandoned them? Were his purposes with Israel over? Has the plan of redemption come to naught? Were the other gods real after all, one of which has defeated Yahweh? As you read this you might think these questions are absurd. The answer to all of them is of course "No!" But to dismiss them so quickly is to miss the weight of the historical moment and, therefore, the power of the text. Those conditions really provoked such fears. It was in *that* context that Jeremiah gave these words of solace. Are they not richer when we reflect for a moment on the historical environment in which they were made? Surely so.

How do I know these were the historical conditions under which Jeremiah wrote? The literary context tells me! For one, the entirety of chapters one through twenty-nine talk about this coming exile. And we learn in 31:31-34 that the ultimate solution to this *covenantal* problem will be a *new covenant*. But equally, we learn a lot simply from the previous verse, Jeremiah 29:10, where the Lord says, "When seventy years are completed for Babylon, I will visit you, and I will fulfill to you my promise and bring you back to *this place*." So Jeremiah 29:11 is not an abstract blessing—a skeletal cliché on which we can hang any existential clothes. It comes in light of the Babylonian conquest, and it is specifically referring to the "promise" Yahweh had made vis-à-vis the land and temple. The whole context invokes the very precise covenant from generations past which loomed large in these people's and Jeremiah's minds. Thus, literary context does double duty for us: careful attention to it can also elucidate historical context!

I hope you can see, therefore, the true significance of Jeremiah 29:11 by looking at it this way. When you do, it makes it hard to apply to individuals in the abstract, because "seventy years" for any individual would certainly place them beyond the grave. What could "plans," "welfare," and "hope" mean, then, except a covenantal promise for the collective people of God across generations? It is a promise that indeed God's purposes with his people are not over, his plans have not failed, and he has not been bested by another deity. It does not apply to individuals who can fill in words like "plan," "welfare," and "hope" with personalized wishes. The application lies in a bigger cosmic vision of God's purposes through the ages, firmly grounded in very detailed covenantal promises to the collective community of God's people in real space and time.

Let us take an example from the New Testament as well. Something had really troubled Paul when he wrote Galatians. In 1:6, he is "astonished" and in verses 8-9 he starts handing out curses! Verse 7 tells us this is all because someone is "distort[ing] the gospel." This is so bad he would even curse *himself* if he ever did that (v. 8). Now, that might be enough to understand the larger sweep of Galatians: Paul is defending the true gospel. But we can go further to really appreciate some of the finer points. Notice in verse 10 he also compares the ministry goal of "seeking the approval of men/to please men" to "seeking the approval . . . of God." Only the latter would make him a true "servant of Christ." Then much later in 6:12 Paul circles back to comment that the motivation for those perverting the gospel is "to make a good showing in the flesh . . . in order that they may not be persecuted for the cross of Christ." Some are twisting the gospel in order to avoid worldly troubles, and even to win the praise of men (v. 13: "that they may boast in your flesh"). So Galatians is not only dealing with a false gospel, but also shining a light on *what sort of temptations* take people down the road of false-gospel proclamation: avoiding worldly troubles and gaining worldly praise.

Understanding something of the historical lay of the land on which the author and original audiences lived helps readers like us—millennia and stadia removed—appreciate a text's rhetorical punch as well as the reason for particular details therein.

Five Ways to Approach the Study of Historical Context

To study historical contexts, we will need to rely on books devoted to the world around the text. But we do not just start reading history books. For efficiency and to achieve the desired results, it is crucial that students of the Bible understand how the various resources are made and what they are designed to accomplish.

With each of the following tools we will move from the most accessible resources, to the more difficult. Equally, that will mean moving from the least time-demanding to the more time-demanding. Yet, as we increase in levels of complexity and commitment we will also increase our depth of knowledge.

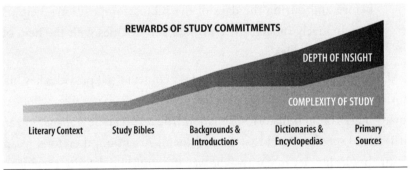

Figure 4.3. More time-intensive historical studies yield deeper insight and more fully orbed interpretations, yet even simple and quick studies remain valuable.

How we approach each resource is directed by how *much* historical context we want, how *much* time we can devote to it, and what *specific questions* we have regarding the historical context. There is never a glowing neon sign telling us what to make of any historical details. A wise study, therefore, depends on the nature of the historical questions readers have, knowing how to use these resources depending on those specific questions, and imaginatively inhabiting the world(s) in which the Bible was written. You can read a lot of material and come away scatterbrained with a lot of diverse factoids that you then do not know how to apply to your study. Rather, you should read your text first and do as much literary context analysis as possible, then come to these resources with historical questions that arise from your literary context work. The main way you should use them is as follows:

1. The literary context itself will start to answer some historical questions.

2. Study Bibles can be very useful for general inquiries.

3. More technical works called backgrounds, introductions, and commentaries can answer questions about specific details of any book, pericope, or verse.

4. Dictionaries and encyclopedias help with big-picture questions that explore the larger historical-cultural issues of the author's and first audience's day.

5. Finally, primary sources—the actual writings of others who lived before and during the days of the Bible's composition—help us imaginatively inhabit their world(s), sometimes with the help of academic articles.

Literary context. First, the very literary context itself provides key historical data. There should be no surprise that texts themselves will bear many marks of their historical situation. The texts can be transparent, as it were, to see the world that created them. Attention, therefore, to an entire book's literary integrity—the way the whole book holds together—can inform the situation in which and to which the book was written. And that, in turn, will influence our understanding of any pericope or verse therein. We saw this above in the examples from Jeremiah and Galatians. No extra resources were needed, but reading the whole gave explicit statements and subtle hints as to why the books were written.

The technical term for this is "mirror reading." It is called that for different reasons than why I used the mirror as an illustration in chapter one. There the text as a mirror was a warning that when we read, we could simply be seeing our own reflection and not what the text truly says. That is bad. This technical kind of mirror reading is when the text mirrors *what was happening at the time it was written*. And that is good. We want to see that. To be clear, however, it is hard to do with every book. Authors assume their audiences already understand their own historical moment. They live in it, after all. So their goal is not to embed little clues that future generations can muse over. And, of course, we could draw conclusions too sweeping from only a few minor textual details. So we should always hold our conclusions from mirror reading provisionally.[6]

Study Bibles (for general inquiries). Next are study Bibles. Note first that not all study Bibles are the same. Some are intended to aid devotional reading. Some have notes that are largely aimed at application. Others are intended as denominational helps (providing comments that represent specific traditions). These can be great as far as they go. The ones I am thinking about here, however, are the ones that give specific attention to historical matters. Let me recommend a few. The *ESV Study Bible* (Crossway, 2008) and the *NIV Zondervan Study Bible* (Zondervan, 2015) are both excellent resources with very helpful maps, charts, drawings, and so on, as well as articles and notes that help the reader imagine the times of the authors and their audiences. Another such resource is the *NIV Cultural Backgrounds Study Bible* (Zondervan, 2016). As the title indicates, the primary focus is the historical landscape on which the Bible was written.

These are good for what I call a "general inquiry." They will answer basic questions of geography and timelines, give insights into customs and patterns of thought, and occasionally show the reader how such matters influence the text. But they are limited because of space and cannot go into too much depth. The serious student of the Bible, therefore, will want to become acquainted with the following resources as well.

Backgrounds, introductions, and commentaries (for text-driven inquiries). The terms "background," "introduction," and "commentary" are all technical terms in biblical studies, and each one means something

---

[6]For the dangers of over-mirror reading, see Andrew David Naselli, *How to Understand and Apply the New Testament: Twelve Steps from Exegesis to Theology* (Phillipsburg, NJ: P&R, 2017), 171-73.

different for how the resource is organized and what it is designed to accomplish. These are not generic terms that publishers could stick on any book cover, but they each mean something very distinct in their structure and purpose. They are good for text-driven inquiries—useful when something in the text raises a question for the interpreter. The texts in question for such inquiries can be an entire testament, a book, a pericope and/or a verse.

A background is a book that explains the customs, worldview, and recent major events in the world at the time the biblical text was written. This is where you can learn about what life was like in Egypt and Palestine and Mesopotamia *for everyone,* not just the people of Israel. What kinds of gods did they worship? What sort of clothes did they wear? What were their political structures? And so forth. And because the New Testament world is in many ways different from the Old Testament world, a background will typically focus on one testament or the other. So a New Testament background will answer a different set of questions: What happened 200 years before Jesus was born? How did Greeks, Romans, and Jews relate to each other? What were the hopes of the Jewish people at that time? What was life like for Jews outside the Promised Land? And so on. Backgrounds, therefore, are great at looking at the larger historical milieu of an entire testament. Like time machines for our imaginations, they help envision the cultural and intellectual environment and *feel* the Old and New Testaments in their original historical eras.

There are a lot that I could recommend, of course. I will comment on just three. For the Old Testament I have found very helpful John H. Walton's *Ancient Near Eastern Thought and the Old Testament* (Baker Academic, 2018). This book does well to paint a picture of how people thought back then and makes use of nonbiblical sources (texts from other cultures, archaeological discoveries, etc.) in a way that is reasonable and accessible. On the specific issue of the various gods among the cultures surrounding Israel, I would point the reader to John D. Currid's *Against the Gods: The Polemical Theology of the Old Testament* (Crossway, 2013). For the New Testament, a bit of a modern classic is Everett Ferguson's

Backgrounds of Early Christianity (Eerdmans, 2003). It too gathers together a lot of sources to paint the picture of what life was like in the Palestine of Jesus' day and throughout the Greco-Roman world of Paul's day, as well as the historical circumstances that created those conditions.

I mention above that I recommend a selective use approach to historical context tools. But for these three resources I would advise the serious Bible student to read them (or similar works) cover to cover. You will not remember every detail, but they will help you imaginatively inhabit the land and times of the Bible. You will develop a historical copiousness, and you will find yourself drawing on it when you read the Bible. Equally, though, these works also have very helpful subject and scriptural indexes. If you have a question about a specific topic, like Nero perhaps, you can look it up in the subject index to see what page Ferguson discusses him and his impact. Or if you are studying Ezekiel 33 and you wonder if there are some historical details of which you are unaware, you can look up Ezekiel 33 in the scriptural index and it will tell you on what page(s) Walton comments on that. If you know how to use these books— to read them straight through or as resources to be consulted at the right time—then you can gain a lot of historical insight from them.

In all, backgrounds operate at "the cognitive environment level," helping us access that shared set of assumptions and shared worldview between authors and audiences that the former expected the latter to know, and the latter used intuitively to interpret.[7]

Introductions are conceptually similar, only they structure their material differently and have a different purpose. Introductions typically look at the historical background (and other issues) surrounding each individual book. If you look at the table of contents the chapter titles will be Genesis, then Exodus, then Leviticus, and so on, or Matthew, Mark, Luke, and so on. They look at each book one by one and address the historical data that pertain uniquely to that particular book. So I always recommend to my students to read a book of the Bible in its entirety in

---

[7]John H. Walton, *Ancient Near Eastern Thought and the Old Testament* (Grand Rapids, MI: Baker Academic, 2006), 21.

one sitting, then read the corresponding chapter in an introduction, and then read the entire book of the Bible in one sitting again. When the student reads the introduction, they will have a good grasp of what is going on because they just read the biblical book in question. Then when they return to the biblical book a second time they will have much more historical data (and other useful material) from the introduction.

As with the previous chapter, introductions are concerned with books as whole texts—they work with the *integrity* of each book—so I cannot commend introductions enough. The two I would recommend are Tremper Longman III and Raymond Dillard's *An Introduction to the Old Testament,* 2nd ed. (Zondervan, 2006) and D. A. Carson and Douglas J. Moo's *An Introduction to the New Testament,* 2nd ed. (Zondervan, 2005). They are not easy reads, but they both cover the most relevant historical data surrounding the interpretation of any book in about twenty-five pages.

We come now to commentaries. As with study Bibles, different commentaries have different goals and, therefore, different results. Some are for devotional reading. Some are to help preachers prepare. And so forth. Such commentaries can be great for those purposes, of course.[8] For this chapter I want to alert you to the commentaries I find to be most helpful to elucidate the historical context.[9] Two commentary series that I recommend to this end are The New International Commentary on the Old Testament (NICOT), and The New International Commentary on the New Testament (NICNT). In any series some volumes are better than others, but these are consistent in targeting matters of historical relevance surrounding the author, the text, and the first audience. They are also easy to navigate and the language is not too technical so as to exclude a wide audience.[10] Less detailed, but also very

---

[8]For help navigating such diversity, see John F. Evans, *A Guide to Biblical Commentaries and Reference Works,* 10th ed. (Grand Rapids, MI: Zondervan Academic, 2016).

[9]I will take this moment, nonetheless, to recommend commentaries from a global perspective and from church history. They can particularly help us see past our biases and presuppositions and make sure the hermeneutical spiral does not become a circle.

[10]The Anchor Bible commentary series (put out by various publishers over the years) and the International Critical Commentary series (T&T Clark) are also good. But they target more highly technical issues for a scholarly audience, and so they assume a high degree of prior understanding and strong discernment skills. Moreover, they can be hard to navigate and know

helpful are *The IVP Bible Background Commentary: Old Testament* (InterVarsity Press, 2000) and *The IVP Bible Background Commentary: New Testament* (InterVarsity Press, 2014).

Now I should emphasize, we come to these with specific questions arising from the biblical text. I had a student once ask me what commentary he should read for Romans. I said "None!" I told him to read Romans many times, over and over. Then, once he felt like he had a strong enough grasp on the whole book's message he should identify key places where he does not understand particular terms, phrases, sentences, how the flow of thought is working, or what historical information would illumine the text. Then, I gave him a list of my three favorite Romans commentators and told him the following:

▶ Read the introduction and preface of the commentary. There you will see the author's assumptions, approach, and general take on the book as a whole. The introduction and preface will also give some big-picture historical data.

▶ Then, turn to the place in the commentary where the author actually addresses the verses about which you have questions. You might find your answer right away. You might be provoked to read other parts of the commentary. You might find that commentary is not helpful at all, and you will never return to it again. That, too, is a great discovery!

In all, the point is if you know how the commentary works, and *why* you are opening it, then you will know where in the book to turn to get your answer and get back to the text of Scripture. If you have the time and want to read an entire commentary cover to cover, go for it. You will learn a lot! If you find a commentary to be a real page-turner and you like the author's style, enjoy! But largely, commentaries should be treated as reference sources, employed when the Bible student has a question arising from their specific engagement with a text.

As a brief example, in studying Mark 4 you might ask about the nature

---

where the truly important material lies if one is not familiar with them.

of storms on the Sea of Galilee. A commentary would be exactly the kind of place that would have some information on an issue specific to that one pericope.

Turn to these resources—backgrounds, introductions, and commentaries —when you have a text-driven inquiry. Specific questions arising from your study of biblical texts push you to these resources. As I mentioned, it is worthwhile to read two backgrounds, one for each testament. Then, when you set out to study a particular book of the Bible, you should read the corresponding chapter in an introduction. Finally, when you have a question about a specific pericope or verse, then you turn to a commentary. Thinking about your study in this way—moving from the broad (a testament) to a specific text (a book) into the details (pericopes and verses in a book)—will focus your study and make efficient use of your time because you will be using the right resource, at the right time, in the right way. So when you have a particular historical question about *texts* (an entire corpus, a specific book, or details of a book) reach for a background, an introduction, or a commentary depending on the nature of said questions and what it is about the texts that interest you.

In the total effort, this too can guard us from the Zeitgeist. The biblical text is driving the question not our own contemporary curiosities.

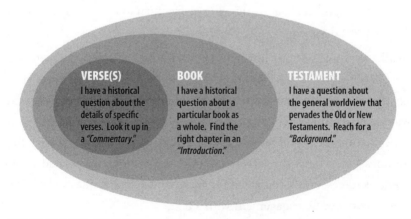

Figure 4.4. The nature of a reader's historical question and the specific level of the text driving the question (a verse, a book, an entire testament) determine what resource is most useful.

Dictionaries, encyclopedias, and atlases (for topic-driven inquiries).
Dictionaries and encyclopedias probably do not need as much explanation. Most people know what they are. Nonetheless, *when* to use them and *how* to use them is less common knowledge. And even less common is the appreciation of them. Here is how a biblical or a theological dictionary or encyclopedia comes together. A publisher finds one or several editors who are well-versed in the field to put together a team of contributors. These contributors write the actual entries. They are chosen by the editors because that are specialists on that particular topic on which they are asked to write. They have been studying that topic for years and often decades! They have read dozens (sometimes hundreds!) of books and articles on the topic and are often conversant in the original languages. Then they compress all that learning into somewhere between three and twenty pages. Think about that: countless hours of research and learning—the devotion of entire careers sometimes—are distilled into a few pages! Then multiply that by the number of entries in the dictionary or encyclopedia and there you have its value in intellectual currency.[11]

But how to use them? Avail yourself of these when you have a topic-driven inquiry. This is a different approach than above. A topic-driven inquiry is when you are studying a text and you suspect there is some sort of broad historical trend that could aid your reading.[12] For example, Psalm 118:27 says, "The LORD is God, and he has made his light to shine upon us. Bind the festal sacrifice with cords, up to the horns of the altar!" Well, what are the "horns of the altar"? What is a "festal sacrifice"? What "light" is this? You could, of course, look this verse up in a commentary (see above) and it will speak to some of these things *in light of Psalm 118 particularly*. But you can also ask broader questions. What were the

---

[11]The accessibility of good Bible dictionaries is why I am not a strong proponent of word studies, notably absent from the previous chapter. Why repeat the hard work that has already been done by trained and experienced scholars? If you are curious about a word, just look it up in a good Bible dictionary; you will get better and quicker results than if you attempted a word study of your own.

[12]To be clear, I am not talking about *theological* dictionaries or dictionaries of church history, or something like that. Those are great too, but for different purposes. I am talking about those specifically aimed at the historical data surrounding the Scriptures, those in the field of *biblical studies*.

"horns of the altar" in general? Where did they come from? What did they look like? What was the point of them? How long in the history of Israel were they used? Were they important elsewhere in the Old Testament, or in other cultures? By looking up "horns of the altar" or just "altar" in a Bible dictionary and/or encyclopedia you will get a broad sweep of their significance across the culture and throughout the Old Testament. Then you can take that knowledge back to Psalm 118 and use your sane imagination to think about what specific details that study adds to understanding Psalm 118. Then, you can do the same thing with "festal sacrifice" and "light." Clearly "light" is a metaphor here. A dictionary or encyclopedia entry on "light" across the Old Testament can go a long way to understanding its possible role in Psalm 118:27. Now, verse 27 may not be one of those loadbearing verses in the flow of Psalm 118, and so you will not make too much of these details. But it *might* be a loadbearing verse, at which point these historical details become all the more important in your interpretation. Either way, verse 27 plays some role in the coherency of the psalm, so these details are worth searching out.

Each publisher seems to have a series of dictionaries and encyclopedias, but the most thorough is *The IVP Bible Dictionary Series*. There is one volume for each genre of Scripture: Pentateuch, Old Testament Historical Books, Jesus and the Gospels, and so on. Specializing like this allows the contributors to really get down into the details.

A Bible atlas is also very handy. The Bible mentions a lot of places. Knowing where they are and their geographical surroundings can go a long way in understanding a pericope. I recommend the *Crossway ESV Study Atlas* (Crossway, 2010).

To be clear, though this context is the world *around* the text, such study does not import foreign ideas into the text, and so compromise its integrity or blur its coherency. To the contrary, historical contextual concerns actually arise out of our literary study of the world *in* the text, for it is the text itself invoking the world around it through the particular cultural details embedded in the text. Pieces of the literary context are asking us to go into that world around the text, and then return to the text for another level of contextual interpretation.

Continuing with our Mark 4 example bears this out. I commented in the last chapter that the literary context draws us into chapter five as well. There you will want to know about the Sea of Galilee in general and what is on the "other side" (5:1), what are the "Gerasenes" (also 5:1), and what is the "Decapolis" (5:20). Commentaries will tell you what these are, specifically

Figure 4.5. "The world around the text" is activated for interpretation by "the world in the text."

in relation to their function in Mark 5. But an atlas will show you where these things are, and a good dictionary or encyclopedia entry will describe them to further fill out your understanding of Jesus' life and times. Your sane imagination can then bring that knowledge to bear on Mark 5 (making you a little less reliant on the commentaries). It turns out these are all marks of Gentile territories. So while the term "Gentile" is not in Mark 5, nonetheless there is a theology in this pericope (coming out of the parables and the stilling of the storm in Mark 4) as it pertains to Gentiles that the astute reader should observe. Despite the threat to the disciples' lives, the mustard seed of the kingdom is already starting to grow *among the Gentiles*. In this way, the *textual* details of Mark 5 have ushered in *historical* details of the first century.

Use these resources for topic-driven inquiries—when you discover in the text an issue in which knowledge about it in the broader historical landscape will fill out your sane imagination, to still better understand your text in question.

Primary sources and academic articles (for worldview-driven inquiries). Finally, you can become a historian! Get an undergraduate degree, then an MA. Then go on to earn a PhD. Hey, what's the next four to twelve years of your life? And the tools of the true historian are primary sources—the actual texts and artifacts from the worlds of the prophets and apostles. Digging into those gets us as deep as we can to truly inhabiting their worlds. The more conversant we are with the primary sources, therefore, the more fluidly our sane imagination works, for we will understand the thoughts of those people on their own terms.

Short of such a lifelong commitment, however, there are accessible compendiums of ancient Near Eastern and Greco-Roman texts. They are already translated for us, and often enough editors have compiled what they discern are the more relevant entries. For the Bible student who would wade into the depths of the prophets' and apostles' conceptual environments, I would recommend starting with *Readings from the Ancient Near East: Primary Sources for Old Testament Study* (Baker Academic, 2002) and *The New Testament Background: Writings from Ancient Greece and the Roman Empire That Illuminate Christian Origins* (HarperOne, 1989).

As you read, however, be aware that some texts represent specific ideas of the writers and their communities, and others reflect general worldview assumptions shared across the culture. Wide reading is the only way to discern which is which.

An illustration might be helpful at this point. If you read enough of the Pseudepigrapha and Dead Sea Scrolls you will start to get the sense that many people (though surely not all) believed that the Babylonian exile was enduring in some sense still hundreds of years after Ezra and Nehemiah's return, and even up to Jesus and the apostles' time.[13] The *Words of the Luminaries*[a] (4Q504) VI, 12-13 asks the Lord to "rescue your people Israel from all the lands near and far where you have banished them." *Testament of Benjamin* 9:1-2 sees the exile end when "the twelve tribes will be gathered together there, as well as all the nations." Here are just two brief examples—one illustrating the understanding that

---

[13]This is not an undisputed point, as one can imagine. An accessible piece that summarizes various views and lays out some primary sources is Nicholas G. Piotrowski, "'Discern the Word and Understand the Vision': Ongoing Exile in Second Temple Judaism and Its Relevance for Biblical Theology," *CTR* 16 (2018): 21-42.

Israelites are still "banished," and another expressing the hope that all will someday be "gathered together."[14]

Did Jesus and the apostles also share this view? Did they too think the exile persisted? That intriguing question is what arises from this study. It turns our antennae on, therefore, to think about what the New Testament authors might mean when they enumerate historical epochs "from the deportation to Babylon to the Christ" (Mt 1:17), or introduced the gospel as the fulfillment of the prophetic expectation of the end of the exile (Mk 1:1-3), or call Christians "sojourners and exiles" (1 Pet 2:11). These are not easy questions, and there are no easy answers. But the window into the culture that primary sources provide can help us discern some of these texts' undercurrents, and access shared understandings (sometimes merely intuitively) between authors and first audiences.

Finally, academic articles are available to help understand the primary sources. These can be found in peer-reviewed journals and on the American Theological Library Association database (which can be accessed at most schools and many public libraries). Buyer beware, however, when it comes to these articles. If dictionaries and encyclopedias house our time-tested knowledge, these academic articles are more experimental. Scholars have hypotheses, write them out, and other scholars evaluate their merits. So time will only tell when an article might carve out a new corner of our knowledge. As you read some, understand that you are not reading *opinion* by any means—these works are backed up with data and argumentation—but you are also not reading undisputed and accepted fact. So make each author prove their point from whatever primary source in question before adopting their views. The quality of each article depends on its own merits, thereby making it hard to recommend one particular journal. But if I must, *Tyndale Bulletin* has a solid reputation for publishing well researched and thoroughly vetted articles on biblical and theological studies.

---

[14]My own translations.

Summary

Attention to historical contexts can guard us from allegory. The more we know of the world *around* the text, the less prone we are to import assumptions from our own world *into* the text. Moreover, attention to historical contexts helps us see more of what is truly in the text. It is the historical details and the shared worldview between authors and original audiences we need to recover if we are going to treat the Bible as it asks to be treated: *historically*.

To do this, we rely on literary contexts and mirror reading first. Biblical texts bear in themselves clear enough marks of their historical circumstances that careful reading can reveal. Yet, additionally, we also have the helpful works of historians and scholars to understand the Bible's cultural landscapes, and to shape a sane imagination for historically

Table 4.1. Distinct resources are designed to answer different questions, as they view/engage biblical texts at various levels. Note: Academic articles can help with any of these questions.

The Aims of Biblical Studies Resources					
	Literary Context	Study Bibles	Backgrounds, Introductions, Commentaries	Dictionaries & Encyclopedias	Primary Sources
General inquiry		√			
Questions over entire testament			√		
Questions related to a specific book	√		√		
Questions related to details of specific verses	√	√	√		
Questions on a topic that stretches across the Bible				√	
Questions on a topic that stretches across a portion of the Bible				√	
Questions on a topic in a book	√			√	
Questions of worldview/ conceptual environment			√		√

minded reading. Study Bibles provide answers for general inquiries, quick answers though not terribly deep, whereas backgrounds, introductions, and commentaries can answer more specific inquiries that arise from a biblical text—either an entire testament, a book, or a given pericope or verse. Dictionaries and encyclopedias add an extra layer of understanding as they address broader historical, cultural, and social trends. Atlases situate us geographically. And finally, there are many accessible translations of primary sources from the cultures in and around Israel and the church that embody both common and specific ideologies. Depending, therefore, on the nature of your question and how deep you want to dive, there are various resources available.

Conclusion

In this chapter we have not exhausted the value of studying historical contexts or detailed all the resources. We have seen, however, some of the value of this sort of contextual study, and I have tried to explain the theoretical reasons behind why certain key resources were made and, therefore, how they can be efficiently used. As an axe can cut through the middle of a tree and see the rings that give much insight into the history of not only the tree itself but also its environment, so too these resources can open up a text to see details of what had been going on in the world around the text both recently and for a long time. Because this was important to Jesus and the apostles, and since history is the dazzling theatre of God's glory, as Calvin put it,[15] this kind of work is both important to good discipleship and close to the very heart of Christianity.

So far, I have argued the theoretical-philosophical (indeed theological) rationale for what is called the historical-grammatical approach to interpretation. By way of the next two chapters, we will expand our approach to what I am calling the historical-grammatical-*christological* approach to interpretation. Again, faithful discipleship calls us to it.

---

[15]Calvin, *Institutes* 1.14.20, ed. McNeill (1:179).

For Further Study

This chapter includes a much longer bibliography. In other chapters I only want to recommend a few resources, so as not to overwhelm. This time, however, I want to list the several resources I mentioned throughout the chapter and a few more. So here in one place, are the books I recommend that the serious Bible student should skip meals to get on their shelf.

Study Bibles

The ESV Study Bible. Wheaton, IL: Crossway Bibles, 2008.

NIV Cultural Backgrounds Study Bible. Grand Rapids, MI: Zondervan, 2016.

NIV Zondervan Study Bible. Grand Rapids, MI: Zondervan, 2015.

Backgrounds, Introductions, and Commentaries

Arnold, Clinton E., ed. *Zondervan Illustrated Bible Backgrounds Commentary: New Testament*. 5 vols. Grand Rapids, MI: Zondervan Academic, 2002.

Carson, D. A., and Douglas J. Moo. *An Introduction to the New Testament*. 2nd ed. Grand Rapids, MI: Zondervan, 2005.

Currid, John D. *Against the Gods: The Polemical Theology of the Old Testament*. Wheaton, IL: Crossway, 2013.

Ferguson, Everett. *Backgrounds of Early Christianity*. 3rd ed. Grand Rapids, MI: Eerdmans, 2003.

Guthrie, Donald. *New Testament Introduction*. 4th ed. Downers Grove, IL: IVP Academic, 1989.

Keener, Craig S. *The IVP Bible Background Commentary: New Testament*. 2nd ed. Downers Grove, IL: InterVarsity Press, 2014.

Longman, Tremper, III, and Raymond Dillard, eds. *An Introduction to the Old Testament*. 2nd ed. Grand Rapids, MI: Zondervan Academic, 2006.

Merrill, Eugene H., Mark F. Rooker, and Michael A. Grisanti. *The World and the Word: An Introduction to the Old Testament*. Nashville: B&H Academic, 2011.

Walton, John H. *Ancient Near Eastern Thought and the Old Testament: Introducing the Conceptual World of the Hebrew Bible*. 2nd ed. Grand Rapids, MI: Baker Academic, 2018.

_____, ed. *Zondervan Illustrated Bible Backgrounds Commentary: Old Testament*. 5 vols. Grand Rapids, MI: Zondervan Academic, 2009.

Walton, John H., Victor H. Matthews, and Mark W. Chavalas, eds. *The IVP Bible Background Commentary: Old Testament*. Downers Grove, IL: InterVarsity Press, 2000.

Dictionaries and Encyclopedias

The IVP Bible Dictionary Series. 8 vols. Downers Grove, IL: IVP Academic, 1993–2013.

Ryken, Leland, James C. Wilhoit, and Tremper Longman III, eds. *Dictionary of Biblical Imagery*. Downers Grove, IL: IVP Academic, 1998.

Tenney, Merrill C., and Moisés Silva, eds. *The Zondervan Encyclopedia of the Bible*. 5 vols. Rev. ed. Grand Rapids, MI: Zondervan Academic, 2010.

Atlases

Currid, John D., and David P. Barrett, eds. *Crossway ESV Bible Atlas*. Wheaton, IL: Crossway, 2010.

Rasmussen, Carl G. *Zondervan Atlas of the Bible*. Rev. ed. Grand Rapids, MI: Zondervan, 2010.

For Advanced Study

Backgrounds, Introductions, and Commentaries

Arnold, Bill T., and Brent A. Strawn. *The World around the Old Testament: The People and Places of the Ancient Near East*. Grand Rapids, MI: Baker Academic, 2016.

Green, Joel B., ed. *The New International Commentary on the New Testament*. 21 vols. Grand Rapids, MI: Eerdmans, 1974–2020.

Green, Joel B., and Lee Martin McDonald, eds. *The World of the New Testament: Cultural, Social, and Historical Contexts*. Grand Rapids, MI: Baker Academic, 2013.

Hoffmeier, James K. *The Archaeology of the Bible*. Oxford: Lion Scholar, 2008.

Hubbard, Robert L., Jr., and Bill T. Arnold, eds. *The New International Commentary on the Old Testament*. 27 vols. Grand Rapids, MI: Eerdmans, 1976–2020.

Wright, N. T. *The New Testament and the People of God*. Vol. 1 of *Christian Origins and the Question of God*. Minneapolis: Fortress, 1992.

Dictionaries and Encyclopedias

Collins, John J., and Daniel C. Harlow, eds. *The Eerdmans Dictionary of Early Judaism*. Grand Rapids, MI: Eerdmans, 2010.

Powell, Mark Allen, ed. *Harper Collins Bible Dictionary*. Rev. and upd. ed. San Francisco: HarperOne, 2001.

Primary Sources

Arnold, Bill T., and Bryan E. Beyer, eds. *Readings from the Ancient Near East: Primary Sources for Old Testament Study*. Grand Rapids, MI: Baker Academic, 2002.

Barrett, C. K., ed. *The New Testament Background: Writings from Ancient Greece and the Roman Empire That Illuminate Christian Origins*. San Francisco: HarperOne, 1989.

Charlesworth, James H., ed. *The Old Testament Pseudepigrapha*. 2 vols. Anchor Bible Reference Library. New York: Doubleday, 1983–1985.

Coogan, Michael, D., Marc Z. Brettler, Carol A. Newsom, and Pheme Perkins, eds. *The New Oxford Annotated Apocrypha*. 5th ed. Oxford: Oxford University Press, 2018.

Elwell, Walter A., and Robert W. Yarbrough, eds. *Readings from the First-Century World: Primary Sources for New Testament Study*. Encountering Biblical Studies. Grand Rapids, MI: Baker Academic, 1998.

Josephus. *The Works of Josephus: Complete and Unabridged.* Upd. ed. Translated by William Whiston. Peabody, MA: Hendrickson, 1987.

Wise, Michael, Martin Abegg Jr., and Edward Cook, eds. *The Dead Sea Scrolls: A New Translation.* San Francisco: HarperOne, 1996, 2005.

Academic Articles

ATLA Religion Database with AtlaSerials. www.atla.com. www.ebsco.com.

Howard, Caleb et. al., eds. *Tyndale Bulletin.* Cambridge: Tyndale House. 1956–present.

5

THE THINGS CONCERNING HIMSELF

The Christological Context, Part 1

FOR MY LAST SEMESTER OF COLLEGE I went to Tasmania, Australia. It was glorious! I saw natural phenomena there that I had never seen before and likely will never see again. Even things as simple as clouds were unique in their subtle nuances. The weather, the plants, the terrain, the angle of the light at dawn and dusk, and of course the stars were all fascinatingly different from my northern hemisphere life.

Toward the end of the semester, my Marine Ecology class took a week-long trip to Maria Island to study the sort of animals (particularly very small invertebrates) that live in kelp forests.

We would scuba dive, collect kelp specimens, and then examine what we found in an onsite lab. When the work was done in the late afternoon, I headed out on my bike to explore Maria Island. It is not a big island, and I could visit all of its popular sites over just a few days. On our last day, I

Figure 5.1. Entire communities of fish and invertebrates live in kelp forests.

woke up very early to hike to the top of Mount Maria, the highest point on the island. If I left early enough and moved quickly, I could spend some time on the top and make it back down to camp before the workday started. When I set out it was very misty as the sun was just stealing over the horizon. As I hiked, the fog did not lift and I was worried that my trek would be for nothing. I wanted to look out over Maria Island and see it all in one glimpse—one 360 degree panorama. But I climbed on in hope, and hope did not disappoint. Just as I summited, the fog thinned and disappeared in what seemed like a fraction of a second. I could see it all!

As I looked out I could also recognize the places I had been, and how the several geological features were connected to each other, even running into each other. There were Riedle Bay and Oyster Bay, and the isthmus that ran between them. There were the Painted Cliffs that glowed at sundown.

To the north were the Fossil Cliffs with innumerable ancient shells. To the west were the slopes on which we often saw kangaroos, sometimes hiding, sometimes showing off. All around was the Tasman Sea where we scuba-dived. It was all laid out before me and I could see how the various geological features were not isolated locations, but all bent and flowed together. In many ways it appeared as though the land emerged seamlessly from the sea and sloped upward through assorted landscapes to the zenith where I stood.

Figure 5.2. Maria Island, Australia

This confluence of otherwise diverse features was only observable from the top of Mount Maria, almost as though Mount Maria was drawing the rest of the island up to itself. Reaching the top of the mountain and looking back allowed me to see unlike I had seen before.

There is, of course, a lesson for biblical hermeneutics here. The Bible is, as we saw in chapter three, a collection of sixty-six integrous and individually cohesive books. Each is interpreted on its own terms and in its own right. We could say that each book of the Bible is like one of those individual geological features on Maria Island. You go to one at a time and enjoy its own local integrity and cohesion. That is what I did each

Figure 5.3. The Painted Cliffs on Maria Island

Figure 5.4. The diverse terrains of Maria Island compose one unified landscape.

day on my bike. Yet, the landscapes, as I tried to illustrate above, do not have hard boundaries. Rather, they touch each other and fit together to create the entire island. So too, the sixty-six integrous and individually cohesive books of the Bible *all come together to comprise the entire testimony of what God is doing in history for the salvation of his people.*

For this chapter, therefore, imagine the Bible like a mountain range. In a mountain range there are several mountains, each with its own name and distinct features. Yet, all those mountains connect and create a distinct landscape. We will look down from above to see the entire mountain range of the Bible in one purview and realize how it all bends and flows together. This is an important step in our consideration of the christological context because in the next chapter we will parachute in and make our way around the terrain.

The Landscape of Redemptive History

While it is largely common that Christians know the major teachings of the Bible and the most iconic verses, it is less common that we understand how all the parts work together to make the Bible what it is in the big picture. We "miss the forest for the trees" as it is often said. The ability to know not just the stories and teachings of the Bible, but how they all come together is what I call "large-scale biblical literacy." The goal of this chapter is to get a glimpse of the contours of the entire Bible just like I saw Maria Island from above. When we zoom out, as it were, and get the big picture we can see more clearly how the parts all fit together and form one beautiful landscape. In short, this chapter is an attempt at developing our large-scale biblical literacy. If we have done our literary context work well, it will now pay off in particular ways. We can now bring together those whole-book metatheologies and understand the broad sweep of redemptive history.

There are many ways to organize this material depending on how in-depth we want to go, or what particular topics attract our attention. I have chosen here an outline that I hope will help readers remember major landmarks across the terrain of Scripture. As expected from the previous two chapters, we will consider redemptive history *book by book*—whole books in their full coherent integrity—in a *historical* order. Thus, we are already applying our hermeneutical knowledge.

Take a moment to look at this outline.

The Creation of God's People
Genesis   Exodus   Leviticus   Numbers   Deuteronomy

The Establishment of God's People
Joshua   Judges

The Crowning of God's King
Ruth   1 & 2 Samuel   1 Kings 1–10

The Worship and Wisdom of God's King
Job   Psalms   Proverbs
Ecclesiastes   Song of Songs

The Disobedience of God's King
1 Kings 11–2 Kings 25   Isaiah   Hosea   Joel   Amos   Obadiah
Jonah   Micah   Nahum   Habakkuk   Zephaniah

The Disestablishment of God's People
Jeremiah   Lamentations   Ezekiel   Daniel

The Re-Creation of God's People
1 and 2 Chronicles   Ezra   Nehemiah   Esther
Haggai   Zechariah   Malachi

God the Son Brings the Kingdom of God
Matthew   Mark   Luke   John
God the Spirit Spreads the Kingdom of God
Acts   Romans   1 and 2 Corinthians   Galatians   Ephesians
Philippians   Colossians   1 and 2 Thessalonians   1 and 2 Timothy
Titus   Philemon   Hebrews   James   1 and 2 Peter
1, 2, and 3 John   Jude
God the Son Reigns over the Kingdom of God
Revelation

What do you notice about this layout? By grouping and organizing the books of the Bible in this way I am trying to show what various books have in common with each other, as well as the progress of redemptive history. Notice that I have taken the first five books of the Bible and labeled them "The Creation of God's People." I will explain more below, but suffice it for now to comment that the overarching concept of those books, taken together, is how God made a people for himself, and what that process entailed. Then straight down from that section is "The Re-Creation of God's People." In those books the dominant concern is remaking his people (and he will remake them again!) in a new way. But why do they need to be "remade" or "re-created"? Well, going back to the second section you will see that I label it "The Establishment of God's People." Those books are all about how God put his people in, and preserved them in, the Promised Land. Then, the great crisis of the Old Testament—it cannot be overstated—is the exile, when Israel was removed from the land by force and lost nearly all its national and religious identity. So I call the books that focus most on that "The Disestablishment of God's People," located directly below is its counterpart. Again, more on this below. We must ask now why they were exiled. Why did God take them out of the land he had initially put them in? In the section called "The Crowning of God's King," we read of how David and his dynasty were raised up to shepherd the Lord's people. But the books in the section "The Disobedience of God's King" record the failures of David's progeny to rule with faithfulness and justice. Basically they (not all, but most) wandered from the ways of the Lord toward other gods. Yet David himself, though by no means perfect, never worshiped false gods. And so, before the decline of his dynasty into exile, we have the heart and lungs of the Old Testament: "The Worship and Wisdom of God's King." These books reflect what kind of wisdom God's king uses to rule his people, and in what manner God's king should lead his people in worship.

With that we come to the New Testament. With the coming of Jesus Christ we see a stunningly beautiful fulfillment of all those Old Testament hopes. I will go into more detail on this below, but it is enough for now to say that with Jesus that kingdom lost under David's sons has returned with breathtaking power. Obviously this is recorded in the books under the heading "God the Son Brings the Kingdom." Then, in Acts and the New Testament letters, this kingdom goes *international* as "God the Spirit Spreads the Kingdom." And finally, the book of Revelation details the current and eternal lordship of Jesus Christ. This section is called "God the Son Reigns over the Kingdom" which returns us to the original intent of creation: a community of every tongue, tribe, people, and nation gathered in the presence of God for unsullied worship, brought there by the perfect image bearer.

Let us now look at some whole-book metatheologies to see how each section coheres and moves into the next.

The Creation of God's People

The first five books, commonly called the Pentateuch or the books of Moses, are all about how God creates a worshiping community that will know him and love him. This idea of creation is evident right from the beginning. Yes, Genesis 1–2 is about the creation of the cosmos, and its climax is when the Almighty "rests" in 2:1-3. But God's last act before "resting" is to make a creature who will bear his image—reflect his glory—and "rest" with him (1:26-27).[1] Thus, humanity's originally intended place in the cosmos is to live in perfect peace with God, with each other,

---

[1] On the connection between the "image of God" and the "glory of God," see Dane C. Ortlund, "What Does It Mean to Fall Short of the Glory of God? Romans 3:23 in Biblical-Theological Perspective," *WTJ* 80 (2018): 128-31.

and with the creation itself. But this "rest" does not mean inactivity. In Genesis 1:28 God tells both the man and the woman to create and spread cultures for human flourishing.

> And God blessed them.
> And God said to them,
> "Be fruitful and multiply and *fill the earth and subdue it,*
> > and *have dominion* over the fish of the sea
> > and over the birds of the heavens
> > and over every living thing that moves on the earth."

That is their calling. They are basically commissioned to act as God has acted: to create and organize. Then chapter two zooms in on those relationships. So, while the Bible starts with the creation of the cosmos, it quickly moves to the creation of God's image bearers who will know him and worship him through living out that creational intent of culture making.[2]

With chapter three things go terribly wrong, however. The man and the woman rebel against the Creator and fall from their felicitous state. Henceforth, their efforts in living out their Genesis 1:28 commission are greatly hindered, and they are expelled from the presence of God. Therefore, issues going forward are ethics, the presence of God, and death: *ethics*, because the problems with the world all originate in rebellion against God; *the presence of God* because humanity was made to enjoy just that but then lost it because of the man's rebellion; and *death* because God is the living God so his image bearers ought to have life, but they die because of that rebellion. As New Testament theologian G. B. Caird summarizes, "Sin separates the human race from God and death is the final severance."[3]

No sooner do they fall, nonetheless, does God promise that one day one of their sons will reverse these conditions and return humanity to that lost place in the presence of God. This is the point of Genesis 3:15. Speaking to the serpent, God says:

---

[2] Andy Crouch, *Culture Making: Recovering Our Creative Calling* (Downers Grove, IL: InterVarsity Press, 2008), 101-117.

[3] G. B. Caird, *New Testament Theology,* ed. L. D. Hurst (Oxford: Oxford University Press, 1994), 83.

I will put enmity between you and the woman,
>   and between your seed and *her seed*;
> he shall strike your head,
>   and you shall strike his heel.[4]

The serpent tempted God's image bearers, and so the defeat of the serpent will open up the door for humanity's return to its original place in the presence of God. This salvation, therefore, will have to address those three problems above: sin and ethics, removal from the presence of God, and death. How exactly this will all happen we do not know yet, but it is this future seed of the woman who will do it. Thus, *returning to the presence of God by overcoming sin and death is the goal of the rest of the Bible*.[5] And how that one seed of the woman will do it is the *overall* drama.[6] This can seem like a reduction of what the Bible is all about, but even within the many twists and turns that the biblical narrative takes, within the diversity of genres and themes, I hope to show in the rest of this chapter that the coming of this one seed of the woman is always in view somehow or another.

To summarize, redemptive history is about how the coming seed of the woman will (1) create a new humanity that will love and obey the Lord, (2) back in the presence of God, (3) with life, and life abundantly.

But the rainbow is far over the hill at this point. Genesis 4–11 describes how humanity rebels more and more against its Creator and the hope of returning to his presence looks hopelessly thin as disobedience and death only increase. But with Genesis 12:1-3 God takes specific steps to that end. He calls one man, Abraham, and says this to him:

> Go from your country
>   and your kindred and your father's house
> to the land that I will show you.

---

[4] Author's translation. The verb "strike" here could also be rendered "bruise" or "crush."

[5] "The Adamic king of the new creation forms the central storyline that is threaded throughout all the various books of the OT" (G. K. Beale, *A New Testament Biblical Theology: The Unfolding of the Old Testament in the New* [Grand Rapids, MI: Baker Academic, 2011], 63).

[6] Two very good surveys of this can be found in T. Desmond Alexander, "Seed," *NDBT*, 769-74, and James Hamilton, "The Skull Crushing Seed of the Woman: Inner-Biblical Interpretation of Genesis 3:15," *SBJT* 10.2 (2006): 30-54.

> And I will make of you a great nation,
>
> and I will bless you
>
> and make your name great,
>
> > so that you will be a blessing.
>
> I will bless those who bless you,
>
> and him who dishonors you I will curse,
>
> > and in you all the families of the earth shall be blessed.

From Abraham, God will create a people for himself through whom he will bless all peoples. It does not say it here specifically, but in the context of all of Genesis it is clear that that blessing will come in the form of the seed of the woman of Genesis 3:15, who will achieve the restoration of humanity.[7] One thing at a time, however. First, God will create a unique people who will know him, love him, and worship him through obedience as Adam and Eve were first called to do.[8]

Here we see the theme of "The Creation of God's People" really come into focus. The rest of the book of Genesis is about the status of those, and related, promises.[9] Will Abraham be more faithful than Adam? Will he have children? If so, through which ones will the promise continue? And so forth, until we get to the end. In Genesis 49:8-12 we read that the promise of a coming savior—who will also be a king as it turns out—will come through the line of Judah. Genesis ends, therefore, with God having created a small group of people, Abraham's grandchildren and their families, through whom he intends to bless the entire world, specifically by giving the world the seed of the woman through the line of Judah to restore rest to the cosmos.

But there are problems. At the end of Genesis, they are not living in the land promised to Abraham, but in Egypt. When the book of Exodus

---

[7] T. Desmond Alexander, "From Adam to Judah: The Significance of the Family Tree in Genesis," *EvQ* 61 (1989): 5-19.

[8] The noun "seed" is both collective and singular. Walter C. Kaiser states that "the word designates the whole line of descendants as a unit, yet it is deliberately flexible enough to denote either one person who epitomizes the whole group . . . , or the many persons in that whole line of natural and/or spiritual descendants" ("zera'," *TWOT* 1:253).

[9] Stephen G. Dempster, *Dominion and Dynasty: A Theology of the Hebrew Bible*, NSBT 15 (Downers Grove, IL: InterVarsity Press, 2003), 55-92; Jared M. August, "The Messianic Hope of Genesis: The *Protoevangelium* and Patriarchal Promises," *Themelios* 42 (2017): 46-62.

opens, hundreds of years have passed and Abraham's descendants, now called "Israel," are enslaved in Egypt. As if it could not get worse, the Pharaoh is also trying to exterminate them! But God remembers his covenant promises to Abraham and his offspring, and so raises up Moses to rescue them. When they come out of Egypt through many signs and wonders they are now a great nation. But the problem remains that no one really knows the Lord; they certainly do not know his laws and what he expects of them. So once they cross the Red Sea, they come to Mount Sinai to receive the Ten Commandments.

Now the creation of God's people is really shaping up. They are a large number and they have the law of God. They can now bless the nations through their righteous obedience. But the goal remains to make of them a worshiping community *in the presence of the Lord*. The rest of Exodus, therefore, focuses on the building of the *tabernacle*, a tent in which God will dwell among his people. Particularly worth noting is that the lead craftsman for building the temple is *of the tribe of Judah* (Ex 31:1-6; 38:22-23). The very end of Exodus, then, is a wonderful climax to the biblical drama so far: the glory of the Lord fills the tabernacle and God is once again dwelling with humanity (Ex 40:34-38)!

Humanity is still sinful, however, and Israel is no different. We have already seen what happens when people transgress the law of God: they are *removed* from his presence and death replaces rest. How, then, can Israel and God dwell together? The answer is, in Leviticus, the Lord sets up a priestly and sacrificial system through which Israel can have their sins atoned for. Thus, God himself has graciously provided the means by which he can still dwell among his people.

The only thing remaining in creating his people is for the Lord to put them in the land he promised to Abraham. But in Numbers the people's trust in the Lord proves to be very weak, and so they do not make it into the Promised Land. So the plan of redemption moves on, though Israel first must wander the desert. Particularly worth noting is the role of Judah during this time, first among the tribes (Num 2:3; 7:12) and leading the nation in battle (Num 10:14).

Numbers ends with a more faithful generation ready to take the Promised Land. Just before they enter, however, Moses gives three sermons in the book of Deuteronomy that interpret how they should apply the law once they enter, and also predict what will happen in their relationship with the Lord. Thus we come to the end of the Pentateuch and God's people are fully created: they have been called out of the mass of sinful fallen humanity, brought together in the form of a great nation, given laws, and given a tabernacle where priests are instructed how to make sacrifices in the presence of God. It has been a lengthy process, but they are now formed as God's worshiping community. Next, they need a *place* to dwell with God.

The Establishment of God's People

The next two books are about God taking his people and putting them in the land and keeping them in the land. These are the overriding concerns of the books of Joshua and Judges. When the people take the land we read in Joshua 21:43-44, "Thus the LORD gave to Israel all the land that he swore to give to their fathers. And they took possession of it, and they settled there. And the LORD gave them rest on every side just as he had sworn to their fathers."

You will notice that "the Lord gave them *rest*." This recalls Genesis 2:1-3. "Rest" is what Adam and Eve had in the presence of God before they sinned. Thus, with the establishment of God's people they have *a semblance* of that original creational experience, and the Promised Land now constitutes the place where God's people live in God's presence. God's goal since Genesis 3:15 was to bring his people back to him and to their creational mission of Genesis 1:28. With Joshua, a significant step in that direction has been accomplished as he *kind of looks like* the seed of the woman.

It is clear, however, that this moment of fulfillment and the reminiscent language of rest is unconsummated, a temporary shadow of what the full restoration to paradise will someday look like. We know this because the very next book, Judges, demonstrates how transitory that rest was. For, as with Adam and the wilderness generation of Numbers, the people are still sinful, and this jeopardizes their ability to live in the presence of God. Judges 2:10-23 concisely describes Israel's life over the next several generations. They forget the good things the Lord has done for them, so they serve other gods, which provokes the Lord, and he raises up their enemies. Each enemy, then, becomes a threat to the people's existence in the land. But the Lord has pity on them and also raises up temporary deliverers called judges "who saved them out of the hand of those who plundered them" (Judg 2:16). All the same, each successive generation turns away from the Lord again, demonstrating how stubbornly entrenched sin and rebellion are in the human heart. This cycle repeats itself seven times in Judges, before two final stories in chapters seventeen to twenty-one reveal the root of the problem. Judges 17–21 starts and ends with the same two sentences: "In those days there was no king in Israel. Everyone did what was right in his own eyes" (Judg 17:6; 21:25).[10] And what is right in the eyes of sinners is wrong in the eyes of God. What could possibly bring the people to righteous obedience? They already have the law. What else do they need? They need a *king*. They need a king that will keep the law and lead *them* in keeping the law as well. Both Judges 17:6 and 21:25 say just that: "In those days there was no king in Israel."

The Crowning of God's King

The book of Ruth is the next step forward in redemptive history, even though it starts on an ominous note: "In the days when the judges ruled" (1:1). By mentioning the judges, we remember the chaos without a king in those days. And there is chaos right away. There is a famine and Israelites have to leave the Promised Land to dwell in Moab (not a friendly nation historically), and then the men of the family all die (vv. 1-5). A slight ray of hope does break over the situation, however, when we are also told in that same first verse that this Israelite family is from *Judah*.

---

[10]Judges 17–21 is a very good example of what we discussed in chap. 3: how multiple pericopes often combine to form larger units of books, and how that combination influences interpretation.

We remember from Gen 49:8-12 that the king will come through the line of Judah.[11] As the story of Ruth progresses there are at times tragic, and at times beautiful, details to observe. But why should this story be part of the Bible? There are a lot of tragic and beautiful stories in the world. What makes this one unique is the way it goes from the chaos of "the days when the judges ruled" (complete with a famine, displacement, death and broken families; the world is truly in chaos) to this blessing in chapter four: "May your house be like the house of Perez, whom Tamar bore to *Judah*, because of the *seed* that the Lord will give you by this young woman" (v. 12).[12]

It turns out that God is bringing order out of the chaos in the book of Ruth by bringing the seed of the woman into the world (Gen 3:15) through the house of Judah (Gen 49:8-12). The last word in Ruth, then, is a genealogy of *David*. And from this point on the Old Testament is steadily fixed on David, "the focus of world genealogy."[13]

First Samuel then commences with the rise of Judah's great son, David, a man after God's own heart. Obviously, other dynamics are at play in 1 Samuel, all of which deserve our attention. For this global summary, nonetheless, the key to understanding 1 Samuel's place in redemptive history is that David comes from the tribe of Judah (cf. 1 Sam 17:12) and he is anointed as king in chapter sixteen. Immediately in chapter seventeen he is already fighting on behalf of his people. That he *decapitates* Goliath (1 Sam 17:51, 54) is reminiscent of Gen 3:15.[14] "The seed of the woman has arrived, and in David's first action as king he is a warrior, an

---

[11]I commonly hear it said that God only gave Israel a king because they begged for one, though God never really wanted a king at all. But the problem with Saul is not the *idea* of a king, but the *reason* why Israel wanted a certain *kind* of king. They wanted a king that would make them like the nations (1 Sam 8:5, 19-20). This constituted a rejection of the Lord's rule over them (1 Sam 8:7; 10:19), who had called them to be distinct from the nations. But the Lord had always intended that his people would have a king, seen in the promises to Judah in Gen 49:8-12. Only the design of the king is to have one who will *mediate* the lordship of the one true God, not subvert it. The people in 1 Samuel 8, however, want the latter (not unlike Adam and Eve).

[12]I have changed the ESV's "offspring" to "seed" in this translation and throughout this chapter to highlight the connections between all these verses. It is the same Hebrew word each time, *zera'*.

[13]Dempster, *Dominion and Dynasty*, 140.

[14]Nicholas G. Piotrowski, "Saul is Esau: Themes from Genesis 3 and Deuteronomy 18 in 1 Samuel," *WTJ* 81 (2019): 214-18.

anointed one who conquers and beheads a monstrous giant, whose speech echoes the serpent's voice."[15]

Within David's biography there are then a lot of fascinating stories and details worth attending to, but one chapter particularly stands out, 2 Samuel 7. In fact, a strong case can be made that 2 Samuel 7 is the most important chapter in all the Bible *for understanding the rest of the Bible*. Of course, it is all God's inspired Word; it is all profitable for teaching, reproof, correction and training in righteousness. But some passages bear more weight and have a certain explanatory power for the rest. So far this brief survey has highlighted such passages. None, however, bear as much weight or explain as much as 2 Samuel 7. *Everything* so far has been building to this moment, and *everything* else will flow out of it. For one, it opens with this statement that the Lord had given David "rest" (vv. 1, 11). Consider here what we said above regarding Joshua's "rest." But the truly unique verses here are 12-16 where the Lord says to David,

> When your days are fulfilled and you lie down with your fathers, I will raise up your *seed* after you, who shall come from your body, and I will establish his *kingdom*. He shall build *a house for my name*, and I will establish the throne of his kingdom *forever*. I will be to him *a father*, and he shall be to me *a son*. When he commits iniquity, I will discipline him with the rod of men, with the stripes of the sons of men, but my steadfast love will not depart from him, as I took it from Saul, whom I put away from before you. And *your house and your kingdom shall be made sure forever before me. Your throne shall be established forever.*

There are two promises here and one requirement for David. First, the Lord promises to David that he will give him a "seed" to rule over an eternal kingdom (vv. 12-13, 16). Second, this descendant will "build a house" for the name of the Lord (v. 13). This means that David's dynasty will produce one heir who will build a temple for the Lord, and his kingdom will have no end. He will even get a special title, God's "son" (v. 14)! The *requirement* of this coming king and temple-builder is that he must keep the law of God (v. 14). If he does not, the Lord will raise up

---

[15]Dempster, *Dominion and Dynasty*, 140.

other nations to discipline him (v. 14). Finally, however, the Lord will never revoke these promises to David and his progeny, even if it requires discipline along the way (v. 15).

It is hard to overstate how important 2 Samuel 7 is to the rest of the Bible. It has all been building up to this moment: The hope for a seed now runs through David's house; the need for a righteous king has never been clearer; the hope to dwell again in the presence of God is the point of the temple. Now the rest of redemptive history will flow out of this chapter: there will be attempts by the enemies of God to stop this Davidic seed from coming into the world, the righteousness or unrighteousness of every subsequent king in the line of David will affect the people over whom he rules, and the temple will come and go and come again. It is impossible to read the rest of the Old Testament and New Testament without constantly looking back to 2 Samuel 7.

Of course the other episodes in David's life are important too. But we can jump ahead to ask, Who was David's son who built the temple? The answer is Solomon. In 1 Kings 8 Solomon completes the temple and praises God for the "rest" they all enjoy (v. 56). Thus, the promises of 2 Samuel 7 seem to be fulfilled (vv. 15-21), as well as all the other goals of redemptive history. Before I said God's presence was in the tabernacle and land of Israel, but now a more particular and permanent presence is in the temple (vv. 13, 27). It is now the place from where God grants forgiveness as in Leviticus (vv. 30-40), and the blessing for all the nations spoken to Abraham in Genesis 12:3 is commencing in 1 Kings 10 as the Queen of Sheba—a Gentile!—comes to Jerusalem to learn wisdom from David's great son.

On the face of it 1 Kings 8-10 could mark the end of redemptive history: David's son is enthroned; the temple-presence of God is experienced; the sacrificial system provides forgiveness; the people have rest; and the nations are blessed.[16] If the Bible ended there, *that* would be

---

[16]In this I agree with Graeme Goldsworthy (*Christ-Centered Biblical Theology: Hermeneutical Foundations and Principles* [Downers Grove, IL: IVP Academic, 2012], 111-69) that Genesis 1–11 theologically frames the entire canon which is then best understood in three parts: (1) the development of the kingdom from Abraham to Solomon provides the paradigm for understanding

salvation: going to Jerusalem to participate in the temple sacrifices and gleaning wisdom from the king. But it does not end there, for juxtaposed with this great moment of fulfillment in 1 Kings 8-10 is 1 Kings 11 where we read the list of Solomon's many other gods. It is sad. And so begins the "chastisement" of David's sons that 2 Samuel 7:14 foretells. Thus, once again, just as we saw in Joshua and Judges, this fulfillment is quite incomplete, but a signal marker on the way to greater fulfillment later. The rise of David is, in a sense, God's affirmation that he is still on track to fulfill his plan of redemption through historical events, and Solomon is a sketch of that salvation still to come. As the remainder of the Old Testament will show us, however, there are still many dangers, toils, and snares.

The Worship and Wisdom of God's King

We will pause our historical overview here to think about the role the poetry and wisdom literature play in redemptive history. There are two things we can say here: (1) The poetic books of the Bible tell this larger narrative in their own right, and (2) they embody "The Worship and Wisdom of God's King."

First, the Psalms themselves tell this larger redemptive-historical drama through poetry. Each individual psalm, to be sure, is its own self-standing poem. Each one reflects something of the wide range of human experience and emotion in response to the innumerable challenges, joys, and heartaches of life while trusting in God. Yet, the way these poems have been put together—in the final collection of these 150 psalms in the order we have them—demonstrates that this is not a loose collection of devotional material. Rather, there is "a theologically motivated framework for the psalms that provides an enduring interpretive context through which to understand the individual psalms and indeed the whole

---

the rest of redemptive history; (2) the prophets then repaint that same paradigm in eschatological terms; and (3) the incarnation, death, resurrection, outpouring of the Spirit, and expectation of the return of Christ constitute the redemptive climax that David's and Solomon's kingdoms foreshadowed and the prophets projected, all of which constitutes a return to Eden.

ensemble."[17] That "theologically motivated framework" is predominantly shaped by, not surprisingly, the Lord's promises to the house of David.[18]

To grasp this, we must first observe that the Psalter is organized into five books. Book 1 (Psalms 1–41) is nearly entirely attributed to David. These psalms express his trials and near-death tribulations. But commonly these psalms also speak of David emerging from his distress— even emerging from the grave as though resurrected—to rule the nations. A very good example of this is Psalm 22. Here David feels forsaken by God (vv. 1-2), is mocked by his enemies (vv. 7-8), and believes himself to be on the verge of death (vv. 15-18). But then, suddenly, he is rescued by the Lord (vv. 19-21), proclaiming his praises (vv. 22-24), and ruling the nations (vv. 27-28)! Here we have a significant clarification to the promises of 2 Samuel 7: the son of David will not only rule Israel, *but the entire world.* At the end of Book 1, Psalm 41:12 remembers this is a promise to the house of David "forever." Having begun with so much creation imagery in Psalm 1 (blessing, man, day and night, tree, rivers of water, fruit), we see David's house in position to restore the entire cosmos.

Book 2 (Psalms 42–72) also ends in a way that remembers 2 Samuel 7's promises. Psalm 72 is a prayer by David for his son Solomon and by extension all subsequent sons in his line, that they would rule with justice and righteousness (vv. 1-7). If they do, the house of David will rule in the land and over the entire earth (v. 8). Verse 9 even echoes the language of Genesis 3:15 ("seed of the woman"), and verses 10-11 echo Genesis 49:10 (Judah)! In the end, if David's house will reign with such justice and righteousness, then "the whole earth [will] be filled with [God's] glory" (v. 19) as in the original creation. Clearly, the entire book is leading to this point, just as the Old Testament builds up narratively to Solomon's temple-building in 1 Kings 8–10.

Book 3 (Psalms 73–89) only finds one psalm attributed to David (Psalm 86), but it ends with a grand overview of 2 Samuel 7 in Psalm 89:1-37.

---

[17]Gerald H. Wilson, "Psalms and Psalter: Paradigm for Biblical Theology," in *Biblical Theology: Retrospect & Prospect*, ed. Scott J. Hafemann (Downers Grove, IL: IVP Academic, 2002), 103.

[18]See O. Palmer Robertson, *The Flow of the Psalms: Discovering Their Structure and Theology* (Phillipsburg, NJ: P&R, 2015), esp. 1-7.

Again, the entire book is leading to this point. The psalmist remembers the eternal nature of the promises to David (vv. 3-4, 28-29, 36-37) and the international scope of his house's reign (vv. 25-27). But then verse 38 takes a shocking turn with "But *now*." The psalmist goes on to describe his great confusion and heartache that the Lord has now "renounced the covenant" and "defiled [David's] crown in the dust" (v. 39; cf. also vv. 44-45)! As mentioned above, and will be emphasized below, this is the dawning of the exile—that terrible moment in Israel's history when David's house was deposed, the temple was destroyed, and the people were removed from the land. This is the disciplining of 2 Samuel 7:14. Thus, the psalmist cries in verse 46, "How long, O Lord?," and pleads in verse 50, "Remember" your promises to David and Israel! This creates the hope that the kingdom vision of Book 2 could still someday be accomplished.

But first, Book 4 (Psalms 90–106) reflects life in exile. The focus, therefore, turns to the eternal reign of God over all. It even starts with "Lord, you have been our dwelling place in all generations. Before the mountains were brought forth, or ever you had formed the earth and the world, from everlasting to everlasting you are God" (Ps 90:1-2). What a fitting and reassuring affirmation for those in exile, for those doubting whether God was still for them or whether the Lord may somehow have been bested by the Babylonian gods.[19] In turn, Book 4 ends with this hope, that the Lord will "gather us from among the nations, that we may give thanks to your holy name and glory in your praise" (Ps 106:47).

Finally, Book 5 (Psalms 107–150) sees the return of a lot of Davidic psalms and casts the hope for a renewed creation—a fitting ending to the book that began with such Edenic imagery in Psalm 1. In fact, it is in this final book of the Psalter that Psalm 110 is found, which speaks of David's "Lord" triumphing over his enemies as an end-times priest-king.[20] Thus, though the Lord has "cast [David's] throne to the ground" (Ps 89:44), the end of the exile

---

[19]Dieudonné Tamfu makes the wonderful observation that Moses' only psalm starts Book 4 to elicit memories of the first exodus in hopes for another ("The Songs of the Messiah: Seeing and Savoring Jesus in the Psalms," [lectures at the Indianapolis Theological Seminary Symposium on the Psalms, Indianapolis, IN, September 8, 2017]).

[20]See esp. David S. Schrock, *The Royal Priesthood and the Glory of God*, SSBT (Wheaton, IL: Crossway, 2022).

will be marked by a reenthronement of the house of David, to the great praise and glory of God throughout a renewed creation (Psalms 146–150).[21]

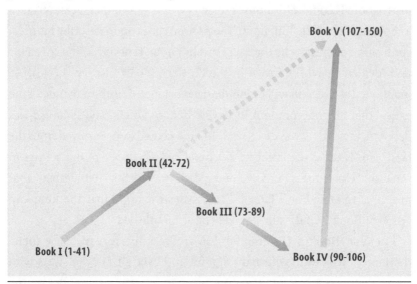

Figure 5.5. The Psalms appear to be organized in a way that addresses the human condition (Pss 1–2) by projecting hopes concerning the House of David (esp. Ps 72) beyond the exile (cf. Pss 89 and 90) to an idyllic future (Pss 146–150).

In all, the book of Psalms poetically retells the story of the entire Bible: the rise of David through fiery trials, the promises of God to bless and rule the nations through the house of David, the high moral calling of the sons of David, their failure and the subsequent exile, and finally the hope for a better and permanent son of David whose "delight is in the law of the Lord, and on his law he meditates day and night" (Ps 1:2). The result of such, consequently, will be the once idolatrous Gentiles coming to worship the one true God, in a renewed creation.

The Proverbs have a similar ethos. *How* will the son(s) of David rule? We have already seen he is (they are) called to rule with justice and righteousness. With Proverbs we see that "wisdom" is required for "righteousness, justice and equity" (Prov 1:2-3). To this end, it is no one less than "Solomon, son of David" giving this instruction to the next "son" in line (Prov 1:1, 8).[22] The book of Proverbs, therefore, lays out the kind of

[21]Tamfu, "Songs."

[22]The term "my son" also occurs in Prov 1:10, 15; 2:1; 3:1, 11, 21; 4:10, 20; 5:1, 20; 6:1, 3, 20; 7:1; 19:27; 23:15, 19, 26; 24:13, 21; 27:11. There are many other references to "son" throughout.

wisdom that is needed for the sons of David to rule in righteousness.[23] Would that they did! The hope is that someday one will.

The same can be said on the macrolevel about Ecclesiastes and the Song of Songs. They both start with introductions describing them as *Solomon's* words. They express the kind of wisdom the ideal king needs with which to rule his people. In turn they become the sort of wisdom his people should hear from him and apply to their lives, a royal wisdom with life-texture.[24]

I conclude, in the big picture, that these books embody "The Worship and Wisdom of God's King." The Psalms represent the *worship* in which the kings should lead the people to God. Job, Proverbs, Ecclesiastes, and the Song of Songs exemplify the *wisdom from God* with which the kings should rule over the people. It is no small thing that more psalms are attributed to David than anyone else, and much of the wisdom literature comes from Solomon.[25] Thus, Israel's two greatest kings are associated with the literature that marks the ideal king and therefore the ideal kingdom.[26] This brings those soaring visions of 2 Samuel 7's promises down to the street level. It is all about David, and *through* the house of David we too can appropriate this sort of wisdom and engage in this sort of worship. Only never without reference to the house of David, never in the abstract from redemptive history.

Of course, as we have seen, neither David nor Solomon lives up to these concepts. So for everything else these great books are, they have a forward-leaning orientation to what the seed of the woman, Judah's final son, will be like and how he will lead and rule over God's people when he comes.[27] The next section of our overview, however, will greatly challenge the hope that he will ever even come at all.

---

[23]O. Palmer Robertson, *The Christ of Wisdom: A Redemptive-Historical Exploration of the Wisdom Books of the Old Testament* (Phillipsburg, NJ: P&R, 2017), esp. 5-8.

[24]While Job is not ascribed to anyone per se, it is helpful to think of this too as part of Israel's wisdom literature, though far more elastic in its genre than the others. More on this in chap. 7.

[25]I realize that Job does not fit this understanding as well as the other books do, but its placement in both the English and Hebrew Bibles associates it with them.

[26]Goldsworthy, *Christ-Centered Biblical Theology*, 29, 125-30.

[27]It should be no surprise, therefore, that in the New Testament we see these psalms on the lips of Jesus so often (Richard B. Hays, *The Conversion of the Imagination: Paul as Interpreter of Israel's Scripture* [Grand Rapids, MI: Eerdmans, 2005], 101-17). "Jesus believed that the Psalms were about him. . . . The apostles and New Testament authors, too, read the Psalms as supplying the lament, thanksgiving, the praises of the Christ and then of all finding refuge in him" (Jason S. DeRouchie, *How to Understand and Apply the Old Testament: Twelve Steps from Exegesis to Theology* [Phillipsburg, NJ: P&R, 2017], 63).

The Disobedience of God's King

We return now to the historical events of 1 Kings 11 and following. With each king in the line of David we see a further and further falling away. With only a few exceptions, the Davidic kings do what is evil in the sight of the Lord *and lead the people into that sin as well* (see 2 Kings 21:9, 11, 16).[28] With this, therefore, an important principle emerges: as the king goes, the people go. The king is responsible for leading the people in righteousness (think of the problems in Judges when there was no king). When he does, the people are blessed. When he does not, he leads by his negative example and provokes the judgment of God on all. The end, therefore, comes with the complete removal of the people from the land: the Babylonian exile.

The end of 2 Kings describes the onset of the exile in alarming detail. Chapter twenty-four tells us that King Jehoiachin reigned for a whopping three months before being taken captive to Babylon (vv. 8, 15). Verse 9 provides that stereotypical assessment of his reign that signals, as seen in the rest of the book, that his story is over. What makes Jehoiachin stand out, though, is that he is the one under whom the Babylonians carry off all the treasures of the temple and destroy its sacred vessels (2 Kings 24:13). As important as the temple's construction was for redemptive history (1 Kings 8), it is absolutely tragic to see it looted like this! But there is more. The king after Jehoiachin is his uncle Zedekiah. But Zedekiah is captured at which time the Babylonians "slaughtered the sons of Zedekiah before his eyes, and put out the eyes of Zedekiah and bound him in chains and took him to Babylon" (2 Kings 25:6-7). This is not just cruel, but think of what it means for redemptive history, for God's plan of salvation. The last king in the line of David is taken off the throne and blinded, and the last thing he sees is not only the death of his sons. That would be bad enough! But their death means *the end of the line of David*. All the promises of God since Genesis that have been channeled through the line of David are now ruined. Without the house of David, all is lost!

---

[28]This principle is applied to the non-Davidic kings of the north as well (inter alia 1 Kings 12:28-30; 15:26; 2 Kings 14:24).

There is a ray of hope at the end of 2 Kings, however. It turns out that Jehoiachin (remember him?) is still alive! He is in prison in Babylon, so he is not exactly reigning as the house of David ought. But he is *freed*, given a seat above the other kings at the table (25:28), and the last word of the book is "he lived" (25:30). So the promises of God still have a chance! The Davidic king is still in Babylon, and right now we do not know of any sons. So redemptive history is hanging by a very, very thin string. But there *is* a string.[29]

During these days of "The Disobedience of God's King," the prophets are busy calling the kings and the people back to covenant faithfulness. The prophetic books that capture this are Isaiah and Hosea through Zephaniah. As with the Psalms, it is hard to categorize all these works briefly.[30] But a common theme is that they place a focus on the leadership, particularly the sons of David. This is clear in places like Isaiah 7 and Micah 3.[31] They are calling the house of David to fulfill its covenant expectations and thereby stave off the coming disaster. Others, like Hosea and Amos, prophesy to the northern kingdom that had long earlier split off from the rulership of the house of David. And still others, like Obadiah and Nahum, are prophecies to other nations altogether. Nonetheless, the solution to the problems in Hosea and Amos is to reunite the people of God under the banner of David's house (Hos 1:11; 3:4-5: Amos 9:9-12; cf. also Ezek 37:19-24). And clearly, in Obadiah and Nahum, the background for those prophecies is still the Lord's works with Judah and Jerusalem. So the prophets are either calling Davidic kings to faithfulness or calling others to submit to David's house. In both functions, the promises and requirements of 2 Samuel 7 and Psalm 2 provide the theological grounding for it all.[32]

---

[29]See esp. Dale Ralph Davis, *2 Kings: The Power and the Fury*, Focus on the Bible (Fearn, Ross-Shire: Christian Focus, 2005), 337-42; Matthew H. Patton, *Hope for a Tender Sprig: Jehoiachin in Biblical Theology*, BBRSup 16 (Winona Lake, IN: Eisenbrauns, 2017).

[30]See Donald E. Gowan, *Theology of the Prophetic Books: The Death & Resurrection of Israel* (Louisville: Westminster John Knox, 1998).

[31]It also seems that the Jerusalem leadership is particularly in view in Habakkuk 1:2-4. Jeremiah 21:12; 22:2-3 would be more examples of this calling on the house of David, but we will save that prophet for the next section. Nehemiah 9:34; 13:17-18 reflects on this *after* the exile.

[32]To be sure, the prophets are concerned with a host of issues; I do not mean to diminish that. My point here is to draw attention to the theological rationale that grounds those issues, and that is

As we read above, however, the Davidic kings continued in their rebellion, leading others into sin as well, and the nations continued to rage. But these same prophets also see a day after the destruction when God will save through David's house again (Is 9; 22; 55; Hos 3:5; Amos 9:11; Mic 5:2-5), and the Spirit will be poured out on all flesh in "the day of the LORD" (Joel 2:28-32).

This new day is described as a second exodus in Isaiah 40–55 as a road (or "way") is prepared for the Lord through the wilderness (40:3; cf. Ex 13:18, 21) and he again reveals his glory (40:5; cf. Ex 14:18). Appropriately, if it was sin that led to the exile, the new exodus out of exile will bring comfort as their "iniquity is pardoned" (40:2). Thus, in the climactic chapters fifty-two and fifty-three we read of the suffering servant who is "crushed for our iniquities" (53:5). Just as the people went out from Egypt with the blood of a lamb, so too in this new exodus the servant is "like a lamb that is led to the slaughter" (53:7), and "stricken for the transgression of [God's] people" (53:8). And this time it will even include Gentiles (e.g., Is 49:1-6). This is how God will bring his people back to him beyond the exile and extend grace to the nations.

The Disestablishment of God's People

It is hard to overstate how terrible the exile was. Everything God had achieved for his people was stripped away. The temple was destroyed. This meant the loss of their priesthood and sacrifices. The Davidic king(s) had been captured (or believed to be dead, certainly nowhere to be found around Jerusalem). There was certainly no experience of rest. They were removed from their land. The Lord even calls them "No Mercy" and "Not My People" in Hosea 1:6-9. In short, all the redemptive-historical progress made from Genesis through 1 Kings 10 is now run in reverse! The books of Jeremiah through Daniel were written during this experience, and so tell the sad tale of the "The Disestablishment of God's People."[33] Jeremiah

---

the covenant with David (Goldsworthy, *Christ-Centered*, 136-48). The social issues particularly stand out; we should see the prophets' concerns for justice derivative of the Ten Commandments and 2 Sam 7:14's calling placed upon the house of David for moral leadership.

[33]Isaiah and Micah could fall in this category. Their writings cross over these time markers. They write before the exile, but also speak in detail of it, while also envisioning the other side of it.

witnesses the destruction of the temple and several waves of exile. Lamentations expresses his sorrow over this, but still his hope is in the Lord. Ezekiel makes it clear that the Lord himself has destroyed his own temple (chaps. 5–10); one should not think the Lord is somehow passive in all this. And Daniel lives through the entire experience in captivity, nonetheless, saying in 4:34-35,

> His dominion is an everlasting dominion,
>> and His kingdom endures from generation to generation;
>> all the inhabitants of the earth are accounted as nothing,
> and he does according to his will among the host of heaven
>> and among the inhabitants of the earth;
> and none can stay his hand
>> or say to Him, "What have you done?"[34]

Thus, even when redemptive history is in tatters, the Lord is still the Lord of all. This gives hope, as these same books also all look beyond the exile. The Lord will again call his people back into his covenant presence. He will again build his temple. He will again forgive. Jeremiah and Ezekiel are particularly clear that this will be through David's house again (Jer 23:5-8; 30:8-9; 33:15-22; Ezek 34:22-24; 37:21-25), in concert with the coming Spirit and the joys of a new covenant (Jer 31:31-34; Ezek 36:16-36).

In the final analysis, the exile is "the rod of men" (Mic 5:1 seems to be a direct echo of 2 Sam 7:14), and it is as though Israel has experienced the same result of Adam's unfaithfulness: death and loss of the presence of God. But for the same reason God gives Adam the promise of Genesis 3:15, so Ezekiel 37 speaks of the coming resurrection of the people (over against their death in exile) and Ezekiel 40–48 promises a new, more glorious temple (over against the loss of the presence of God in the exile). God has also indelibly promised David, "but my steadfast love will not depart from [your son] . . . your house and your kingdom shall be made sure forever before me" (2 Sam 7:15-16).

---

[34]These words are actually found on the lips of Nebuchadnezzar, but it is clearly Daniel's theology as the rest of the stories in the book revolve around these ideas.

The Re-Creation of God's People

Our final section of the Old Testament is the "The Re-Creation of God's People." After seventy years of captivity many (but not all) come back to the land, they rebuild a (much smaller) temple, and they reinstall (at least for the time being) a Davidic heir, Zerubbabel (Ezra 1:1-3; 3:1-2). It seems, however, that this restoration is not as sweeping or grand as the prophets had foreseen.[35] In Ezra 3 the returnees lay a foundation for a new temple (v. 10). As expected, many people shout and sing and praise the Lord (v. 11), for this is a wonderful step back in the right direction. But verse 12 tells us that many of the "old men who had seen the first house wept with a loud voice when they saw the foundation of this house being laid." They had seen the old temple, Solomon's temple, and this was nothing of the sorts.[36] As we have seen elsewhere, the fulfillment of redemptive-historical expectations also comes with longings for something better. Alas, this is not a full restoration. Later on, Ezra even comments that they have experienced only "a little reviving" (9:8-9). Nehemiah also says, despite being back in the land, that they are still "slaves this day" (9:36). Haggai and Malachi still look forward to a better temple while Zechariah longs for a future and better son of David. Finally, 1 and 2 Chronicles recounts the same historical span covered by 1 Samuel 16 through 2 Kings 25, but it does so from a *post*exilic vantage. It looks back to how the exile came about, but equally looks ahead by remembering that God's promises to the house of David will somehow surely endure.[37]

While these books narrate "The Re-Creation of God's People," they are nothing like 1 Kings 8–10. They still leave a lot to be desired in fulfilling the promises of 2 Samuel 7 or Genesis 12. The Davidic dynasty is not ruling over all. The nations are not blessed. The temple is not the place where Gentile idolaters come to find the true and living God. There is still no rest. Thus, while these books look back to the failures of the

---

[35]The prophets had described the restoration from exile as the exodus relived (e.g., Isa 40:1-11; 43:16-21; 51:9-11; Jer 16:14-15; 23:7-8; Hos 11:1-11).

[36]To compare Solomon's temple to the postexilic temple, see the *ESV Study Bible*, 595, 604-605, 813, 828-29.

[37]Esther is set, of course, while a community of Jews are still living abroad, and the Lord is still with them.

Davidic kings and rejoice in a modicum of restoration, they lean forward in hope for the full coming of the kingdom: only a new David who will build a new temple with a new sacrifice can lead humanity back into the presence of God.

To summarize our Old Testament survey, the overarching principles are that

▶ God is creating a worshiping people

▶ By *overcoming sin and death*

▶ Through sacrifice and resurrection,

▶ *Leading back to the presence of God*

▶ To know him, love him, obey him and enjoy him forever.

This plan has been carried forward by

▶ The seed of the woman who crushes the head of the serpent,

▶ Who will come from the line of Abraham,

▶ Will be a king in the line of Judah,

▶ And will be the climactic son of David

▶ To rule and bless the nations

▶ With all righteousness and wisdom.

This will all result in

▶ An end to the exile in the form of a second exodus,

▶ A renewal of the covenant,

▶ Forgiveness of sins,

▶ A righteous and just king,

▶ The gift of the Spirit,

▶ A new and glorious temple where God can dwell with his people,

▶ Blessing for all peoples of the earth,

▶ An experience of rest for the cosmos,

▶ And the image of God in humanity again reflecting the glory of

God to the creation.

God's original creational purposes that were lost with Adam, and hinted at but finally lost again in Israel, will be restored full-scale. It is with that hope that the reader turns to the New Testament.

God the Son Brings the Kingdom

The New Testament opens with a bold and exhilarating claim. The first sentence announces that Jesus Christ is "the son of David, the son of Abraham" (Mt 1:1)! The point is even made that he is born in "Bethlehem, in the land of Judah" (Mt 2:6), the same town David is from. Jesus' miracles and teachings cause people to ask "Can this be the Son of David" (Mt 12:23)? And when he enters Jerusalem the people shout "Hosanna to the Son of David" (Mt 21:9, 15). It is clear that the Gospel of Matthew sees Jesus as the fulfillment of God's promises to David![38] Under this banner, Jesus' words—"Come to me, all who labor and are heavy laden, and I will give you *rest*" (Mt 11:28)—are a manifesto that he is the one who leads humanity back to its original creational status in the presence of God.

To accomplish this, as mentioned above, necessitates resolving humanity's two great problems: sin and death. Thus, Jesus "save[s] his people from their sins" (Mt 1:21) which is accomplished when he "give[s] his life as a ransom for many" (20:28). He himself becomes the sacrifice of atonement for his people! He makes this clear in the Last Supper when he says, "This is my body" and "this is my blood of the covenant, which is poured out for many for the forgiveness of sins" (Mt 26:26-28). When Jesus dies on the cross, therefore, he is not a hapless martyr or a revolutionary who got himself in too deep. He is giving himself as the ultimate and final sacrifice to bring humanity back to God (Mt 27:45-54). But that only resolves one problem, that of sin. What of death? Three days later Jesus is also raised to new life (Mt 28:1-10). Thus, the new David has resolved humanity's two great problems of sin and death, and opened the path back to God, back to rest, with his own atoning death and life-giving resurrection.

---

[38]See esp. H. Daniel Zacharias, *Matthew's Presentation of the Son of David*, TTCBS (London: Bloomsbury, 2017).

Additionally, because Jesus is the Son of David, per 2 Samuel 7, he is also the king to rule the nations righteously. That is why he can say in Matthew 28:18, "All authority in heaven and on earth has been given to me." What an audacious claim! But Jesus can make it because that is exactly what God promised to David *forever*. Thus, what was lost in the exile is now regained. Moreover, this son of David is also, as we saw above, the son of Abraham. Jesus is also, therefore, the one who will bless the nations per Genesis 12:3. This is why after making that claim to all authority in heaven and earth, he then immediately tells his disciples to "go therefore and make disciples of all nations, baptizing them in the name of the Father and of the Son and of the Holy Spirit, teaching them to observe all that I have commanded you" (Mt 28:19-20). The way God is blessing the nations is by giving them Jesus' teachings on the lips of his followers.[39] And it is those teachings that Jesus himself lived out, full of the wisdom and righteousness expected of the Davidic king, the exemplar for his people.[40]

All this and more is what Jesus means when he says "the kingdom of heaven is at hand" (Mt 4:17; cf. also Mk 1:15; Lk 4:43). By the end of only the first New Testament book, therefore, we see so much of God's Old Testament purposes coalescing around Jesus! "The redemptive-historical clock has struck the final hour, bringing the major covenants to their climax."[41]

In Mark we get even more as we are told that all this amounts to a new exodus, "the way" of the Lord through the wilderness (Mk 1:1-3) in fulfillment of Isaiah 40:3.[42] Jesus giving his life as a ransom for "many"

---

[39]Nicholas G. Piotrowski, "'After the Deportation': Observations in Matthew's Apocalyptic Genealogy," *BBR* 25 (2015): 189-203.

[40]This is, of course, also the obedience expected of Adam, now seen in Christ (Brandon D. Crowe, *The Last Adam: A Theology of the Obedient Life of Jesus in the Gospels* [Grand Rapids, MI: Baker Academic, 2017], 23-81, 139-50).

[41]Nicholas Perrin, *The Kingdom of God: A Biblical Theology*, BTL (Grand Rapids, MI: Zondervan, 2019), 224.

[42]Rikki E. Watts, *Isaiah's New Exodus in Mark*, BSL (Grand Rapids, MI: Baker Academic, 2000; repr. from WUNT 2/88; Tübingen: Mohr Siebeck, 1997), 53-136, 221-94; Nicholas G. Piotrowski, "'Whatever You Ask' for the Missionary Purposes of the Eschatological Temple: Quotation and Typology in Mark 11–12," *SBJT* 21 (2017): 97-99.

(Mk 10:45) is also an echo of Isaiah 52:15's "so shall he sprinkle many" and Isaiah 53:12's "he bore the sin of many," while the "astonishment" at the servant in Isaiah 52:14 is echoed time and again in Mark (e.g., 1:22). Jesus is the suffering servant, the sacrificial lamb, of the new exodus.

Luke makes it all explicit when he says, "The Lord God will give to [Jesus] the throne of his father David . . . and of his kingdom there will be no end" (Lk 1:32-33), a very clear echo of 2 Samuel 7. In Jesus, the Lord

> has visited and redeemed His people and has raised up a horn of salvation for us in the house of his servant David, as he spoke by the mouth of his holy prophets from of old, that we should be saved from our enemies and from the hand of all who hate us; to show the mercy promised to our fathers and to remember his holy covenant, the oath that he swore to our father Abraham . . . to give knowledge of salvation to his people in the forgiveness of their sins. (Luke 1:68-73, 77)

A step further, those verbs, "visited" (also 7:16; 19:44) and "redeemed" (also 24:21), are particularly *divine* activities in the Old Testament (Ex 4:31; Ps 106:4; 80:14; Is 41:14; 43:14; 44:24; 49:7).[43] In Jesus, the Lord *himself* is visiting and redeeming. Luke "subtly but insistently portrays Jesus as the embodied presence of Israel's Lord and God."[44]

John returns us to the language of creation (Jn 1:1-8), signaling that a new world begins with Jesus.[45] He says he has come to "accomplish" the work of his Father (4:34; 5:17), and on the cross, victoriously cries, "It is finished" (19:30). God's purposes in the created world have reached their apex with the coming of Christ. John is even the clearest on the language of the temple: Jesus *himself* is the temple (1:14), which after its destruction on the cross, will be permanently rebuilt in the resurrection (2:17-22). Thus, *in Jesus,* people meet with God to know, love, and enjoy him.

You cannot miss the redemptive-historical excitement as these evangelists introduce us to Jesus and describe what his life, death, and resurrection accomplish. They are the great fulfillment (in fact the Gospel

---

[43]Richard B. Hays, *Reading Backwards: Figural Christology and the Fourfold Gospel Witness* (Waco, TX: Baylor University Press, 2014), 66-74.
[44]Hays, *Reading Backwards*, 58.
[45]Jeannine K. Brown, "Creation's Renewal in the Gospel of John," *CBQ* 72.2 (2010): 275-90.

writers love saying, "Thus fulfilled") of God's purposes through re-demptive history in the sending of his Son. As Paul would later remark, all the promises of God are yes and amen in Christ (2 Cor 1:20). In this way, "God the Son Brings the Kingdom of God":

- ▶ Jesus is the son of Abraham who blesses the nations.
- ▶ Jesus is the son of Judah and the son of David who rules over all.
- ▶ Jesus leads his people on a new exodus back to God.
- ▶ Jesus inaugurates the new covenant.
- ▶ Jesus lives a wise and righteous life.
- ▶ Jesus is the atoning sacrifice for sins.
- ▶ Jesus is the beginning of the resurrection from the dead.
- ▶ Jesus is the head of the new creation.
- ▶ Jesus is the temple of God, the meeting place on earth between God and sinners.
- ▶ Jesus is God himself, visiting his people.
- ▶ And in all this Jesus is bringing rest to the cosmos.

It is simply awe-inspiring the way Jesus draws so many Old Testament expectations onto his shoulders.[46] Indeed, the hopes and fears of all the years are met in Jesus Christ.

God the Spirit Spreads the Kingdom

The Gospels, however, are but the beginning of fulfillment. Jesus also creates an international worshiping community through the sending of the Spirit. This is what we see in the book of Acts, a story unlike anything else in the Bible. In the book of Acts, the story of how the Jewish God has acted through the Jewish Messiah in fulfillment of the Jewish Scrip-tures is now spreading over the entire world, as both Jews and Gentiles come into this end-times community called "Christians." Nothing like this has ever happened before. Sure, Jonah convinced one generation of

---

[46]For an especially insightful read on this, see Perrin, *Kingdom of God*, 99-116.

Ninevites to repent. And there are more than a handful of Gentile converts in the Old Testament (we considered one above, Ruth). But what we see in Acts is attributable only to a new push forward in redemptive history as the Spirit pours out of heaven into Jerusalem and starts overflowing into the rest of the world, as Jesus' followers take the gospel with them everywhere they go. All this, Peter tells us, is the fulfillment of Joel 2 (Acts 2:14-21) and God's promises to David (Acts 2:22-36).[47]

And the *letters* of the New Testament! It should not be lost on us that these are written to places like Rome, Corinth, Ephesus, Thessalonica, Cappadocia, and Bithynia (1 Pet 1:1). God is working *internationally* now. His sights are set on the ends of the earth, as Jesus takes the throne of David "to bring about the obedience of faith . . . among all the nations" (Rom 1:3-5). Thus, in these letters Paul tells *Gentiles* that it is "those of faith who are the sons of Abraham" (Gal 3:7; cf. also Rom 4:16). Jesus is the one "seed" (Gal 3:16), and those who are in Christ are "heirs according to [the] promise" to Abraham (Gal 3:29). He tells the church in Ephesus, a community of Jews and Gentiles, that *they* are, by their union with Christ, "a holy temple in the Lord" (Eph 2:21; cf. also 1 Cor 3:16), the place where God now dwells on earth by his Spirit! And Peter says to the church, "Once you were not a people, but now you are God's people; once you had not received mercy, but now you have received mercy" (1 Pet 2:10), clearly echoing Hosea 1:6-11 discussed above.

Yet larger still, his redemptive purposes extend to the entire cosmos through Jesus, the perfect "image" of God and preeminent head over all things (Col 1:15-20)—the new man who completes Adam's mission. God is now breaking out of the historical places of his presence (temple and land) to accomplish his original creational purposes for *all* humanity and *all over the world*. In this way "God the Spirit Spreads the Kingdom":

- ▶ The Spirit falls on all flesh, great and small, Jew and Gentile.

- ▶ The Spirit creates an international worshiping community.

- ▶ All of this constitutes the new Adam's success as the true image of God.

---

[47]Dennis E. Johnson, *The Message of Acts in the History of Redemption* (Phillipsburg, NJ: P&R, 1997), 53-69.

God the Son Reigns over the Kingdom

Finally, a word on Revelation. It is important to note that "revelation" does not mean "future stuff." Rather, "revelation" means showing readers *present truths* that might be hidden for one reason or another. And so, the book of Revelation is appropriately named. While of course there are predictive prophecies in Revelation, the primary thrust of the book is *current realities that first-century cultural pressures might cause first-century Christians to miss.*[48] Thus, John is *revealing* true and current things about Jesus that we need to see. Just a few of those things can detain us here. For one, Jesus is "the ruler of the kings on earth" (Rev 1:5). Second, he has "freed us from our sins by his blood" and "he is the firstborn of the dead" (Rev 1:5). Thus, again, the emphasis is on atoning for sins and bringing immortality to life. This is emphasized again in 5:9-10, where all creation sings,

> Worthy are you to take the scroll and to open its seals,
>> for you were slain,
>> and by your blood you ransomed people for God
>>> from every tribe and language and people and nation,
>> and you have made them a kingdom and priests to our God,
>>> and they shall reign on the earth.

Third, we learn that Jesus is that long expected seed of the woman who defeats "that ancient serpent . . . the deceiver of the whole world" (Rev 12:9). And fourth, he is finally the one who rules and judges in complete righteousness (Rev 19:11).

All of these current realities are also anticipatory of the final defeat of the serpent, when Jesus returns and establishes the eternal presence of God on earth (Rev 21:22) in a new and glorious creation (Rev 21:1). Thus, the universe will be renewed and a redeemed humanity brought into the eternal new Eden (Rev 21:22–22:5). In the end, image bearers are brought back to creation's pre-sin and pre-death state, and the glory of God is all in all. As Genesis 1:28 had commissioned the first Adam, the last Adam has subdued and filled the earth with his people, his teaching, and his

---

[48]Richard Bauckham, *The Theology of the Book of Revelation*, NTT (Cambridge: Cambridge University Press, 1993), 1-22.

righteousness. In this way, already and still to come, "God the Son Reigns over the Kingdom":

▶ Jesus is the King of kings and Lord of lords.

▶ Jesus is the one seed of the woman who triumphs over the serpent/ Satan/devil.

▶ Jesus is the ransom for sins and beginning of the resurrection.

▶ Jesus will finally and completely restore the cosmos to its original creational intent.

▶ And so the people of God will be with him forever, as his presence and glory fill the cosmos (i.e., all of creation becomes God's temple)!

In the final analysis, all those temporary and partial fulfillments that we saw in the Old Testament have given way to the decisive inbreaking of the kingdom. Jesus has come, taught in righteousness, died for sinners, was raised to indestructible life, and set on the eternal throne of David. Now his Spirit-empowered people fill the earth with the blessing of Jesus' teachings, all in anticipation of the complete and entire restoration of the cosmos to its original Edenic conditions.

Summarily, we can say the Bible is a long detailed away-and-home-again story. The goal of redemptive history is to create an international worshiping community in the presence of God. That is what Adam and Eve were in Eden before sin and death. That is what Israel was expected to be in the land. And that is what the church is today the world over. That is what all those freed from their sins by Jesus' blood will be in the new heavens and the new earth.

What *Is* the Bible?

It is important to see these overriding themes so that we can understand how all the individual stories of the Bible are contextually situated. Put another way, seeing these larger purposes in the progress of redemptive history orients us to know how to deal with the details. The pericopes that comprise these books are not just disconnected and divergent stories. Rather, the individual stories come together to make this larger mosaic as redemptive history heads toward its goal: the rewelcoming of humanity into the original creational presence of God to again enjoy rest in fulfilling its Genesis 1:28 commission. Each of these sections of the Old Testament leans necessarily to that end, and each individual story helps fill out the larger section and makes it what it is.[49] This was admittedly brief and I had to leave out a lot of details. But the goal is not to be reductionistic or ignore the details. Rather, the goal was to give an accurate big-picture overview of the sweep of the whole *so that we can appropriately deal with the details* as they are situated in their final christological context.

The Old Testament is christotelic. Looking at the Bible as a whole, therefore, we can say that the Old Testament is *christo*telic. That suffix, "telic," comes from the word *telos* meaning the end or the goal. Where is the Old Testament going? What is the final horizon of all its content? It is flowing and bending toward all those fulfillments in Christ. As at the beginning of this chapter, we can compare the Old Testament to a mountain range with one dominant peak. The pinnacle is the cross and resurrection (which brings with it the ascension and giving of the Spirit, and therefore also the creation of the church), the destination to which the entire slope is climbing. As we read the Old Testament, we should see how everything is heading to this summit. Just as when climbing a mountain, sometimes the terrain is clearly upward toward the peak, and

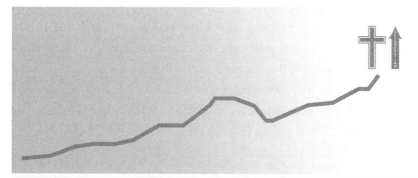

Figure 5.6. The OT metanarrative is trajecting toward Jesus' person and work; in this way the OT is "christotelic."

---

[49]In this respect, I like John Goldingay's understanding of "middle narratives" giving shape to the "grand narrative" (*Do We Need the New Testament? Letting the Old Testament Speak for Itself* [Downers Grove, IL: IVP Academic, 2015], 69-90), but I of course see more continuity across the whole than he does.

sometimes it is flat or even downward sloped. So too, some parts of the Old Testament are very clearly angled toward fulfillment in Christ. At other places, it is unclear where it is going at all. But the big picture shows a net upward trajectory to the climax in Christ.

To employ a different metaphor, think of a satellite launched from Earth to explore Saturn (which NASA did in 1997). As the satellite heads toward Saturn, one might say it is Saturno*telic*. Its launch angle and velocity away from the Earth are intentionally designed so that it will reach Saturn. But it does not go on a straight line, instead it has to arc past Venus twice and Jupiter once, and once more back past the Earth, each time changing its course and speed. Sometimes it is decidedly going *away* from Saturn. But to be sure, despite the seeming regression at times, it does get there. In this way, the Old Testament is christo*telic*.

Before moving on to the New Testament, I should make a clarifying comment here about this word, "christotelic," because scholars have used it in a variety of ways with different meanings (as is common when a new word is coined). Some have used it to mean that the overall sweep of the Old Testament is heading toward Christ even though there are contradictions between some Old Testament quotations in the New Testament and their original Old Testament contexts.[50] In other words, the New Testament authors clearly thought Jesus was the climax to Israel's story, and in their zeal to show that, they overreached and applied texts to Jesus that were originally not messianic nor predictive at all.[51] Others mean that there are large Old Testament contexts that have nothing to do with christology, and so New Testament authors had little contextual awareness, but "at the same time, all of the Old Testament is herding us toward Christ."[52] Still others, that the Old Testament does not *intend* to

---

[50]Peter Enns, *Inspiration and Incarnation: Evangelicals and the Problem of the Old Testament* (Grand Rapids, MI: Baker, 2005). In my view, Enns has not thoroughly examined the Old Testament contexts in question, and therefore makes hasty conclusions.

[51]Matthew seems to be accused of this the most. See Nicholas G. Piotrowski, *Matthew's New David at the End of Exile: A Socio-Rhetorical Study of Scriptural Quotations*, NovTSup 170 (Leiden: Brill, 2016) for the counterthesis.

[52]John H. Walton, *Old Testament Theology for Christians: From Ancient Context to Enduring Belief* (Downers Grove, IL: IVP Academic, 2017), 5-6, 276-82; quote from 6. I think the issue here is too narrow a definition of christology.

move toward Christ, but readers of the New Testament can see it only retrospectively.[53] In this case, the Old Testament authors either wrote more than they knew, or the New Testament authors simply gave the Old Testament a new interpretation in light of the Christ event. I do *not* mean christotelic in those ways. I mean it to speak of the *goal* of the Old Testament, the intentional destination to which *all contexts* are heading— that upward slope to Christ's incarnation, death, resurrection, his ascension, giving of the Spirit, and creation and gifting of the church.[54] New Testament authors, for their part, took the history of Israel and the Old Testament in context, and still preached Christ as the climax of all God's purposes. In fact, it is this combination of *history, literary contexts,* and *christology* that makes hermeneutics what it is. Never one without the other, the central thesis is this work.

To these other scholars the term is, it seems to me, reactionary to those who would speak of the Old Testament as christo*centric*. I agree that the Old Testament is not christo*centric*; it does not *revolve* around Jesus, but *leads to* Jesus. So christo*telic* is a better word to describe the Old Testament, only I should be clear to disambiguate my meaning from that of others.[55]

The New Testament is christocentric. Turning now to the New Testament, indeed we *can* call this collection of books christo*centric*. Here the idea is that fulfillment of those Old Testament expectations has been reached and so now all *revolves* around the decisive cross and resurrection.

---

[53]Richard B. Hays, *Echoes of Scripture in the Gospels* (Waco, TX: Baylor University Press, 2016), 1-3. In this case I think Hays is reacting to an overemphasis on how conscious the Old Testament authors were of predicting Christ. First Peter 1:10-11 notwithstanding, it seems irrelevant to get into the prophets' psyche; the *texts* of the Old Testament surely lean forward to *something* future. Of course, details await the New Testament.

[54]For a strong case that the recurring patterns in the Old Testament evince that typology is not only seen retrospectively, or forced onto the Old Testament by New Testament authors, see Francis Foulkes, "The Acts of God: A Study of the Basis of Typology in the Old Testament," in *The Right Doctrine from the Wrong Text?: Essays on the Use of the Old Testament in the New,* ed. G. K. Beale (Grand Rapids, MI: Baker, 1994), 342-71.

[55]The adjective "christiconic" has also been suggested (Abraham Kuruvilla, *Privilege the Text!: A Theological Hermeneutic for Preaching* [Chicago: Moody, 2013]), where all Scripture portrays various characteristics of Christ that can be learned and applied. This too is helpful, but it does not quite capture the flowing and developmental nature of the Scriptures that christo*telic* does.

To return to our illustration of a satellite bound for Saturn, once it arrives (which the NASA probe did in 2004) it then becomes Saturno*centric*. It revolves around Saturn, never to leave its orbit again.[56] It can then focus on all the beautiful details of the planet.[57]

The gospel of Jesus' atoning death and life-giving resurrection is like a magnetic weight in the New Testament that organizes all the rest of its details. If we misunderstand the centrally organizing effect of the gospel in the New Testament, all our other doctrines become detached and lose their proper orientation. Of course, there are predictive elements of the New Testament as well, looking forward to the return of Christ. But even there such forward glances are premised on the *completed* work of Christ on the cross and in the resurrection. It is as though all the glories of the coming

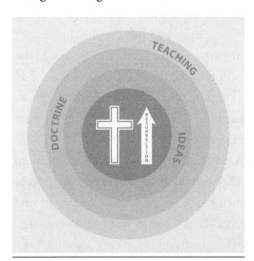

Figure 5.7. Everything in the NT revolves around Jesus' person and work; in this way the NT is "christocentric."

new creation are amplifications of the myriad of good things Christ has already accomplished for his people in his first coming. Thus, taken as a whole, the New Testament is christo*centric*.

Altogether the Bible is christological. In all, it is the *logic of the gospel* that ties the diversity of the Bible together. Thus, the entire Bible is christo*logical*. Just as tectonic plates move the crust of the Earth around to create the landscapes on which we live, so the gospel is the substructure on which everything in the Bible is finally grounded. We cannot see tectonic plates, but they are surely there, and their movements make the

---

[56]No illustration is perfect, however. The satellite called "Cassini" crashed into Saturn in 2017.

[57]Again, no illustration is perfect. The satellite to Saturn only gathered information once it got there. I am arguing that the *pathway* to Christ matters as well. The journey through the Old Testament and *how* it arrives at the New Testament greatly influences the reading of both.

terrain of the Earth what it is, which we of course *can* see. Everything from the highest mountains to the deepest ocean trenches owe their existence to the movement of these plates. Equally, the gospel is like the plate-tectonic stratum under the whole of the Bible. It cannot be found in every passage, but every passage of the Bible is part of the landscape of the whole. And that landscape is shaped distinctly as it is *because* of the gospel. Everything ultimately makes sense—the parts in light of the whole and vice versa—because of the underlying gospelness of the Bible's final form.

By way of visual illustration, a house foundation works the same way. However it is laid down will determine the shape of the house and the dynamics of its various parts. There is a certain *logic* to any house that must work within the foundation's capacities.

This is why an interchangeable term for redemptive

Figure 5.8. The entire Bible, with all its literary and theological variety, is unified by Jesus' person and work; in this way the entire Bible is "christological."

history is "christological context." It is the largest context possible, the one that orients everything else and binds everything else together—the large-scale sweep of what God has been doing in history for the redemption of his people. And since it all finally coheres through the person and work of Christ, all the Scriptures can be called christological. The logic of the gospel of Jesus Christ is what gives redemptive history its distinctive shape and brings unity to all the diversity. Thus, the entire scope of redemptive history now becomes the christological context for any individual verse, pericope, passage, or book. When, therefore, we study any verse, pericope, passage, or book we need to understand where in redemptive history it is located and, from there, deal with its christo-logic in different ways.

To tie off our space exploration metaphor, the entire design of the satellite is Saturno*logical*. It is everything about Saturn—its size, density, gravitational pull, rings, orbit, speed, location at the time of launch, and so on—that determines the design of the satellite and how it would be launched. What it takes to get to Saturn (the Saturno*telic* part) and what it takes to stay in Saturn's orbit (the Saturno*centric* part) are all controlled by what Saturn is and how it functions in space, the *logic* of Saturn.

It is important for our hermeneutical considerations to understand what the Bible is, what kind of book we are dealing with and how its parts work together to form the whole. The Old Testament is christo*telic*. The New Testament is christo*centric*. All of it is christo*logical*. Appreciating this will help us handle it ethically and legitimately.

Conclusion

This overview has been necessarily selective, but crucial in order to "take account of the full drama of redemption."[58] The Creator's original intent for the cosmos, though disrupted by sin and death, will come to fruition; he will rule the nations through a righteous king. That is promised in Genesis 3:15 and slowly developed through the Old Testament, climaxing in the person and work of Christ who atones for our sins and is raised to incorruptible life. Seeing this larger landscape of redemptive history will allow us to navigate it ethically and legitimately with any text we might study. In conclusion I would say, therefore, that in their entirety *the Scriptures are the Spirit-inspired record and interpretation of God's historical acts of redemption that climax in the death and resurrection of Jesus Christ and his ongoing work among the nations.* That death and resurrection is the fulfillment of God's redemptive purposes to bring humanity back to its Edenic relationship with God and the world. It is what the Old Testament looks forward to. It is what the New Testament revolves around. It is the fulcrum on which all else hangs and turns. Reading the Old Testament with this *telos* in mind, and the New Testament with this *centrality* in mind, as well as any verse, pericope, or passage with this *logic*

---

[58]Edmund P. Clowney, *Preaching Christ in All of Scripture* (Wheaton, IL: Crossway, 2003), 11.

in mind, is an essential hermeneutical consideration. Showing what that actually looks like is the burden of the next chapter.

For Further Study

Alexander, T. Desmond, Brian S. Rosner, D. A. Carson, and Graeme Goldsworthy. *New Dictionary of Biblical Theology: Exploring the Unity and Diversity of Scripture.* IVP Reference Collection. Downers Grove, IL: IVP Academic, 2000. I cannot recommend this book enough. It is such a helpful collection of essays on the Bible's major themes. It also has entries for each book of the Bible, so it is helpful for literary context studies as well.

Clowney, Edmund P. *The Unfolding Mystery: Discovering Christ in the Old Testament.* Phillipsburg, NJ: P&R, 1988. A bit of a modern classic on the topic.

Goldsworthy, Graeme. *Gospel and Kingdom.* Carlisle: Paternoster, 1981. Goldsworthy lays out a tripartite structure to redemptive history that gives orientation to the biblical-theological process: the kingdom revealed in (1) Israel's history, (2) prophecy, and (3) Jesus Christ, the contours of Eden serving as the essential theological outline for all.

Roberts, Vaughn. *God's Big Picture: Tracing the Storyline of the Bible.* Downers Grove, IL: InterVarsity Press, 2002. Giving credit to Goldsworthy for his influence, Roberts describes the flow of the Bible's metanarrative in terms of God's people in God's place under God's rule and blessing. One stage at a time, Roberts develops a heuristic diagram for understanding redemptive history.

For Advanced Study

Alexander, T. Desmond. *From Eden to the New Jerusalem: An Introduction to Biblical Theology.* Grand Rapids, MI: Kregel Academic, 2008. This is a very rich work that explores not just related themes in Genesis and Revelation, but the dynamic of those themes in Israel and the church as well. Alexander is particularly strong on the role of the temple across the biblical narrative.

Beale, G. K. *A New Testament Biblical Theology: The Unfolding of the Old Testament in the New.* Grand Rapids, MI: Baker Academic, 2011. No other New Testament theology gives as much attention to the Old Testament background.

Gentry, Peter J., and Stephen J. Wellum. *Kingdom Through Covenant: A Biblical-Theological Understanding of the Covenants.* 2nd ed. Wheaton, IL: Crossway, 2018. Covenant is another major theme that should be included in this chapter, but it is really too big and deserves too much nuance to fit into a survey. This work is as thorough an examination as you will find.

Goldsworthy, Graeme. *Christ-Centered Biblical Theology: Hermeneutical Foundations and Principles.* Downers Grove, IL: IVP Academic, 2012. In this work Goldsworthy both defends the discipline of biblical theology and argues for his understanding of the structure of redemptive history.

Perrin, Nicholas. *The Kingdom of God: A Biblical Theology*. Biblical Theology for Life. Grand Rapids, MI: Zondervan, 2019. The arrival of the "kingdom of God" was the central message of Jesus' preaching. Perrin explores very clearly and helpfully the who, what, where, when, how, and why of the kingdom.

Robertson, O. Palmer. *The Christ of the Covenants*. Phillipsburg: P&R, 1980. Robertson demonstrates how the structure of redemptive history is best understood through the relationships between the various covenants of the Bible.

Vos, Geerhardus. *Biblical Theology: Old and New Testaments*. Grand Rapids, MI: Eerdmans, 1948. Also taking on both testaments, Vos's work is a classic in the discipline.

THROUGH THE TEXT

The Christological Context, Part 2

WHEN I WAS IN SEVENTH GRADE, I had a homework project where I had to describe how to get to the mall from my house. I needed to look at a paper map, interpret the symbols in the key, and write out the directions, distances, lights, turns, roads, ramps, and so forth so that someone could take my directions and get to the mall. It was an exercise in understanding how maps work. No one ever used my directions. But my teacher could tell if I understood the logic of maps based on what I wrote. It was tricky. For example, if you are traveling south and you want to go to the right on your map, you actually have to take a left in the car. As seventh graders we struggled a bit, but we caught on.

When I got into my ecology program in college, however, I was a little stunned by the maps I was given in my first lab. Where were the lines of different color and thickness indicating various road types? Where were the numbers and names of the roads? Where were the symbols for fire and police stations? Why was the map all one bland color? I was used to counties and/or states designated by varying colors. All this map had was a bunch of misshaped "circles" and incomplete squiggly lines. I was told it was a map of the area we were going to study, but I was lost before we even got there.

It turns out, of course, it was *topographical* map. Topographical maps describe the *lay of the land*, not the cultural objects (roads, fire stations, etc.) that humans have built on the land. *Road* maps typically do not show the terrain (at least not with any detail). They just show how to get

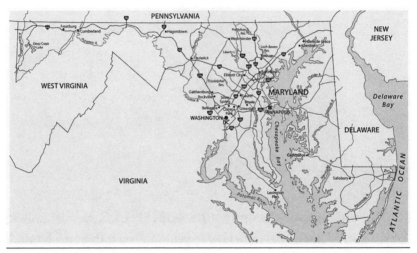

Figure 6.1. A road map of Maryland shows how to cut across the landscape to arrive quickly at the desired destination.

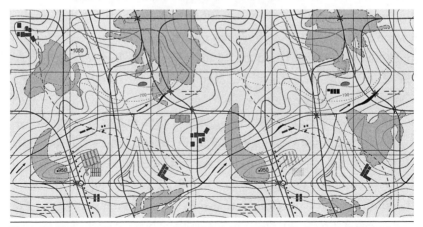

Figure 6.2. A topographical map shows detailed elevations and complex features within a landscape.

from point A to point B if you follow the manmade roads. Stay on the road, and you are fine. Indeed, road maps are great! *But those roads must have been built with the topography of the land in mind.* If not, roads will go up and down inclines that are too steep or lead into a swamp. The topography of the land *must first be considered* so that we can lay down roads from point A to point B in the right way, in a way that works with the terrain, with the natural lay of the land.

In the previous chapter I described the Bible's content from an aerial view, as though we were looking down on it from a high enough peak to see it all in one vista. You could say we created a topographical map of the Bible as we attended to the terrain of redemptive history.

I made the case that *in their entirety the Scriptures are the Spirit-inspired record and interpretation of God's historical acts of redemption that climax in the death and resurrection of Jesus Christ and his ongoing work among the nations.* All the terrain, in other words, bends and flows toward the gospel. And this is not accidental. It is intentional on God's part. It is imperative, therefore, that when reading any portion of Scripture we understand where we are on that landscape and *the right way to get to the gospel.* Roads can rarely make straight lines from point A to point B; they have to follow the natural terrain. In the same way, as we read any book, pericope, or verse we need to let the Bible's terrain lead us to where we need to go. Now that we have that topographical map of the Bible's major contours, we need to navigate it properly. We need to know where we are at any given time, what is around us, and the path to get to the gospel *legitimately.*

Some interpreters get nervous when we talk about a path to the gospel. It can ignore the details of Old Testament passages and actually flatten out the gospel. For example, John Goldingay is concerned that the spirituality of the Old Testament and the character of God—as just two examples—are diminished when the "First Testament" is somehow subordinated (intentionally or not) to the New Testament.[1] I agree! And I will

---

[1] John Goldingay, *Do We Need the New Testament? Letting the Old Testament Speak for Itself* (Downers Grove, IL: IVP Academic, 2015).

critique some slightly misleading language at the end of this chapter. All the same, I am insisting on giving weight to the larger biblical theological conclusion that "Jesus brings the fulfillment of God's purposes for Israel" and that through him "we know *how* God's self-giving came to a climax," and what that larger metanarrative realization does to our reading any part of the Bible.[2] To be clear, therefore, I am proposing a path that gives full consideration to all Old Testament dynamics and provides "textual controls" for *how* that path is trod to Jesus. Such an approach will accomplish what Goldingay suggests: "When [interpretation] seeks to set in a wider context the theological insights expressed in a text it will operate in a way that recognizes how Jesus is the decisive moment in God's fulfilling his purpose in the world, but it will expect to find that the texts also nuance our understanding of Jesus' significance."[3]

This chapter, therefore, focuses on what lines of meaning are running "through the text," those ideas that originate in the earlier parts of the Bible and develop through subsequent books on their way to their climax in Christ.

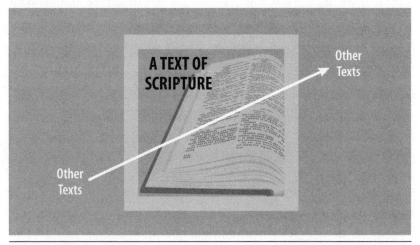

Figure 6.3. Biblical hermeneutics is unique because there are "worlds running through the texts"—interpretative lines that originate in prior texts and climax in subsequent texts.

---

[2]Goldingay, *Do We Need the New Testament?*, 32, 47; emphasis added.
[3]Goldingay, *Do We Need the New Testament?*, 175.

Sometimes texts lead directly to the gospel (indeed there are some very straight roads in the world). But more often they wend to the gospel (there certainly are more winding roads that also require bridges and tunnels). It is important, therefore, that we do not force texts to be more direct than they are, nor that we get clever, nor bulldoze the terrain. The key is to let the terrain direct us to the gospel *on its own terms*. The text itself will tell us how to get there. In short, we let the *literary* context and the *historical* context lead the way.

Allow me to change the metaphor slightly from roads to train tracks. If you lay down tracks, but do not have a train, what good are the tracks? It is the train that carries the freight. But equally the train *needs* the tracks. Christological context is like the train. It is the necessary component of hermeneutics because it gets us to where we need to go, to the gospel. It carries the freight of the gospel. But it needs tracks. The literary context is the left rail, and historical context is the right rail. The train needs *both* to travel, or else the train derails. So what will stop us from crashing the interpretive train on the rocks of allegory, speculation, fancy, cleverness, or any other many dangers? The answer is *the rails of literary and historical context*. Just as with roads, train tracks are also laid down with respect to the lay of the land. In the same way therefore, these rails of literary and historical context will keep our christological train *on the right path*—appropriately laid down on the redemptive-historical terrain—lest we are tempted to jump the rails and take shortcuts. We have to get to the gospel because that is how Jesus and the New Testament authors understood things. We have to drive the interpretive train to that decisive destination, or else we just have rails and nowhere to go. Yet, it is those rails that keep the train on course. If our path to the gospel violates something in the literary context, our train has crashed. If our path to the gospel ignores something in the historical context, our train has crashed. But careful attention to these contexts will give more stability to our christological train. In short, literary and historical contexts make our christological interpretation ethical and legitimate.

Thus, literary contexts and historical contexts are servants of the christological context. Every pericope, of course, has a *meaning* in its literary context alone. We could call this a pericope's "first level meaning." And every pericope *meant* something in its original historical context. We can call this the pericope's "second level meaning." The two cannot contradict, but work in symbiosis for the *text* was created *in history*. And yet, sometimes those literary and historical meanings might not *in and of themselves* have anything to do with Christ. But the moment we realize that the pericope is part of the Bible—part of redemptive history—then this new christological context must be given its due weight. When we take this last hermeneutical step, we can say that we are exploring a pericope's "climactic meaning." This might look different, or even unexpected, from the first and second level meanings, but not contradictory or implausible. In fact, a lot of New Testament uses of the Old Testament are surprising. In hindsight, though, the New Testament brings coherency to *the whole canon*. Surprising or not, it is coherent. In this way, meaning is running through the text.

In this chapter we will explore five ways that the terrain bends and flows toward the gospel, five ways the rails of literature and history are set up to run on the redemptive-historical landscape, taking the interpretive train to Christ. Each way depends on the text in question. That is, different texts at different places on the lay of the Bible's terrain direct us along different paths to the gospel.[4] Just as different roads have different shapes depending on the landscape, so too our literary and historical rails will take the christological train along different routes. The five ways are as follows: (1) through Old Testament quotes, echoes, and allusions in the New Testament; (2) through prophecy; (3) through typology; (4) through major recurring themes; and (5) through whole-book contexts. As we go through this, we should remember how we discussed in the previous chapter that the Old Testament is christo*telic*: the Old Testament has an overall slope and goal toward the gospel. The

---

[4]See esp. David S. Schrock, "From Beelines to Plotlines: Typology That Follows the Covenantal Topography of Scripture," *SBJT* 21 (2017): 35-56.

New Testament is christo*centric*: everything in the New Testament revolves around the gospel. And thus, the entire Bible is christo*logical*:
everything makes sense finally only in light of the gospel. The gospel
pulls together the entire canon to give it its coherency. In this way we are
"thinking *with* the Bible rather than merely *about* it."[5]

Old Testament Quotations, Echoes, and Allusions in the New Testament

Direct references to the Old Testament in the New Testament can be the
simplest and most difficult at the same time. It is simple because it is
obvious when New Testament passages quote Old Testament verses.
They will commonly introduce it with "Thus fulfilled what was spoken
by the prophet," or "For the Scripture says," or "As it is written." It can be
difficult, however, to understand *why* the New Testament author has
invoked that Old Testament verse. Moreover, it is more common that
Old Testament language is employed *without* such introductions, and
therefore can sometimes be missed. What to do?

Quotations. To begin, when we see an Old Testament quote in the
New Testament, something very interesting is happening. The New
Testament author is grabbing part of another literary world (the Old
Testament book) and bringing it back into his own. Thus, the New Testament book now has a shard of the Old Testament book in it. The New
Testament book, in other words, embeds into its own integrous text a
portion of another. That Old Testament text is now part of the New Testament text, and that Old Testament text now has to be considered in
discerning the New Testament book's coherency. Thus, when we see an
Old Testament quote we have to read the Old Testament *context* (no
surprise here!) from which it comes. A good study Bible (see chap. 4) will
have cross references that will tell you exactly where to turn in the Old
Testament to find the verse being employed in the New Testament.[6]

---

[5]Kevin J. Vanhoozer and Daniel J. Treier, *Theology and the Mirror of Scripture: A Mere Evangelical Account*, SCDS (Downers Grove, IL: IVP Academic, 2015), 100.

[6]Be careful with these cross references, however. Sometimes they merely point you to another verse or passage that happens to discuss the same theological concept. That is all well and good

Read at least the Old Testament pericope. If it is a loadbearing pericope, then read more of the larger passage. In fact, the best practice is to do an entire contextual study of the Old Testament book from which the quote comes (see chap. 3). Then ask yourself, What is this verse contributing to its original Old Testament book, particularly its immediate pericope? Then revisit the New Testament book where it is used and ask yourself the same question. What is the Old Testament context contributing to the New Testament book that now employs it? What similar themes do you see *between* the contexts? You will discover that more times than not, the New Testament author is not just quoting *a single verse* that suits his purposes, but indexing *a larger theological point* from the Old Testament context (maybe the entire book).

This is not a violation of the New Testament book's integrity, because we are not importing foreign ideas. The idea *is* there in the New Testament text. The New Testament author has put it in there and asked readers to consider the Old Testament idea *as part of the New Testament text* now. The quote creates a direct path from the New Testament text to the Old Testament text and back again. The New Testament author is telling readers to take the round trip. We call this "intertexture." Like an interstate highway that goes between states, so too this is a communication channel between texts, an "intertext."[7]

Let us take an example. Ephesians 4:8 quotes Psalm 68:18—"When He ascended on high he led a host of captives, and he gave gifts to men."

---

if you are trying to do a general thematic study of the entire Bible. But remember, each book has its own integrity and coherency. Any verse should be interpreted in light of the whole book and does not need the teachings of another book to supplement it. So, while it is fine to look at other verses in the Bible on a common theme, do not grab cross references and import them *back* into the primary book under consideration if it is not being called for by that book (as in a direct quote). Let each book have its own distinct voice; do not violate any book's integrity or disrupt its coherency.

[7]The term "intertexture" is frowned upon by some biblical scholars because originally it carried the suggestion that the meaning of texts is constantly fluid (see Stefan Alkier, "Intertextuality and the Semiotics of Biblical Texts," in *Reading the Bible Intertextually*, eds. Richard B. Hays, Stefan Alkier and Leroy A. Huizenga [Waco, TX: Baylor University Press, 2009], 3-7). The reader should simply be aware that different definitions of "intertexture" exist, but I am using the term here to speak of the communication channel between texts that are opened up when one text references another.

When you see this you could just keep reading, but you will be confused as the flow of thought just becomes strange. But if you take the effort to turn to Psalm 68 and study it, interpretive angles open up. The psalm is about God's salvation in the exodus that eventuated in God's dwelling with his people in the tabernacle and then the Jerusalem temple. Well, Ephesians has a lot to say about salvation in Christ, and the church as the new temple-dwelling place of God (2:19-22). Thus, the gifts the Egyptians gave—gold and silver—to build the tabernacle *are compared to the spiritual gifts Jesus now gives to build the church!* The upshot of seeing this is that we get a more lucid theology of the church and spiritual gifts along the Bible's larger narrative arc vis-à-vis the temple—not just some vague Old Testament language dropped into Ephesians 4 for unclear reasons. A lot more could be said about this intertexture and its effect on reading Ephesians, but that is enough for now to illustrate the point of how necessary it is to explore the Old Testament context of verses quoted in the New Testament.[8]

In this case, our study of the literary context became a challenge that only attention to the christological context could resolve. To be sure, it seems impossible to do the former without the latter. The latter is now part of the former as the entire context of Psalm 68 is drawn into Ephesians 4, making itself necessary to understand if we are to appreciate Ephesians's coherency.

Conversely, when we read the Old Testament and come across a verse that we know is quoted in the New Testament, we should explore that New Testament context. Again, a good study Bible will have the New Testament verses in a margin or footnote. The New Testament context then becomes for us a Spirit-inspired interpretation of the Old Testament text. The New Testament provides that "climactic meaning" of the Old Testament pericope. Let us say, for example, you are studying Habakkuk and you arrive at 2:4, which gets a lot of airtime in the New Testament.

---

[8]This example also illustrates the way some New Testament quotes are not exact word for word quotes of the Old Testament. For such matters see G. K. Beale and D. A. Carson, eds., *Commentary on the New Testament Use of the Old Testament* (Grand Rapids, MI: Baker Academic, 2007).

It is quoted in Romans 1:17, Galatians 3:11, and Hebrews 10:38. When you see that, you will want to explore some of the context around Romans 1, Galatians 3, and Hebrews 10. If you really want to get your hands dirty, study all of Romans, Galatians, and Hebrews. But *first,* do all your literary and historical work in Habakkuk! Here is the problem: people see Habakkuk 2:4 used in Romans, Galatians, and Hebrews, and they just run off to those New Testament texts and forget about the rest of Habakkuk. Let Habakkuk 2:4 do its work in the literary and historical contexts of Habakkuk first. Understand it well in its original textual and cultural home. Then take that knowledge to Romans, Galatians, and Hebrews. Understanding what Habakkuk 2:4 contributes to the whole of Habakkuk will go a long way to also understanding Romans 1, Galatians 3, and Hebrews 10 all the more.

Echoes. More commonly, however, New Testament authors do not signal when they are employing Old Testament language. They just seamlessly knit it into their discourse.

A nice example is, again, in the parable of the mustard seed. In Mark 4:32 Jesus comments that the fully grown plant puts out "large branches" so that "the birds of the air can make nests in its shade." Why this extra detail? It is more than just vivid storytelling. That same language of *birds* in the *shade* of *large branches* is also found in Ezekiel 17:23 and 31:6. The context of Ezekiel 17:23 speaks of God planting Israel after the exile. It is a restoration promise. And Ezekiel 31:6 outright explains the metaphor of the birds: they represent all the nations. Thus, it seems Jesus' parable was not drawn up on the spot. But he is echoing the language of the Lord's promises of restoration that will bless Israel *and* the nations. He is helping his audience make the connection that his mustard-seed-like kingdom is the fulfillment of Ezekiel's vision. This makes even more sense of why Jesus then goes into *Gentile* territory immediately thereafter in Mark 5:1-20 (see comments in chap. 3). The movement into Gentile territory is the first branch being put out; the healed demoniac is the first "bird" so to speak. But there is more. Ezekiel himself may have drawn that sort of language from creation. Psalm 104 is a hymn of praise for how effortlessly—and for his own glory—God created the cosmos. In verses 12 and 17 the psalmist speaks of how God made trees for *birds of the heavens* to make *nests* in their *branches*. The value in hearing this additional echo is that it brings with it that notion of the sovereign effortlessness with which God created. Jesus seems to be evoking that language to double down on his confidence that the mustard seed will indeed grow into the biggest of all plants. How can Jesus be so confident in this? Just as God sovereignly, and for his own glory, did effortlessly create the world, so too will God sovereignly, and for his own glory, grow this mustard seed into the largest of all plants—whatever obstacles may come. Perhaps this suggests something of why Jesus performs a nature miracle in the next pericope (4:35-41), linking together the kingdom and new creation (as we saw often in chap. 5). Now our interpretation of Mark 4:30–5:20 has a deep and rich theology full of the themes of creation, the sovereignty of God, the glory of God, the restoration of the Israel, and the salvation of the nations.

But how do we know the theologies of Ezekiel and Psalm 104 are really part of Mark 4–5? It is common that readers imagine such links. That results in eisegesis, and we do not want that. How do we know when we have a genuine echo and we are not hearing voices, fanciful musings in our minds but not truly a point of the text?

When we believe there could be an Old Testament echo in a New Testament verse, there are two questions we can ask.[9] First, are there enough keywords that this is not just coincidental?[10] The link between Mark 4:32 and those Old Testament verses does not hang on one term, but several terms. The language of birds, branches, nests, and shade in trees make for a lot of similarities.

Another example of this is in Galatians 1:15-16, where Paul says "it pleased God, who separated me *from my mother's womb* and called me

---

[9]Richard B. Hays has a fuller list in *The Conversion of the Imagination: Paul as Interpreter of Israel's Scripture* (Grand Rapids, MI: Eerdmans, 2005), 34-45.

[10]Admittedly we have to be careful here for two reasons. An English Bible may use the same or similar words but different Greek or Hebrew words actually lie behind the translation. Or an English Bible may use different words that are actually translations of the same Greek or Hebrew word. Again, a good study Bible can point these things out.

through His grace, to reveal His Son in me, that I might *preach Him among the Gentiles*" (NKJV). This sounds somewhat like Jeremiah's calling: "Before I formed you *in the womb* I knew you; Before you were born I sanctified you; I ordained you *a prophet to the nations*" (1:5 NKJV). We have the mention of the *womb*, the *ordaining (or setting apart)*, and to minister among the *nations (or Gentiles)*. That is a lot of similarity. We might have an echo.

The second question is, Is there enough thematic similarity between the two contexts? If we find significant commonalities in the contexts of both pericopes (or passages) then the intertexture will illuminate something significant in the New Testament text. The Old Testament context will help pull together the logic of the New Testament context (or even the entire New Testament book). The author has drawn on that Old Testament context to make his own point. As mentioned above, the invoking of creation followed by a nature miracle, and the image of birds representing the nations with Jesus' immediate voyage into Gentile territory, show how both Psalm 104 and Ezekiel are similar to themes already in Mark 4–5, such that the Old Testament echo highlights and/or reinforces those themes all the more, providing more depth to our understanding of Mark 4–5. Equally, Paul's apostleship seems to be in question in Galatians. What better way to help establish that than to invoke the language of one of Israel's prophets?

Equally, when reading the Old Testament and something is later echoed in the New Testament, take the effort to go to that New Testament context and read through it. There in that New Testament context you have a Spirit-inspired application of the Old Testament text you are studying. Of course, we should avail ourselves of that, but do your literary and historical analysis of the Old Testament text first. Do not run off too quickly to the New Testament, but equally, do not forget to attend to this climactic meaning.

Let us take an example starting with the Old Testament. In the previous chapter we looked at the crucial place of Psalm 72 in the Psalter. After doing that literary contextual work, understanding it as the pinnacle of God's purposes for the cosmos through the house of David, we should also observe how it is echoed at the beginning of the New Testament. When magi arrive in Jerusalem at Jesus' birth, Matthew 2:11 echoes the tribute of the nations in Psalm 72:10-11.[11] We have also already seen how Matthew 1 is so focused on David's house. Thus, both the number of keywords and thematic similarities strongly suggest that Matthew sees these magi as the beginning of the fulfillment of the Psalm's expectations. These observations, therefore, tie off our study of Psalm 72, showing us its climatic meaning: the kingdom of righteousness and justice envisioned for David's house dawns with Jesus' birth.[12]

To navigate this sort of redemptive-historical terrain, the same hermeneutical principles apply, and the same steps can be taken as we saw with quotations. We have to read *both* contexts. The reason this can work is the same reason why quotes index larger passages: intertextures open up communication channels wherein both texts are forever hermeneutically linked.

Allusions. Making a difference between echoes and allusions might be hairsplitting, but I think there is a difference worth mentioning. My definition for "allusion" is when a New Testament text references or points to an Old Testament context without any of the particular language of the Old Testament. While quotes and echoes use specific wording, allusions are more like direct instructions to go explore the Old Testament context.

An example will demonstrate what I mean. In John 3:14 Jesus mentions, "As Moses lifted up the serpent in the wilderness." While that is not a quote or an echo, it is a direct reference to an event. Thus, we have to turn to Numbers 21:4-9 (again, a good study Bible is enough to point you there) and wrap our minds around that story in its original context before we go any further in John.

---

[11]Robert H. Gundry, *The Use of the Old Testament in St. Matthew's Gospel, With Special Reference to the Messianic Hope*, NovTSup 18 (Leiden: Brill, 1967), 129-30.

[12]It should be pointed out, all the same, that there is an already-not-yet dynamic to this kingdom, and so Rev 19:11 and 21:26 also appear to echo Psalm 72:2, 10-11, 15 as Jesus the righteous judge accepts the glories of the nations into his eternal kingdom.

The same would apply if we were studying Numbers. When we get to chapter twenty-one we should take the effort to explore John 3 as well. Jesus' comparison between the snake and himself provides the climactic meaning, the final redemptive-historical horizon to which Numbers 21 points. Again, study Numbers 21 in its original literary and historical contexts first. Do not run off to the New Testament too fast, but get there nonetheless.

A less explicit allusion—but equally present and equally important— occurs in the stilling of the storm in Mark 4:35-41. We have looked at this pericope and its surrounding contexts a lot, as well as the Old Testament echoes in the foregoing parable. Could there really be more? There is. In the episode Jesus is asleep in the boat when the storm stirs up, the disciples think they are going to die, divine intervention stops the storm, and then verse 41 says the disciples were filled with "great fear." Well, where else do you read of someone asleep on a boat when a storm arises, those on board think they are going to die, the storm is stopped by God, and the people fear *more* after the miracle? My second-grade son can tell you that one: it is Jonah! The parallels are clear. Mark has told this account in such a way as to allude to that famous story. (In fact, there is some echoing here to help readers out: both Jonah 1:4 and Mark 4:37 speak of a "great wind" and both Jonah 1:16 and Mark 4:41 speak of "great fear.") But why? What does it add to our reading of Mark to notice the Jonah-shaped outline of the stilling of the storm? It surely has something to do with the question the disciples ask in Mark 4:41: "Who then is this, that even the wind and the sea obey him?" In Jonah the answer to that was the Creator Lord God (cf. Jon 1:9). In Mark, the answer is Jesus! No wonder the disciples "feared" during the storm (Mk 4:40) but were filled with "great fear" afterward (Mk 4:41); the Creator Lord God is in the boat with them! Again, as mentioned above with the echo of Psalm 104, that realization will do a lot to increase our confidence in the parable Jesus just told. It was uttered by God himself!

I hope you are appreciating the depth of insight available when we slow down and read the Old Testament contexts of quotations, echoes, and allusions in the New Testament.[13] If we remember that the Old Testament is christotelic, that it has an overall uphill slope toward the gospel, then quotes, echoes, and allusions in the New Testament are like backward glances that recall the journey and celebrate the arrival at the climactic meaning.

Prophecy

Commonly an Old Testament quote contains a particular prophecy, as is often the case when a New Testament author says something has been "fulfilled." These can seem simpler than echoes and allusions because the concepts of prediction and accomplishment are more intuitive. But there are two characteristics of prophecy to consider: (1) Old Testament prophecies typically operate in a near-and-far dynamic, and (2) there are, as expected, contextual matters in both Old Testament and New Testament to navigate. Thus, prophecy is rarely as simple as "this fulfills that."

First, biblical prophecy commonly operates with a near-and-far dynamic. The Old Testament often calls the prophets "seers" because God has shown them the future, and it is common that their descriptions of what they saw of the future plays out over multiple events. Yet, they give just one description. It seems they are looking over multiple horizons of time but seeing only one thing. As Walter Kaiser illustrates, it is as though prophets are looking to the future with just one eye and so have no depth perception. They speak, therefore, of a singular future event while actually "seeing" multiple horizons of fulfillment without any specific comment on the distance between those horizons.[14] We can call this "prophetic telescoping," where events' similarities evince their conceptual and theological alignment. So while prophets give *one* prophecy, the fulfillment actually plays out over several future events. Commonly enough, it could even look like the point of the prophecy is exhausted in

---

[13]Of course, a lot more could be said about quotations, echoes, and allusions. For the eager student, I would point to G. K. Beale's *Handbook on the New Testament Use of the Old Testament: Exegesis and Interpretation* (Grand Rapids, MI: Baker Academic, 2012).

[14]Walter C. Kaiser, *The Uses of the Old Testament in the New* (Chicago: Moody, 1985; repr., Eugene, OR: Wipf & Stock, 2001), 61-76.

the first fulfillment, only to see later there was actually more to it, each subsequent fulfillment building intensity toward the final fulfillment. We saw this sort of dynamic in our survey of redemptive history as well. We saw several episodes that looked in *some way* like God's purposes in redemption were coming to pass, but we also knew that could not be the full extent—Joseph, the exodus, Joshua, David, Solomon, second temple, and so forth. Likewise, the prophets would see the future, and the first horizon of fulfillment would come very soon, all the while holding out the expectation that that first fulfillment is but the shape of something greater still to come.

To illustrate, Matthew 1:23's quote of Isaiah 7:14 is famous enough: "Behold the virgin shall conceive and bear a son" So says the prophet and, lo and behold, so says Matthew. Prophecy and fulfillment. Simple, right? Well, not so simple. As always we need to read Isaiah 7:14 in its original literary and historical contexts. When we do, we see why Isaiah made that prediction in the first place. In Isaiah 7:1-13 David's house is under siege: Two kings from the north want to join forces and assault Jerusalem, topple the house of David, and install their own puppet-king (vv. 1, 5-6). The promise of this miraculous birth in verse 14 is a sign to reassure Judah and Jerusalem that God will not abandon them, but save them yet again from this historical threat. Then in Isaiah 8 a child is born (v. 3) and before he is old enough to even lisp "mama" or "papa," these two northern kings are already plundered (v. 4)! It seems, in the context of Isaiah alone, that 7:14's prediction is accomplished in chapter eight. But alas, Matthew 1:23 shows us how Isaiah 8 was a down payment along the way to the full and final fulfillment in Jesus' birth as "he will save his people from their sins" (Mt 1:21).

The second characteristic of Old Testament prophecy is its contextual nature. When the New Testament claims the fulfillment of an Old Testament verse, the issues mentioned above regarding *quotations* remain— the Old Testament context also needs to be explored to fully grasp the New Testament flow of thought. Rarely do the New Testament authors quote Old Testament verses in fulfillment to simply say, "See, *this* fulfills *that!*" Rather, even prophecies bring with them larger Old Testament contexts. Let us return to the quote of Isaiah 7:14 in Matthew 1:23 to think about this as well. If attention to near-and-far dynamics helped us see *why Isaiah* made the prophecy, then comparing Old Testament and New Testament contexts will help us see *why Matthew* drew upon the prophecy. Looking at the context of Matthew 1 we see the evangelist's concern is more than simply Mary's virginity (though it is not less than that either). The fact that Mary was a virgin does not exhaust the significance of the fulfillment of Isaiah 7:14 in Matthew 1:23. As just mentioned in Isaiah 7, Jerusalem is under siege. The specific focus, however, is on the house of David (vv. 2, 13). A *coup d'état* is imminent. Why focus on the house of David like this? As discussed in the previous chapter, God had promised David an *eternal* throne (cf. 2 Sam 7:12-13). And we can see that this is Isaiah's concern in what he calls the king in verses 2 and 13: "house of David." He does not call him by his name, Ahaz, but by the redemptive-historical entity he represents. This is no run-of-the-mill war story, therefore. It is through the house of David that the Lord will accomplish his saving work, or not at all. To attack David's throne, therefore, is to fight against God himself, and specifically to fight against God's purposes in redemptive history. And the Lord's provision of the "Immanuel" sign-child in Isaiah 8, followed by the quick demise of the northern kings, shows all Jerusalem that his purposes in redemption will indeed continue, and specifically through the house of David.

When we bring such larger contextual issues to bear on Matthew 1 many things jump off the page. Davidic themes are all over Matthew 1. We have in Matthew, therefore, a typological appropriation of an old story. The house of David was spared in Isaiah 7–8. And while it was eventually dethroned (2 Kings 24–25), and the promises of God had gone unfulfilled for centuries, Matthew suddenly brings the focus back to the house of David. The point is profoundly this: just as the Lord had saved the house of David from near death, a greater salvation is now coming forth as the Lord *resurrects* the house of David from the grave! Now a true virgin bears the son of David and the Lord is proven true to his word! The concern in Matthew 1, then, is not just that Jesus had no earthly father (though it is not less than that either), but the hope that the house of David will be remade.[15] The rest of the Gospel of Matthew is the exciting story of how that happens. So considering the contextual theologies of Isaiah 7 and Matthew 1 has brought depth to our interpretation that can now influence our reading of the rest of Matthew.

These two characteristics of biblical prophecy—their near-and-far nature, and their contextual embeddedness—are important to keep in mind to *legitimately* navigate the redemptive-historical terrain to the gospel. When reading a prophecy in the Old Testament its near-and-far dynamic must be explored *before* running too quickly to where it is quoted, echoed, or alluded to in the New Testament. Equally, when reading the New Testament and an Old Testament verse is fulfilled, it is not just an apologetic check box to tick. But the Old Testament context must be explored for a more thorough understanding of the theology of both the original prophetic utterance and its fresh New Testament use.

If we remember that the Old Testament is christotelic, that the Old Testament has an overall, uphill slope toward the gospel, then prophecy is like signposts along the way pointing us to the summit.

Typology

We thought a lot about typology in chapters one and two. We saw two things there: (1) it has a long history in the church, and (2) it is different than allegory. It has such a long history because the church has always recognized that the Bible bends and flows toward Christ (this is not new with us), and typology is a common path to that end. And, as we have seen, the Bible teaches us the idea of typology and gives us very clear examples of it. Yet, there are ways to "get to Christ" that are not textually determined, or bypass Christ altogether and jump to "application." That is allegory. So let us turn to a legitimate and ethical appropriation of typology.[16]

---

[15]Nicholas G. Piotrowski, *Matthew's New David at the End of Exile: A Socio-Rhetorical Study of Scriptural Quotations*, NovTSup 170 (Leiden: Brill, 2016), 33-59.

[16]I would note also that even though I am listing typology as one of many ways to travel through the text, I actually agree with Goldsworthy that typology provides the "underlying structure or

"Typology" can be defined as the hermeneutical study of *God's sovereignty in Old Testament people, institutions, and events that prefigure the person and work of Christ in concert with literary genre and history*. As we saw in chapter two, it gets its name from Romans 5:14, 1 Corinthians 10:6, Hebrews 8:5, and 1 Peter 3:21 where the Greek words *typos* and *antitypos* are used to speak of recurring patterns in redemptive history that climax in the person and work of Christ. A "type," then, is the historical person, institution, or event, and an "antitype" is the corresponding element of Christ's person and work that provides the climactic meaning of the type.

By "person and work" of Christ I mean who he *is* (his person) and what he has done (his work). His *person* includes his humanity but also his deity, as well as the various roles he filled such as prophet, priest, and king. His *work* includes his teaching and miracle-working ministry, his sacrifice on the cross, his coronation in his resurrection and ascension, and his giving of the Spirit to create and build up the church. Typology is when an Old Testament person, institution, or event prefigures some aspect of any of that.[17] As Jean Daniélou states, "All the outstanding persons and leading events of Scripture are both stages and rough outlines to prepare and prefigure the mystery which is one day to be fulfilled in Christ."[18]

Figure 6.4. Diamonds of the same cut showcase a particularly prominent one. In like manner, typology explores biblical patterns that prefigure the preeminent work of Christ.

---

matrix of Scripture that generates the variety of connections" like quotes, allusions, echoes, prophecies, themes, and so forth (*Christ-Centered Biblical Theology: Hermeneutical Foundations and Principles* [Downers Grove, IL: IVP Academic, 2012], 189). Thus, this section on typological reading contains elements and instructions that can be applied in all reading. In that sense, typology is not one among many interpretive tools, but more like the entire shop.

[17]Poythress helpfully suggests Old Testament symbols and plots for typological consideration as well (*Reading the Word of God in the Presence of God: A Handbook for Biblical Interpretation* [Wheaton, IL: Crossway, 2016], 275-78).

[18]Jean Daniélou, *From Shadows to Reality*, trans. Dom Wulstan Hibberd, Studies in the Biblical Theology of the Fathers (Westminster, MD: Newman, 1960), 11.

For example, what Old Testament people prefigure some aspect of the person and work of Christ, even in the smallest way? Consider Adam, Noah, Isaac, Joseph, Moses, Joshua, Samson (yes even him!), David, Solomon, any of the prophets, or priests—even Cyrus! This is just a handful of some of the obvious examples. It is not as though their entire lives prefigure Christ, but some aspects of their lives do. Adam was the "image of God" who brought sin and death; Christ is the "image of God" who brings righteousness and life (Rom 5:12-21). Joseph was left for dead by his family and came back to save and rule the world; Jesus was entirely dead after which he came back to save and rule the world. Samson is called a "savior"; Jesus is the Savior. All the prophets were persecuted; Jesus was persecuted (Mt 23:29-32; Acts 7:52). Cyrus allows the exiles to return and rebuild the temple (Is 44:28; 2 Chron 36:23); Jesus permanently ends humanity's alienation from God and makes the church his temple (1 Pet 2:4-10). It is just endlessly fascinating the way God has called and used individuals (quite flawed individuals) in the history of Israel to sketch little outlines of what the Savior would someday be and do.

What *institutions* prefigure some aspect of the person and work of Christ? In Deuteronomy 18 we learn of the office of the prophet, but someday there will be a singular final prophet to whom all must listen (v. 15). This makes every prophet a type of Christ, *the* prophet. For example, Samuel was Israel's next prophet after Moses. In 1 Samuel 1–7 he is described in the language of Deuteronomy 18's prophet. Thus, simply filling the role of a prophet makes Samuel a type of the expected great *one* prophet to come (cf. Jn 6:14). God had always intended to give the world the great Deuteronomy 18 prophet in Christ, and sovereignly provided little patterns of *the* prophet throughout Israel's history, described in Israel's texts.[19] Equally, Jesus is our great high

---

[19]David Schrock calls these little patterns, "ectypes" ("What Designates a Valid Type?: A Christotelic, Covenantal Proposal," *STR* 5 [2014]: 17-24). Adam is the "prototype," Moses the "type," subsequent prophets "ectypes," and Jesus the "antitype." A step further, the church becomes the "supratype" (Schrock, "From Beelines to Plotlines: Typology That Follows the Covenantal Topography of Scripture," *SBJT* 21 [2017]: 45-46) that "share[s] covenantal attributes with and carr[ies] out the offices assigned by Jesus Christ" (36).

priest (Heb 4:14 and throughout); each priest in the Old Testament pre-figures Jesus' greater ministry.[20] Each Old Testament king in the line of David points forward to the King of kings.[21] The prophetic office, the priesthood, and the kingship are all institutions in Israel, as are the temple and its sacrificial system, the Passover and the Sabbath. All play a tangible and crucial role in the history of Israel, and in God's provi-dence they were installed to prepare the way to meet their typological fulfillment in Christ: He is the ultimate temple dwelling of God on earth (Mt 12:6; Jn 1:14); he is the final sacrifice for our sins (Heb 10:10); he is "the Lamb of God who takes away the sin of the world" (Jn 1:29); he is the "lord of the Sabbath" (Lk 6:5).

Finally, what *events* prefigure some aspect of the person and work of Christ? Isaac came back alive after nearly dying, Christ came back alive from literal death (Heb 11:19). The exodus was the means by which God's people came out of the land of idolatry and slavery. All four Gospels present Jesus' life, death, and resurrection as a new exodus (Mt 3:3; Mk 1:2-3; Lk 3:4-6; Jn 1:23) from all sorts of idolatries and our slavery to sin (cf. esp. Jn 8:34-36). Joshua gave the people rest; Jesus gives the greater "rest" (Mt 11:28; Heb 4:8). The destruction and rebuilding of the Old Tes-tament temple prefigure Jesus' death and resurrection (Jn 2:19-22) and creation of the church (Eph 2:18-22; 1 Pet 2:4-10). We could go on, but you get the point. God has sovereignly organized the history and liter-ature of Israel so that Jesus could step onto the stage of redemptive history, and his teachings and actions be filled with tremendous imagery and significance.

The value here is to fill out our understanding of Jesus' person and work with more detail as well as to marvel at God's covenantal faith-fulness as he brings all his many purposes of redemption to coalesce around the one Messiah. It is simply beautiful to see the way God has

---

[20]And again, the church serves a priestly function to the world (see Jason S. DeRouchie, *How to Understand and Apply the Old Testament: Twelve Steps from Exegesis to Theology* [Phillipsburg, NJ: P&R, 2017], 370-74).

[21]On the church as kings, see T. Desmond Alexander, *From Eden to the New Jerusalem: An Intro-duction to Biblical Theology* (Grand Rapids, MI: Kregel Academic, 2008), 89-97.

been piecing together very intricate details of his purposes in Christ from the very beginning of creation and throughout redemptive history. As Paul says, it shows the depths of the riches of God's wisdom and knowledge, his unsearchable judgments, his inscrutable ways, his aseity, his sovereignty, and his glory (Rom 11:33-36). The end result is to know the Father better through the person and work of the Son, with the power of the Holy Spirit, in the fellowship of the church, as we glory in the grand tapestry of the Trinity's work across redemptive history and our lives.

To spot legitimate types we need to be guided by the *text*, not our imaginations.[22] We need to look in the Old Testament and New Testament texts for strong linguistic and thematic connections between types and their antitypes, just as we did with possible echoes and allusions.[23] This will help us avoid allegory. Even allegory that says something about Jesus and the church is still allegory if it gets there without following the appropriate literary and historical topographies of the Bible. Moreover, such textual attention will give us confidence that our typological interpretations are legitimate and ethical because the text has pointed us to these conclusions.

Again, if we remember that the Old Testament is christotelic, that the Old Testament has an overall uphill slope toward the gospel, then each type is like a pair of binoculars found along the way; looking through them we can see some intriguing details of the summit.

Major Recurring Biblical Themes

The fourth path brings the previous three together for some big-picture synthesis. The paths we have considered so far—quotes, echoes, allusions, prophecy, and typology—have something in common. They are different ways of describing the way we see repeated themes throughout the Bible. There are about two dozen major themes in the Bible that regularly repeat. Quotes, echoes, allusions, prophecies, and types are how we see

---

[22]See Beale, *Handbook*, 19-22; Schrock, "Valid Type," 3-26.

[23]Above I called the use of Numbers 21 in John 3 an "allusion." But typology is also at work there. "Allusion" is the *literary device*, but typology provides the *logic* whereby Jesus can compare the snake in Numbers 21 to himself.

them. Prophecies speak of initial fulfillments of the themes, just to have more fulfillments later. Types embody these themes over and over again. These themes seem to be like magnetic forces that pull all the details of redemptive history together into its discernable shape. And, no surprise, all these repeated themes escalate in the gospel of Jesus Christ.[24]

For example, the exodus was the event by which the Lord led his covenant people along "the way" through the wilderness out of the land of idolatry and slavery (e.g., Ex 13:18 and throughout). It became a paradigm of salvation that many subsequent biblical authors would reemploy in fascinating ways. The book of Joshua, the Psalms, and end-of-exile prophecies in the Prophets are just a few examples. Then throughout the Gospels the imagery is powerfully taken up to describe Jesus' life and ministry (e.g., Mt 2:15; Mk 1:2-3; Lk 1:68; Jn 1:14). These authors saw in the person and work of Jesus God's greatest act of redemption; there is nothing greater to compare it to than the original exodus. When we see the theme and the language of the exodus, therefore, in the rest of the Old Testament (spotted in echoic language, types, etc.) we can think back to the original event and forward to the climactic second exodus in the New Testament (where more echoes, types, and so on appear). Equally, when New Testament authors look back to the exodus they do so through the lens of Christ (e.g., 1 Cor 10:1-4), and in turn understand the person and work of Christ through the lens of the exodus (e.g., 1 Pet 2:9).[25]

These themes can be wide-ranging, elastic, and sometimes come in combinations. Have you ever noticed how Daniel's story is reminiscent of Joseph's. Joseph was shipped away by his brothers yet remained faithful, imprisoned, and interpreted dreams in Egypt where he rose in power. Daniel is exiled, remains faithful, trapped with lions, and interprets dreams in Babylon where he rises in power. What is the upshot of observing such connections? As God acted to deliver Joseph *and his people*

---

[24]Sidney Greidanus calls these various "roads" from the Old Testament to the New (*Preaching Christ from the Old Testament: A Contemporary Hermeneutical Method* [Grand Rapids, MI: Eerdmans, 1999], 203-77).

[25]See Alastair J. Roberts and Andrew Wilson, *Echoes of Exodus: Tracing Themes of Redemption through Scripture* (Wheaton, IL: Crossway, 2018).

once before, God will act again to deliver Daniel *and his people* in a new way. Thus, here we have themes of exile from home, divine revelation, and the rise of the persecuted pious one all revolving around these figures. It is not hard to see the outline of Jesus in both.

Other major themes include creation, re-creation, judgment, sacrifice, salvation, temple, land, seed, blessing, covenant, Spirit, kingdom, the Day of the Lord, all the typological persons, institutions and events mentioned above, and the list goes on.[26] Some books focus on a few of these themes, other books focus on others. Some emerge and then lie dormant for a while across redemptive history, but they all come back in the gospel. This drawing tries to represent this.

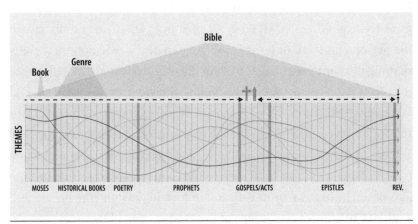

Figure 6.5. The various books of the Bible are united by a central christologic (see ch. 5) as well as diverse themes that begin in the Pentateuch, weave through the strata of redemptive history, and climax in the NT.

Each vertical rectangle represents one book of the Bible. As argued in chapter three, each one is an integrous and coherent work in its own right and should be interpreted as such. Yet, as this and the previous chapter consider, these sixty-six books come together in a beautiful symbiosis to lay out the whole of redemptive history and its climax in Christ. Everything in the Old Testament is climbing up to the cross and resurrection,

---

[26]The *New Dictionary of Biblical Theology: Exploring the Unity and Diversity of Scripture*, eds. T. Desmond Alexander, et al. (Downers Grove, IL: IVP Academic, 2000) is a great resource for studying these themes.

and everything in the New Testament looks back to the same while also anticipating Jesus' return. And while each book, *considered in its entirety,* comprises an individual steppingstone in the larger gospel-plot, there are also individual *themes* woven throughout the books (some more than others) and running between books, often playing off each other.[27] Nearly all of them start in Genesis and finalize in Revelation; they all coalesce in the gospel.[28]

Thus, books often pick up on a previous theme and develop it so that the next book can run further with it. There had been little of prophecy or mention of kingship since the books of Moses. Then those themes are taken up in 1 Samuel afresh and further developed through the rest of the Old Testament, leading into the New Testament. The theme of God's presence takes a big stride forward with the construction of the tabernacle (Ex 40) and then a *leap* forward with the building of the Jerusalem temple (1 Kings 8). Sadly, it also takes two steps back when that temple is destroyed (2 Kings 24:12-13). Then the prophets talk up the new temple to come (Ezek 40–48). In this way, the theme of God's presence rises and falls and rises again. It is just beautiful, then, when Jesus is called *Immanuel* ("God with us") in Matthew 1:23, and when Jesus calls himself the temple in John 2:19, and when the church is called the temple in 1 Corinthians 3:16.[29] As we saw in the last chapter, rest and seed are important themes running through Genesis, David's story, and elsewhere, that then tie off in the New Testament. They reach their climactic meaning in the New Testament.

One particular theme worth highlighting is the recurring cycle of *sin, judgment, and grace*. It seems to be everywhere. Adam and Eve sin, they are expelled from the garden, but God also clothes them and gives them the Genesis 3:15 promise. All humanity sins, God sends the flood, but

---

[27]On the helpfulness of both plots and themes, see Daniel J. Brendsel, "Plots, Themes, and Responsibilities: The Search for a Center of Biblical Theology Reexamined," *Themelios* 35 (2010): 400-412.

[28]"The truth—as this may sound shocking—is that almost every important church doctrine is found in 'seed' form in the book of Genesis" (John D. Currid, *A Study Commentary on Genesis,* 2 vols. [Darlington, CO: Evangelical Press, 2003–2004], 1:17).

[29]Again, such *christology* immediately leads to *ecclesiology*.

God also delivers one family. The nations rebel at the tower of Babel, God scatters them, but God then calls Abram through whom God will again bless the nations. Israel sins in carving the golden calf, God declares judgment on them, but Moses intercedes so that God will again be gracious to them. The wilderness generation does not believe, so they will not enter the land, but God brings his people into the land in the next generation. The episode with the snakes in Numbers 21 embodies this theme well: The people grumble, God sends poisonous snakes, but God also heals them. The larger sweep of Israel's history is described as such in Deuteronomy 27–30 as Moses foretells the exile and restoration. Throughout Judges the people forget the Lord and chase other gods, so the Lord raises up Israel's enemies, but then the Lord also gives them saviors. Throughout the Historical Books this basic sin-judgment-grace cycle shows up in various ways, as it does in the Psalms as well. The prophetic books are also intriguing. The recurring basic structure of *every* prophetic book (either in parts of the book or as its macro-outline) is the (1) accusation against Israel and Judah for sin; (2) promise of judgment; (3) call to repent; (4) grace toward the covenant people. It is nothing short of amazing how consistently that outline structures the prophets' many oracles.[30]

Why such a pervasive theme throughout the Old Testament? The quintessential moment of sin-judgment-grace is, of course, at the cross. This is Paul's point in Romans 3:26 where, because of the atoning death of Christ, God is revealed to be "just and the justifier" of believers. In the cross God is *just*—he is righteously judging sin. But in his great wisdom he is also able to *justify* sinners—he righteously declares them innocent of sin! What a paradox! How can this be? Christ has borne the sins of his people and thus *they* have been judged *in him* (the point of Rom 5:12-21 is to explain how one man's righteousness, life, and death can be applied to those in covenantal union with him). So judgment has been met and sinners no longer have any accusation against them (Rom 8:33). It has

---

[30]Such common structuring is likely built off the shared prophetic commitments to law and covenant (see O. Palmer Robertson, *The Christ of the Prophets* [Phillipsburg, NJ: P&R, 2004] 121-87).

been atoned for. The just one has justified them. And this is all of grace (Rom 3:24). The sin-judgment-grace cycles build to this moment of the cross. The recurring theme causes readers to meditate on the end. To put it another way, each sin-judgment-grace cycle in the Old Testament is a type (a pattern) of the cross.[31]

Once again, if we remember that the Old Testament is christotelic, that the Old Testament has an overall uphill slope toward the gospel, then these themes are little hills along the way whose shape strikingly resembles the main peak to which we are headed, none more so than the Old Testament's sin-judgment-grace cycles. That hill looks like it was carved in miniature to resemble the main peak, and then placed throughout the mountain range.

Whole-Book Contexts

This next path I do not hear discussed too much, but I would advocate that it is essential. It is a consideration of whole-book contexts as a necessary intermediary step between any verse or pericope, and its christological significance. To be clear, I am advocating an approach to hermeneutics that we should always attend to the larger literary context of every passage, based on the very idea that the Bible is not just one long book of disconnected stories and poems, but comprised of dozens of whole books that stand on their own right and yet build upon each other. Thus, situating any pericope in its whole-book context is the necessary intermediary step to discerning its location on the terrain of redemptive history. That intermediary step—from text, *to context,* to Christ—should always be taken.[32]

When we think of the Old Testament it is not clear how *every* passage has something to do with Christ. It is not even clear how every pericope in the New Testament teaches the gospel particularly. Take Isaiah 12:6 for example. It says, "Shout, and sing for joy, O inhabitant of Zion, for great

---

[31]See esp. James M. Hamilton, Jr., *God's Glory in Salvation through Judgment: A Biblical Theology* (Wheaton, IL: Crossway, 2010).

[32]This is also argued by Gerhard Hasel, "Proposals for a Canonical Biblical Theology," *AUSS* 34 (1996): 33; Hasel, "Biblical Theology: Then, Now and Tomorrow," *HBT* 4 (1982): 79-80.

in your midst is the Holy One of Israel." It does not seem that this verse is a prophecy nor is there a type at work. It is not quoted, echoed, or alluded to in the New Testament. And it is not contributing to any major recurring biblical theme. How do we understand its place on the redemptive historical landscape, nonetheless, and how does that part of the landscape still bend and flow toward Christ's person and work?

The first answer to this question should be obvious: we would never treat Isaiah 12:6 in abstraction. This verse was not written to be read alone, but it is the conclusion to a larger passage: all of Isaiah 12. It should not be interpreted, therefore, apart from the rest of the chapter. Here is the rest of Isaiah 12:

> You will say *in that day*:
>> "I will give thanks to you, O LORD,
>>> for though you were angry with me,
>>> your anger turned away,
>>> that you might comfort me.
>>> Behold, God is my salvation;
>> I will trust, and will not be afraid;
>>> for the LORD GOD is my strength and my song,
>>> and he has become my salvation."
> With joy you will draw water from the wells of salvation.
> And you will say *in that day*:
>> "Give thanks to the LORD,
>> call upon his name,
>> make known his deeds among the peoples,
>> proclaim that his name is exalted.
>> Sing praises to the LORD,
>>> for he has done gloriously;
>> let this be made known in all the earth.
>> Shout, and sing for joy, O inhabitant of Zion,
>>> for great in your midst is the Holy One of Israel."

When we observe the immediate context, we notice that it is a prophecy after all. Verses 1 and 4 above both have this line: "You will say in that day" (emphasis added), indicating a future rejoicing and thanksgiving.

But when is that day and why will people rejoice and give thanks? And why is God's holiness particularly emphasized?

Just as verse 6 should not be read in isolation, neither should chapter twelve for that matter. *It too* is part of a still larger context. Isaiah 7–12 (some interpreters say 6–12) is all part of one full oracle. Thus, chapter twelve itself is the *conclusion* of the running discourse for several chapters. When we take that into consideration, we get an idea of what "that day" is in 12:1 and 4. It turns out that the phrase "that day" is also in Isaiah 7:18, 20, 21, 23; 10:20, 27; 11:10, 11. A thorough study of the "day" Isaiah has in view seems really necessary for understanding Isaiah 12 at all, let alone its concluding comment in verse 6. If we want to know the reason for rejoicing and thanksgiving, or what makes "the Holy One of Israel" so great, we would need a running start from chapter seven (or even chap. 6). In the course of that study, we would need an understanding of near-and-far prophecy, but all the same, it would be clear to see that the coming "day" consists of a son born within the "house of David" (7:2, 13) of whose "government" and "peace" "there will be no end" (7:2, 13; 9:1-7; 11:1-10), and who will lead an exodus-style salvation "a second time" (11:11).

It is those events of redemptive history that the prophet foretells and therefore calls the people of God in 12:6 to rejoice, give thanks, sing, and shout because of that salvation through David's house in a second exodus. Furthermore, the sin of chapters one through five is also in view. Thus, the specific emphasis on the Holy One of Israel. It is this second exodus through the House of David "in that day" that will resolve the unholy problem of sin.

Now it is a lot easier to see what Isaiah 12 has to do with Jesus. Matthew 1:20-23 quotes Isaiah 7:14 at Jesus' birth, and Matthew 4:13-17 quotes Isaiah 9:1-2 at the beginning of Jesus' public ministry. There is also likely an allusion to Isaiah 11:1 in Matthew 2:23.[33] All this goes to show that Matthew understood "that day" as the coming of the Messiah to save his

---

[33]Nicholas G. Piotrowski, "Nazarene," in *Dictionary of Jesus and the Gospels*, ed. Joel B. Green, 2nd ed. (Downers Grove, IL: IVP Academic, 2013), 624-25.

people from their sins (cf. Mt 1:21). "That day," says Isaiah, will be for praise, thanksgiving, singing, joy, and shouting to the holy God.[34]

Thus, when we do our literary context work well, it sets us up for legitimate and ethical christological readings too. Take Joshua 6 as another example. What does the fall of Jericho have to do with Jesus? I have no desire to force Jesus (or the gospel) into passages where he is not there in his own right. But Joshua 6 contributes to *all of Joshua*. It is integral for the development of the entire book. In fact, *every* chapter in Joshua is integral for the whole. Every piece of the book fits together to make the message of Joshua what it is. If a single chapter were missing, or moved to a different part of the book, the larger message of Joshua in its coherent integrity would be changed. We need to understand, therefore, *what role does Joshua 6 play in the metatheology (the overall point[s]) of Joshua.* Once we understand Joshua as a whole text in its full integrity— not treating Joshua 6 or any part of it as standalone stories—we can then ask *what is Joshua, as a complete narrative, contributing to the development of redemptive history.* From there, it is a bit easier to see the whole book's contribution to the upward slope of the Old Testament toward the gospel of Jesus Christ. We will understand both Joshua 6 better as well as the gospel better when we do this.

No, there is no direct prophecy that says, "the coming Messiah will be like Joshua in this way and that." But Joshua and Christ are compared in Hebrews 4: In some way Joshua gave the people of God "rest"; yet, a greater and permanent "rest" remains for the people of God which Jesus alone can provide. Thus, Joshua's "rest" prefigures Jesus' eternal "rest"—it is a *type*. So is Joshua 6 *about* Jesus? Joshua 6's first level meaning has to do with the text of Joshua, all of Joshua, and nothing but Joshua. And the second level meaning has to do with life and conquest in the ancient Near East. But why do we care about Joshua's conquest? We care because it is part of the warp and woof of God's purposes in redemption which find their telos in Christ. Thus, we can say yes, Joshua 6 is *climactically* about

---

[34]It is also worth pointing out that Is 12:2 might be echoed in Heb 2:13 and Is 12:3 might be one of a couple verses echoed in Jn 7:37.

Christ. The climactic meaning—that meaning toward which the divine author in his providence has always patiently pointed—concerns how all humanity will attain true *rest*.

In short, I am proposing a path for understanding any pericope's climactic meaning in Christ when it is understood within its larger book-wide context first. *Each pericope is necessary for each book's coherency, and each book is necessary for redemptive history's progress toward Christ.* And this is not an extra add-on to our hermeneutic, as though now we place the Jesus-cherry on top of our interpretation. Nor am I saying this is optional for those who are particularly inclined toward big-picture readings. Rather I am saying that the Old Testament was laid down to prepare the context for the coming of Christ, and so the Bible is asking to be read this way. Observing the upward slope of redemptive history toward the gospel, the bending and flowing of all the terrain toward Christ with an appreciation of whole-book contexts, is to respect the integrity and coherency of the entire Bible.

Commonly we hear of "finding Jesus in every verse" of the Old Testament, which makes some people nervous, and understandably so. We could insert Jesus into any verse; with enough force we could jam any square peg into any round hole. Or some speak of "the gospel on every page." Again, this makes people nervous because it comes across like we are forcing Old Testament texts to say something of the gospel when they really do not. The end result is to misunderstand the Old Testament text in question and draw false conclusions about the gospel.

Am I doing the same here? No. Rather than saying Jesus or the gospel are in every verse or pericope, I am saying that every verse or pericope *is in the Bible*. And the Bible is climactically about Christ's person and work. We are asking not only what is in the pericope (chap. 3) but also what is the pericope *in* (chap. 5). It is in an integrous, individually coherent book, and that book is in the christological Bible. Thus, we are looking for each pericope's contribution to the development toward the gospel, not reshaping every pericope to fit the gospel. Every text is within its own integrous book, and each integrous, coherent book is in the flow of redemptive history. This understanding should prevent us from forcing Jesus into every verse, and also stop us from running roughshod over the literary and historical terrain of the Old Testament, but all the same arriving at christological interpretations legitimately and ethically.

Let us return to our drawing. Here is an additional amplification to demonstrate the dynamics between verse, pericope, whole-book context, and redemptive history.

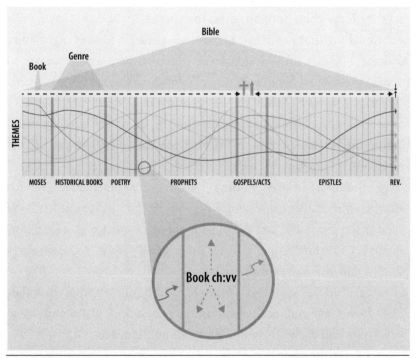

Figure 6.6. We can discover any pericope's christological context by observing its place in a book's metatheology, and in turn that book's place in the warp and woof of redemptive history.

With major biblical themes running into each book and out the other side, there is also a connection between any pericope and the rest of its book. Then each coherent, integrous book contributes to the upward slope of redemptive history that climaxes in the birth, teachings, miracles, death, resurrection, and coronation of Christ as well as the outpouring of the Holy Spirit and preaching of the gospel. Interpreting any verse or pericope in the Bible, therefore, necessitates locating it within its book-wide context, and understanding what the pericope contributes to the whole book. *Careful attention to whole-book context is, therefore, the necessary intermediary step between the details of a specific pericope and the Bible's final horizon that, in turn, gives hermeneutical legitimacy to reading Christ from all the Scriptures.* So we see again how attending well to literary context helps us immensely with another context, the christological context.

Finally, if we remember that the Old Testament is christotelic, that the Old Testament has an overall uphill slope toward the gospel, then attending to whole-book contexts is like paying attention to the smaller mountain we are on at any moment, and the contribution it makes to the much larger mountain range. Equally, it is like summiting small mountains within the range (coming to understand their whole book coherency) whereby the vista is clearest to see what it takes to get to the main peak.

Conclusion

In the previous chapter we saw how the Old Testament is christo*telic*, book by book climbing to the climax of revelation: the person and work of Jesus Christ. We also saw how the New Testament is christo*centric*, revolving around Christ in all things. In all, we concluded that the entire Bible is christo*logical*, the gospel providing the unifying rationale for everything. In this chapter we sought to look at the various ways this is observed, and considered how to navigate such redemptive-historical terrain in a way that is ethical and legitimate. The New Testament quotes, echoes, and alludes to the Old Testament, all of which call for contextual considerations of both the original Old Testament text and its new New Testament home. Prophecy is commonly observed in the Old Testament as is its fulfillment in the New Testament, but we also saw how its near-and-far dynamic keeps us in the Old Testament a bit longer before heading too quickly to the New Testament. Typology has been a constant theme throughout this book because it is not just a technique, but a theological conviction about the nature of redemption and revelation. As redemptive history progresses under God's sovereignty, the Antiochenes observed, there are several types that repeat and develop through the pages of Scripture until they reach their antitypes in the New Testament. Similarly, we saw how themes rise and fall throughout the Old Testament, also on their way to the full expression in Christ and his people. The sin-judgment-grace cycle especially stands out. Finally, we thought again about how every book is an integrous whole, and every pericope therein contributes to its full coherency. Insofar as each whole book contributes to that christotelic nature of the Old Testament, we saw how whole-book context is a critical steppingstone between any pericope and its climactic meaning in Christ.

In sum, christological context is like a locomotive, where literary context and historical context are the rails that keep the train properly tied to the Bible's topography. All three contexts working together, therefore, keep us from abusing the Old Testament in an excessive zeal to "see Jesus everywhere," but still do get us to the Bible's own redemptive-historical destination in the gospel.

For Further Study

Goldsworthy, Graeme. *According to Plan: The Unfolding Revelation of God in the Bible.* Downers Grove, IL: InterVarsity Press, 1991. This introduction to biblical theology starts with a very helpful methodological section, then focuses on the themes that run through the Bible beginning to end.

Hunter, Trent, and Stephen Wellum. *Christ from Beginning to End: How the Full Story of Scripture Reveals the Full Glory of Christ.* Grand Rapids: Zondervan, 2018. The basic content of this book can also be accessed in video lectures by the authors at www .thegospelcoalition.org. Part one of this book (which is, however, not in the videos) has a very helpful summary of paying attention to contexts when reading christologically.

Johnson, Dennis E. *Walking with Jesus through His Word: Discovering Christ in All the Scriptures.* Phillipsburg: P&R, 2015. Johnson also uses the metaphor of roads and paths; some lead directly to the city, some take a tortuous path but end up there all the same. Travelers need skills to understand the geography and use landmarks and signals along the way. The leading question of the book is "How can we follow the paths and roads and highways that *God has actually embedded* in the Bible, rather than blazing our own trails in flights of invention and imagination?" (55).

For Advanced Study

Beale, G. K. *Handbook on the New Testament Use of the Old Testament: Exegesis and Interpretation*. Grand Rapids, MI: Baker Academic, 2012. Beale discusses twelve ways the New Testament uses the Old Testament, and lays out a nine-step process for analyzation.

Beale, G. K., and D. A. Carson, eds. *Commentary on the New Testament Use of the Old Testament*. Grand Rapids, MI: Baker Academic, 2007. A true one of a kind, this work provides commentary on every Old Testament quote and most echoes and allusions in the New Testament. It also addresses several technical issues the curious reader can also explore.

Carson, D. A., and H. G. M. Williamson. *It Is Written: Scripture Citing Scripture: Essays in Honour of Barnabas Lindars*. Cambridge: Cambridge University Press, 1988. Many experts assemble to deal not only with Old Testament in the New Testament issues, but Old Testament in the Old Testament and intertestamental issues as well.

Dodd, C. H. *According to the Scriptures: The Sub-Structure of New Testament Theology*. London: Nisbet & Co., 1952. A work that deserves a republication, this book has been very influential in the contemporary awareness of Old Testament contexts underlying New Testament quotes.

Hays, Richard B. *Reading Backwards: Figural Christology and the Fourfold Gospel Witness*. Waco, TX: Baylor University Press, 2014. While I see more of a prospective element to the Old Testament than Hays, this is a great book, nonetheless, on discerning those echoes and allusions.

7

IN, AROUND, AND THROUGH THE TEXT

Genre Considered

I WAS NEVER AFRAID OF JELLYFISH until I visited Australia. Growing up in Maryland I often saw jellyfish in the ocean and bay. My sister and brothers and I would stay away from them, sure. But sometimes we also got stung; it was no big deal. The sting wore off in a few minutes, then back into the water. That is why I was quite surprised when I saw signs on the Australian beaches that read "Warning: Box Jellies. Emergency kits here." Then there was a series of instructions ending with "seek medical attention." What? We need a caution sign and supplies because of *jellyfish*? No sign for sharks, mind you, just *jellyfish*. Then we need to go to the ER? I was not so sure I wanted to swim any longer. Well, it turns out these were a different *kind* of jellyfish. While related—still jellyfish—they were different enough that swimmers have to think about them and deal with them in quite different ways.

Again, as in ecology, so too in hermeneutics. There are different *kinds* of texts in the Bible that demand readers think about them and deal with them in different ways. Though they are all biblical texts to which pertain all the matters of the previous chapters, the various books of the Bible are written in diverse *styles*, called "genres." By writing in one genre (or a combination of several) the author actually communicates to the reader *how* to deal with the text. Thus, genre is not just a writing style or mode of textual communication, but also a way to guide readers interpretively through the text. By using a certain genre and not others, the text is telling the audience, "Read me like this, not like that." It is the content, the details of the text itself, that both clues the reader in to the genre employed and instructs the reader how to read such a genre.[1]

The problem with all this, however, is that a piece of literature (biblical or otherwise) rarely comes with a decoder that gives point-by-point instructions on how to deal legitimately and ethically with the genre in question. Rather, authors use a certain genre and *simply expect* readers to know how to navigate it intelligently. For their part, readers typically succeed in such navigation *intuitively* if they live within

Figure 7.1. Moon jellyfish, commonly found in the Chesapeake Bay

Figure 7.2. Box jellyfish, found off Australia's northern coasts

---

[1]Jeannine K. Brown, *Scripture as Communication: Introducing Biblical Hermeneutics* (Grand Rapids, MI: Baker Academic, 2007), 76-77, 139-41.

close historical proximity to the author. That is, they just know how the genre works because it is familiar to them. Readers who encounter a new genre may not understand it at all at first. But after a while, after some repeated exposure to the genre, readers begin to understand.

A few illustrations will make this point clear. If you have ever read comic books, you know what all the bubbles mean and that there is a certain order to follow as to which bubble comes first. How did you figure this out? After reading three or four you saw how the stories made sense (you discovered their coherency) when you read in a certain order. This may be a simple illustration because comics are kids' books; they are designed, of course, to be easily navigated. But therein lies the point: even children intuitively think in terms of genre because texts have tacitly taught them to. And yet, even more sophisticated writings can become easy to navigate as well. The front pages of newspapers are commonly cluttered with a lot of print, yet you know the most important story is the one given the most space and the biggest headline. Right there, that is interpretation by attention to genre. The size of the font and location on the front page leads you to draw the hermeneutical conclusion that this is what the editors think is most important. Moreover, you likely discerned that the headline itself gives the main point of the story in a few pithy words. Then the article is the details filling out the main point. Not so in a novel, right? The title does not necessarily broadcast the main ideas. Rather, novelists are coy with their titles to draw you in, not give away too much about the contents. Also, those contents are fictitious and entirely controlled by the author. It is to be regarded and handled in a completely different way than the newspaper. All this to say nothing about other genres: love letters, biographies, screenplays, periodicals, poems, lyrics, government briefings, sacred texts, emails, text messages, and so on. Each one is written differently, handled differently, read differently, and interpreted differently. And all for the same reason: they look different and use different rhetorical techniques. The authors choose a particular genre for many different reasons. But readers understand the genres for one reason: they have seen those genres before and are familiar enough with them to know what to do with them.

Therein lies the problem with *biblical* genres, however. All those genres just mentioned are common in our world. You see them everywhere. Yet it is those we are less familiar with, like maybe the poem, that are more difficult to interpret. When it comes to biblical genres we are far removed from their common use. Read any good law codes lately? Or perhaps an acrostic poem without rhyme or meter? Or a nice apocalypse? Because the Bible uses genres that are far less common today, we are less familiar with them and do not know instinctively how to navigate them. I had seen Chesapeake Bay jellyfish many times and my experience with them informed me how to deal with them. But once I was in Australian box jelly territory, I was perplexed.

To draw out the point, issues of genre are both a literary concern as well as a historical concern. They are different writing styles, and therefore attention to each genre's unique characteristics is vital for discerning a text's flow of thought (as discussed in chap. 3). Equally, genres function as they do because of certain *historical conditions* surrounding authors and audiences. In fact, it was often historical trends that gave rise to the development of new genres. All the while, I will argue in this chapter that genre is also a redemptive-historical circumstances. It is no coincidence that we see the Bible's diverse genres grouped together at unique moments in redemptive history. One clear difference between Chesapeake Bay jellyfish and Australian box jellies is that *they live in different parts of the world.* And one easy way to adapt to them is to know what part of the world you are in at any time. So too, matters of genre will greatly depend on knowing *where* in redemptive history any given genre is (predominantly) employed, *why* those genres are employed per se, and *what* it means that they are. This is why we saved the more thorough discussion of genre for now: attention to genre means attention to all three literary, historical, and christological contexts at the same time.

The genres we will consider are (1) covenantal history; (2) covenantal genealogy; (3) covenantal law; (4) covenantal poetry; (5) covenantal wisdom; (6) covenantal prophecy; (7) kingdom parables;

(8) missiological epistles; and (9) apocalypse. Consideration of each one is important because the *medium* by which the Scriptures communicate leads us to the *message*.

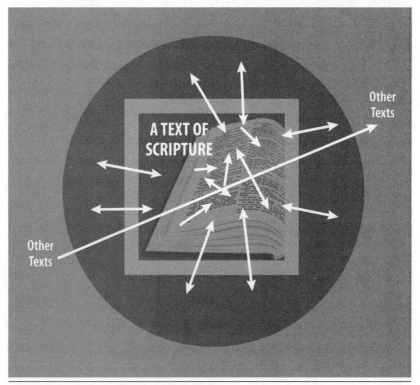

Figure 7.3. Genre is an integrative study of the "the worlds in the text, around the text, and running through the text."

Covenantal History

The genre most commonly found in the Bible is the historical narrative. The following books are predominantly narratival accounts of historical events: Genesis–Exodus, Numbers, Joshua–Esther, parts of Isaiah, Jeremiah, Hosea, most of Daniel, Jonah, and Matthew–Acts. Now in calling these *narratives*, or even stories, is *not* to say they are fiction. Rather the point here is that the telling of history is never (and certainly not in the Bible) a list of factoids from the past. Historians put the data into a storyline that *narrates* what happened. So we call these historical narratives.

Additionally, we must observe that biblical authors are not only concerned with *what happened* but also with *what it means*. They do not just recount the story, but in telling the story they have an interpretive agenda. Through the story or narrative, a *theological* point is being conveyed. When reading such theological history, therefore, we need to understand why any given story is important in the first place. Biblical authors do not tell us everything about Israel, or everything about Jesus or the early church. They select what material to communicate and what details about the story matter the most, then arrange it all to convey the theological takeaway. For example, you may want to know more about Moses' childhood, or how Abraham felt at times, or what exactly David did in battle. We may want to know more about Jesus' motives or the disciples' reaction, or particular details of what the church did and how. But the authors are getting at a point and the point is never "Here are all the details about this historical episode to sate your curiosity." The authors may have well suspected that readers would want to know more about certain details, but they told us what is *theologically* important. We have to resist the temptation, then, to fill in the gaps and pay all the more attention to the details that *are* provided.

We can go a step further, though. What is the overriding theological concern of such biblical narratives? The answer is *covenant*. With any historical narrative in the Bible we should ask, "What is the most recent covenant God has entered into and what is the current status of that covenant?"[2] This is a very helpful question to keep in mind. Again, why are some stories from Israel's history or Jesus' life included and not others? Why are some details emphasized and others ignored? The answer is, of course, the author has a point to make and is telling the story theologically to do so. And commonly enough, the point is in reference to the most recent, and therefore most immediately operative, covenant God has made. Biblical authors are unflinchingly focused on God's covenantal promises and so the stories of Israel and Jesus are

---

[2]This is akin to Richard Lints's "epochal horizon" of interpretation (*The Fabric of Theology: A Prolegomenon to Evangelical Theology* [Grand Rapids, MI: Eerdmans, 1993], 293-95, 300-303).

basically answers to the question, "How are things going in the covenant?" The narratives are the outworkings of the current state of the covenant.[3] For this reason, I call this genre "covenantal history."

For example, the story of how Abraham almost sacrificed his son Isaac (Gen 22) operates on so many levels of intrigue, and it is very tempting to opine over all the various layers of human drama in the story. All the while, however, it is important to never lose sight of what Genesis 22 is doing in the overall flow of the book of Genesis, or Genesis's role in redemptive history. Particularly, this near sacrifice of Isaac is significant because God had just said in 21:12, "In Isaac will your seed be called" (NKJV).Therein lies the real drama the author wants you to feel! In Genesis 15 God covenants with Abraham and promises him a great multitude of descendants ("seed"; cf. esp. 15:3-5). So 21:12 must be read in that light: Isaac is the first descendant through which the rest of the "seed" will come. If Abraham kills Isaac in chapter twenty-two, then what becomes of the covenant promises? Equally, as we saw two chapters ago, the success of God's entire plan of redemption (Gen 3:15) depends on the success of the covenant with Abraham.

In fact, once God enters into a covenant with Israel (Ex 24), Deuteronomy 27–30 basically projects the rest of the Old Testament as the result of their covenant faithfulness or disobedience: The people will break the covenant, the Lord will discipline them, but finally he will restore them. This explains what is going on in Judges. This explains Israel's life under king Saul. And ultimately it explains the exile and restoration. These events are all barometers of the state of the covenant.

Yet, once David is promised an eternal throne in 2 Samuel 7, the Old Testament historical narratives hone in on his sons. Bringing the 2 Samuel 7 promises to fulfillment becomes the focus of the rest of the Old Testament (the entire Bible actually), so the stories of Solomon and David's subsequent grandchildren come center stage. Their stories are

---

[3]There are many good works that explain the relationships between biblical covenants. I have found O. Palmer Robertson's *The Christ of the Covenants* (Phillipsburg, NJ: P&R, 1980) and Peter J. Gentry and Stephen J. Wellum's *Kingdom Through Covenant: A Biblical-Theological Understanding of the Covenants*, 2nd ed. (Wheaton, IL: Crossway, 2018) to be most helpful.

not a mere historical survey, but test cases of the covenant, indicators on the status of the covenants and signs for the future.

Now, how do we discern the flow of thought through covenantal history narratives? As argued in chapter three, each pericope has a beginning, middle, and end, and each individual pericope needs to be understood in the scope of the entire book in which it is situated. So we need to read in and out: discrete self-contained pericopes and larger passages that see how individual stories work together. Thus, before we dig into any particular story, we read entire books in one sitting—which will also have their own beginning, middle, and end—to see how they develop to their climax. The basic structure of any book of covenantal history, therefore, might approximately be represented as such:

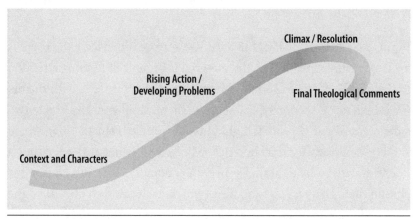

Figure 7.4. Historical narratives commonly follow a dramatic pattern as seen here.

The books begin by introducing readers to important themes and people. Then those themes are woven in and out of the narrative as the characters face more and more problems. Finally, it all comes to a head and the themes reach their full development as the story resolves itself. Commonly, there will be a postscript of sorts that ties off any remaining theological threads. Think of the description I gave of Genesis in chapter five. All the major concerns of the book are set up in chapters one through three, and the rest of the book follows the line of the seed to its climax with Judah in chapter forty-nine.

Additionally, large sections of some books may be structured as follows.

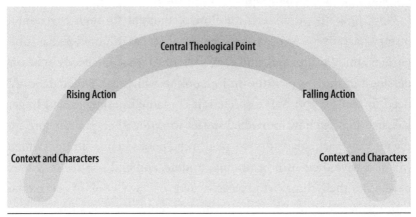

Figure 7.5. Some historical narratives organize material to emphasize a central pericope, with mirroring elements on both sides.

In this case the first half of the narrative mirrors the back half. There is no single climax per se, but the material is organized to draw attention to the middle of the material. We saw this in chapter three with the historical narrative section of Daniel 1–9. There, similar stories create two sides of a massive chiasm. It highlights the middle (Dan 4:34-35), which is not the narrative's crescendo per se because it is not at the end, but it does draw the individual stories in Daniel onto its axis. Both ends of the chiasm then, chapters one and nine (which itself could still be called the crescendo), provide the trying context for the powerful words of chapter four in the middle of the chiasm. Though the people of God are oppressed, all history is still in the hands of their covenant God who will act again in history to deliver his people once more. Seeing this narratological structure helps us recognize the points of emphasis and relate the stories to the metatheology.

Sometimes a book will combine these two structures. Exodus would be an example of this. Chapters one through eighteen exhibit the first style where the crossing of the Red Sea and Moses' song in chapter fifteen represents the long-awaited finale. Then the second half of the book begins with the glory of the Lord on the mountain (chaps. 19–20), followed by instructions to build the tabernacle (chaps. 25–31). That is then mirrored by the actual building of the tabernacle (chaps. 35–40), concluding with the glory of the Lord now dwelling among his people (40:34-38). Punctuating the middle of it all are chapters thirty-two through thirty-four where the people break the covenant, and Moses intercedes so that the covenant is renewed. It all accentuates the Lord's glory on the ends of the chiasm and his covenant grace in the middle.

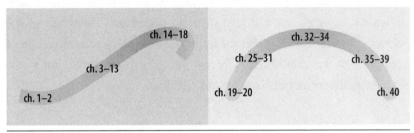

Figure 7.6. The book of Exodus utilizes both macrostructuring techniques.

Each individual story also operates much the same way on a smaller scale. Usually these smaller stories are divided nicely by the chapters in our English Bibles.[4] They too either rise to a point of resolution, or rise and fall to accentuate the middle. Careful reading will reveal which is structuring any story.[5] Take Genesis 17 for example. It begins and ends with Abram's age (vv. 1 and 24), then the actions of Abram and the speeches of the Lord mirror each other in verses 1-8 and 15-23. In the middle sits the covenant of circumcision in verses 9-14, highlighting those verses as the main point of the chapter. Seeing this allows readers to focus on the part of the text that the text itself accentuates.[6] It also helps situate verses 25-27 which stand *outside* the chiasm. Examples of the former structure—rise to the resolution—are more common. Take

---

[4]This is not always the case though, as in 1 Sam 28:1-2 which seems to be the ending of the story in the previous chapter. So we have to read carefully for ourselves to see where one pericope ends and another begins.

[5]There are, of course, a variety of slight nuances to these basic patters (see Richard L. Pratt, Jr., *He Gave Us Stories: The Bible Student's Guide to Interpreting Old Testament Narratives* [Phillipsburg, NJ: P&R, 1990], 179-202).

[6]David A. Dorsey demonstrates how Genesis 17 is not only a chiasm, but itself sits in the middle of an even larger chiasm covering chaps. 12–21 (*Literary Structure of the Old Testament: A Commentary on Genesis–Malachi* [Grand Rapids, MI: Baker Academic, 1999], 56-57).

the David and Goliath story in 1 Samuel 17. No one will fight Goliath. David comes along (recently anointed king in the previous chapter). Insults are thrown back and forth. David then wins the victory. And finally, the people of Israel are emboldened to fight whereas before they cowered.

The point here is that the sweep of an entire book and/or large sections of a book take individual stories and stitch them together to convey the metatheology. The individual stories therein also have their points to make, but readers need to see how the smaller contributions of each individual story fill out and give shape to the whole. The whole of the narrative is, after all, the integrous singular message of each coherent text. So, taking covenantal history's micro- and macrostructures under consideration, an entire book might look like this:

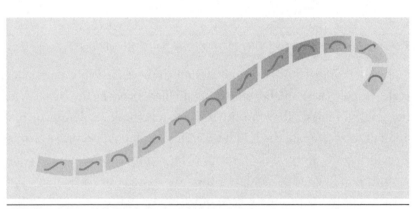

Figure 7.7. Individual pericopes in a historical narrative book also demonstrate these common structures, as they work together to fill out the book's macrostructure.

The book rises to its resolution while the individual stories that make it up exhibit these sorts of structures in their own right. Of course this is just an artificial example to give readers a sense of things. The wise reader will look for combinations and variations on these general patterns.[7]

Flow of thought is crucial. The biblical authors do not present us with a collection of disparate stories from which we gather isolated teachings and morals. Rather, "redemptive plots in the Bible are . . . not *merely*

---

[7]For example, Judges seems to have a cyclical nature to the book as a whole, even while using these linear structures in the smaller narratives.

illustrations or symbols of something else . . . but one step and one phase in the totality of history."[8] Each individual story builds on the prior that collectively form whole books whose metatheologies can easily be lost if we atomize things.

Covenantal Genealogy

Let us turn the corner to another genre: covenantal genealogy. Again, the prefix "covenantal" is important. These genealogies are not aimed to satisfy our interest in family trees. In fact, the logic of biblical genealogies is not strictly genetic. But since they are embedded within covenantal history they continue to carry that attribute. They can be found in the following: Genesis, Numbers, Ruth, 1 Chronicles, Ezra, Matthew, and Luke. They serve as transitions and orienting pericopes to the larger sweep of these covenantal history books.[9] Take Ruth for example. Ruth ends with a genealogy of Boaz. But why is Boaz so special that we need his genealogy? Well, it turns out that Boaz is an ancestor of *David*. Thus, the story of Ruth is not a love story as we typically think of them, or even an example of redemption primarily. Rather, as we saw in chapter five, it is the narratival account of how God is bringing his redemptive purposes through "the days when the judges ruled" (1:1) to the time of Israel's great King David (4:22). Equally in Matthew, the genealogy that starts the narrative is not just a list of ancestors. But each name invokes their stories wherein Abraham and David are particularly highlighted (see Mt 1:1 and 1:17). This is Matthew's way of saying, "All the promises to Abraham and David that have languished for years *are now coming to pass*. Just read the rest of my story; you'll see!"

Thus, genealogies bring order out of the chaos of history. The years of the judges had been disastrous, but now we see God had been at work all along to bring David onto the scene. Likewise, it had looked like the

---

[8]Vern Poythress, *Reading the Word of God in the Presence of God: A Handbook for Biblical Interpretation* (Wheaton, IL: Crossway, 2016), 278; emphasis original.

[9]Marshall Johnson, *The Purpose of the Biblical Genealogies: With Special Reference to the Setting of the Genealogies of Jesus*, 2nd ed., SNTSMS 8 (London: Cambridge University Press, 1969; repr. Eugene, OR: Wipf & Stock, 2002), 77-82.

covenantal promises to Abraham and David would never come to fruition, but now Matthew's genealogy reveals that God had never lost sight of his plan, even during the terrifying time of exile. First Chronicles begins with a very long genealogy, nine chapters worth! What could be the point of that? Family record keeping? No, but a testimony of God's providence, as a people look back on their history after the confusing time of exile. Genealogies show how God has things in control even when all seems lost from the human perspective. Thus, they should be read as little stories in and of themselves, and commonly they have their own structure. Pay attention to the names and what stories from Israel's history they invoke, and pay attention to the extra details in addition to the names.

Again, discerning a book's flow of thought is the goal here. It is easy to treat genealogies in the abstract, and/or simply skip over them because they feel like the antiquated concerns of people long gone. But they are not just family trees stuck in conspicuous places in various texts. They are integrally wrapped into the surrounding narrative and serve to orient the reader to the major concerns of the rest of the narrative. They provide context for the narrative and help the narrative in its larger presentation of its metatheology. Seeing how they interface with narrative texts, therefore, is essential for better understanding that narrative's flow of thought.

Covenantal Law

We come now to covenantal law. This can be a tricky genre to consider because the question always arises: Are we to keep these laws today? If the answer were simply yes, then we would scratch our heads as to how some of them even apply. If the answer is no, then how do we understand that the Bible is God's Word? Can we just ignore part of it? Of course not. But if the answer is sometimes yes and sometimes no, then we need a legitimate and ethical way of discerning when it is yes and when it is no, lest our Bible reading become arbitrary, in which case what is the point of reading the Bible at all? And we damage our witness if we believe and obey only part of God's Word. How authoritative can it be if we get to pick and choose what applies and what does not? In that case it would seem our preconceived notions and personal dispositions are actually the authority—the hermeneutical spiral run amuck.

Let us begin like this. The Bible itself indicates that there are *different* kinds of laws. So, when considering the law genre, we need to understand there are subgenres in play: (1) prescriptive law, (2) descriptive law, and (3) ceremonial law.[10]

Prescriptive law. First, there is what can be called "prescriptive law." These are laws that are binding all the time in all places on all people. God is the Creator and from him comes all knowledge of right and wrong. This is why they are called "prescriptive." God has *prescribed* them for us, unchanging because his own character is unchanging. We find them in the Ten Commandments: Exodus 20:1-17 and Deuteronomy 5:6-21. These stand out from other biblical law texts for a few reasons. They were originally spoken directly by God himself (see Ex 20:1). Then they were *literally* written in stone, engraved on both sides of tablets by God himself (Ex 32:15-16; see also Ex 31:18). Being written in stone attests to the unchanging nature of this law. And being written on both sides attests to the *completeness* of this law. Thus God himself, without a mediator, has given a law that is unchanging and totalizing.[11] These are the Ten Commandments, God's moral will for all humanity. These attributes seem to be important because Moses repeats all this in Deuteronomy 9:10-11. Moreover, they appear to be embedded in creation itself.[12] So, when it comes to the Ten Commandments, yes, we should keep all these laws.

---

[10]Some readers will notice that I am not using the traditional tripartite division of the law: moral, civil, and ceremonial. That has been critiqued recently as being more heuristic than biblical. While I agree with that critique (civil does not seem to be an adequate description, and it is all moral), there are still, nonetheless, different types of laws that the Bible does itself delineate. Here I make that case for prescriptive, descriptive, and ceremonial.

The law is also sometimes described in terms of its *uses*: to curb sin; to reflect God's moral perfection and in turn highlight our sinfulness (thus driving sinners to Christ); and to guide the Christian in holy living. I have no qualms with these uses. We should only note that they are matters of *application*, and I am trying to arrive at *hermeneutical* categories.

[11]On all these points, so John D. Currid, *A Study Commentary on Exodus,* 2 vols. (Darlington, CO: Evangelical Press, 2000–2001), 2:33-34.

[12]Jared C. Hood, "The Decalogue of Genesis 1–3," *RTR* 75 (2016): 35-59. That they are given to Israel does not speak against their universality but *for* it because it is through Israel that God intends to reestablish his original creational purposes through an obedient humanity (see chap. 5).

Descriptive law. No sooner are the Ten Commandments thundered from Mount Sinai, however, that Moses then goes on to describe the rest of the laws in Exodus in a different manner. Notice that in Exodus 21:1 the Lord tells Moses that *he* is to set the following "rules" before the people (see also Ex 24:4, 7).[13] The word for "rules" here is *mishpat* which is a judgment or decision based on prior case law.[14] That is, the "rules" in Exodus 21–24 are a *description* of how Moses is to apply the Ten Commandments at his moment in redemptive history. Most of Deuteronomy operates the same way. In Deuteronomy 1:5 we read, "Beyond the Jordan, in the land of Moab, Moses undertook to explain this law." Explain *what* law? After reiterating the Ten Commandments in chapter five, chapters six through twenty-six *explain* how the Ten Commandments can be applied once the children of Israel come to live in the land.[15] It is the *description* of the *prescription* for their moment in time. So, with the exception of the Ten Commandments (Deut 5), most of Deuteronomy is laws that are not timeless, but descriptive applications of the written-in-stone prescript.

Descriptive law is found in Exodus 21–24 and Deuteronomy 6–26. These are designed to serve the people of Israel at that unique moment in redemptive history, but later the exile will throw everything into upheaval. We have a new descriptive law (based on the same prescriptive law): the teachings of the apostles in the New Testament epistles. More on that below. Suffice it for now to emphasize the different nature of Exodus 21–24 and Deuteronomy 6–26 from the Ten Commandments, and therefore how they are to be interpreted differently. The Ten Commandments are given directly by God on tablets of stone, forever binding. The rules are mediated through Moses and serve a time in redemptive history that is now over.

By emphasizing that God gave the Ten Commandments and Moses gave the other laws is not to diminish the authority or inspired nature of

---

[13]Some translations say "judgments" or "ordinances."

[14]Currid, *Exodus*, 2:56-57.

[15]John Calvin, *Commentaries on the Four Last Books of Moses: Arranged in the Form of a Harmony*, trans. Charles William Bingham, 2 vols. (Grand Rapids, MI: Baker, 1979), 1:417–2:196.

the latter (indeed Ex 21:1 says God told Moses to write it down). Rather, it differentiates the *application* of these subgenres. The former is authoritative as forever-binding prescript. The latter is still inspired and authoritative as a description of the former. There is still value, therefore, in reading Exodus 21–24 and Deuteronomy 6–26 if only we handle them rightly. They remain great examples of how to think through and apply the Ten Commandments. So, for example, we learn that the fifth commandment, to honor one's mother and father, actually applies to all kinds of authorities God places over us (see Deut 16:18–18:22), mother and father being but the first layer of authority. We see that the sixth commandment, not to murder, actually applies to hurting people at all (see Deut 19–21), and conversely calling for ways to help people and promote life. The seventh commandment, forbidding adultery, actually applies to all kinds of sexual sins (see Deut 22:13–23:14). So we can read descriptive law as an exposition of the prescriptive law, to help us think better and more thoroughly of how prescriptive law might be applied in our own day and age.

Ceremonial law. The third kind of biblical law is a bit easier to identify and understand. It is called ceremonial law. It is found largely in Leviticus. It is called "ceremonial" because it pertains to the specifically liturgical activities of the people, the priests in particular. It has to do with purity of worship, duties of priests, sacrifices, and festivals. The book of Hebrews makes clear that these are all fulfilled in the coming of Christ, and so have reached their redemptive-historical intent. They are not to be repeated. They are worth studying because they tell us much of the nature of Christ's person and work. But they apply *through* Christ, not as a list of ongoing ritual commands.

Can you see, therefore, how the law codes of the Bible should be understood as *covenantal* law? They are not just a list of timeless dos and don'ts, but situated at a certain moment in redemptive history, they serve the covenant people in creating the cultural space for them to live out their commission as a "kingdom of priests" (Ex 19:6), the new Adam, and moral exemplars to the world.

Covenantal Poetry

As we come to biblical poetry, there are two crucial considerations. One is how it is covenantal. The Psalms occupy a crucial place in redemptive history, particularly shaped after the Lord's designs with the house of David. Thus, the Psalms are covenantal, and that helps us remember not to take the Psalms as simply generic spiritual poems. We do not want to treat them in the abstract from their christological context by ignoring any psalm's location in the Psalter, or running around Jesus to make Christ-less application to ourselves.

The other crucial consideration is the unique way biblical poetry structures flow of thought. When we think of poetry, we are accustomed to look for rhyme and/or meter.

> Roses are red.
>> Violets are blue.
> I love hermeneutics,
>> And clearly you do too.

This beautiful piece of poetry has a four-four-six-six meter: four syllables on each of the first two lines, six syllables each on the next two. It also has rhyme: "blue" rhymes with "too." We know from our youth to look for such things in English poetry. Well, go ahead and forget all that for Hebrew poetry! Hebrew poetry does not use rhyme or meter, but it does have other characteristics that are necessary to observe. The most important characteristic is the use of "parallelism." Parallelism is when an author will say something, and then says the same thing again with a different emphasis. Usually, that different emphasis amounts to a heightening of the intensity of the previous statement, or to reverse the viewpoint of the previous statement. A simple example of this would be Psalm 6:1,

> 1a O Lord, *rebuke me* not in *your anger,*
> 1b nor *discipline me* in *your wrath.*
>> 1c Be *gracious to me,* O Lord, for *I am languishing;*
>> 1d *heal me,* O Lord, for *my bones are troubled.*

Notice that what I am calling lines 1a and 1b basically say the same thing, even though 1b is more intense. The terms "rebuke" and "discipline," as well as the ideas of "anger" and "wrath," capture the same concept. Yet, "wrath" is more severe than "anger." So the author has said the same thing twice, with stronger imagery the second time. The same is true with 1c and 1d. "Gracious to me" parallels "heal me," while "languishing" is in parallel with "bones are troubled." Yet to speak of troubled bones is more expressive than the nondescript concept of just "languishing."

We could say more though. If you group 1a and 1b, connected as they are through the parallelism, and do the same with 1c and 1d, then we see that the unit 1a-1b is in parallel with the unit 1c-1d by way of *reversal*. Notice that 1c-1d reverses 1a-1b. In 1a-1b the author fears the Lord's "anger" and "wrath" but in 1c-1d he pleads for the Lord's "grace" and "healing." The verse has, therefore, two layers of parallelism to vividly capture one basic thought: "Please forgive me, Lord." Poetry, therefore, has an artistic beauty in its animated language that can arouse deeper feelings in readers, and hit more powerfully than just simply "Please forgive me, Lord."

The further value of observing these parallels is to think with the author in blocks of thought instead of line-by-line details. We can really spin our interpretive wheels if we were to make a big deal about the difference between a "rebuke" and "discipline." Or spend too much time and energy on differentiating what it means for the Lord to be "gracious" or to "heal." Or to get too specific and try to suggest the actual kind of grace the author seeks is specifically physical healing. So instead of thinking lineally—like we do with covenantal history—we track poetic discourse in *blocks* of thought (more on this in just a moment).

Sometimes the parallelism can get quite sophisticated, wherein a line could have multiple parallels or a parallel may not be in the very next line. Here is Psalm 32:3-5:

> 3aWhen *I kept silent* about my *sin*,
>> 3bmy *bones wasted away* through my groaning *all day long*.
>> 4aFor *day and night* your *hand was heavy upon me*;
>> 4bmy *strength was dried up* as by the heat of *summer*.   Selah
>
> 5aI *acknowledged* my *sin* to you,
> 5band *I did not cover* my *iniquity*;

> [5c]I said, "*I will confess* my *transgressions* to the L<small>ORD</small>,"
> 　　[5d]and *you forgave the iniquity of my sin.*   Selah

I have indented the parallel lines and italicized key concepts that show the parallelisms. You can see that lines 3b-4b are all in parallel; they all speak of physical exhaustion for increasing durations of time. And lines 5a-5c are also in parallel; they each speak of confession. Yet 3a does not seem to have a parallel. But it does. The parallel to 3a is all of 5a-5c, wherein 5a-5c is the *opposite* of 3a. First he keeps *silent* about his sin, then he *acknowledges* his sin. Unexpectedly, then, 5d has no parallel, giving it a particular punch as it breaks from that expectation.

Again, we should not get hung up on the differences between "sin," "iniquity," and "transgressions." There is no difference in these poetic lines (though there could well be elsewhere depending on how they are used in other genres); lines 5a-5c are simply diverse poetic expressions of the same idea. So too with 3b-4b; there is a poetic heightening from line to line (the timespans get longer) but no real difference in meaning. All this brings out the beauty of the poem and helps us wrap our minds around the flow of thought without getting lost in details abstracted from the *way* the rest of the psalm is working. Thus, while sometimes the psalms can feel like a twisted collection of emotions going in every direction, they do have a structure and an order to their thoughts. Spotting parallels help us see that order.

On the larger scale as well, the *concept* of parallelism has influence on the way whole psalms are sometimes organized. Occasionally large units (several verses thematically working together) parallel each other, and, as we just saw, such parallels do not have to be back-to-back in the text. The chiasm we saw in Psalm 2 (chap. 3) would be an example of this. A chiasm is actually a sophisticated set of parallels, not one right after another but spread out in a mirroring design. Here is an example in Psalm 42:

T<small>O THE CHOIRMASTER</small>. A M<small>ASKIL OF THE</small> S<small>ONS OF</small> K<small>ORAH</small>.

> [1]As a deer *pants* for flowing streams,
> 　so pants my soul for you, O God.   } A

²My soul *thirsts* for God, for the living God.
  When shall I come and appear before God?
³My tears have been my *food* day and night,
  while they say to me all the day long, *"Where is your God?"*

⟩ A

⁴These things *I remember*, as I pour out my soul:
  how I would go with the throng
    and lead them in procession to the house of God
      with glad shouts and songs of praise,
  a multitude keeping festival.

⟩ B

⁵Why are you *cast down*, O *my soul*,
  and why are you in turmoil within me?
    ***Hope in God*;**
      for I shall again praise him,
        my salvation
          ⁶and my God.

⟩ C

My soul is *cast down* within me;
    therefore *I remember* you from the land of Jordan
      and of Hermon, from Mount Mizar.
      ⁷Deep calls to deep at the roar of your waterfalls;
      all your breakers and your waves have gone over me.
      ⁸By day the LORD commands his steadfast love,
      and at night his song is with me,
      a prayer to the God of my life.

⟩ B′

⁹I say to God, my rock: "Why have you forgotten me?
  Why do I go mourning because of the oppression of the enemy?"
¹⁰As with a deadly wound in my bones, my adversaries taunt me,
  while they say to me all the day long, *"Where is your God?"*

⟩ A′

¹¹Why are you *cast down*, O *my soul*,
  and why are you in turmoil within me?
    ***Hope in God*;**
      for I shall again praise him,
        my salvation
          and my God.

⟩ C′

You can see the parallelism in the lines I have indented to the same margins. I have also labeled the blocks of thought with letters A, B, and C, and their parallels A´, B´, and C´. To show this structure (it is not just made up) I have also italicized the repeated words and phrases, and bold-faced the repeated blocks. "Where is your God?" concludes A and A´. "I remember" leads B and B´. And block C is simply repeated at the middle and the end. The larger point of this psalm is, therefore, at the center of the A-B-C-B´-A´ chiasm: "Hope in God!" which is also repeated at the end to double down on it. The upshot here is to navigate through all the details of this beautiful work of poetry to the *main* ideas and understand the way the details lead up to and support those main ideas, rather than getting confused amid so much imagery.

While I have mentioned the Psalms only so far, poetry as a literary genre can actually be found in a lot of books: Job–Song of Songs and throughout the prophetic books. Moreover, the Hebrew poetic style also seems to have influenced other genres too. We see this anytime an author speaks in parallel concepts. You can easily see this in the way the lines of prophecy are laid on the page. So when we consider Old Testament prophecy below and all its unique distinctives, we will need to remember that the prophets often employ poetic parallelism in addition to whatever else they are doing. Additionally, while we may not see clear individual lines of poetry in historical narratives or the epistles, nonetheless the practice of stating and restating something in a heightened form seems to have caught on in other genres as well. So, we should look for parallel concepts all over the Bible in addition to the obvious parallel *lines* in true-blue poetry.

Taking care to observe parallel lines and thought units is very important for discerning the flow of thought in biblical poetry. It teaches us to think in *blocks* of text rather than line by line. In the examples above, if a reader were to think each line were something new to add to the previous (the way epistles do as we will shortly see) then we will get bogged down trying to differentiate the significance of various details, when those details are all actually getting at the same point. The poets want us to take the parallel thoughts together, poetically bound concept by poetically bound concept, not line by line individually or separate from its parallel. In observing this we come a lot closer to discerning a poem's flow of thought.

Covenantal Wisdom

The books that comprise the Bible's wisdom literature are Job and Proverbs–Song of Songs. In explaining these works, it is easiest to take the proverbs as the most basic example because they are actually very much like our own proverbial sayings today. Ironically, however, we seem to treat them differently! We treat the proverbs often enough as though they were law or divine guarantees. But they are, well, proverbs. A proverb is a wise saying that helps people navigate the Creator's world by thinking his thoughts after him and valuing the things he values. And while the proverbs provide wisdom, they equally *require* wisdom to know when and how they apply.[16] That is, the proverbs should not be read like *promises* from the Lord or incantations for sure results, but divine *wisdom* we humans can appropriate for living the good life *as God so defines the good life.*[17]

Demonstrating a use of parallelism as well, here are a few examples. Proverbs 15:27 says,

> Whoever is greedy for unjust gain troubles his own household,
> but he who hates bribes will live.

Well, is that *always* true that the greedy and the unjust trouble their families? Not always. Sadly, sometimes the greedy and the unjust actually make their families rich. And is it *always* true that "hating a bribe" will result in life? Again, it is sad but true that there are parts of the world where rejecting a bribe, while the right thing to do, could bring trouble.

---

[16] As stated, this is the way our own everyday proverbs work too. One needs wisdom to know when to apply "A bird in the hand is worth two in the bush," or "Nothing ventured nothing gained." Wisdom is needed to know when "fortune favors the bold," or to "look before you leap." Do "birds of a feather flock together," or do "opposites attract"? None of these are universal laws but sayings that the wise know when they apply.

[17] Hence, one's "best life now" is what the Creator says is best, not defined by our own fallen creaturely ambitions.

But that is exactly the point: while greed and injustice sometimes pay off, *that is not the kind of person you want to be, not the way to live well in the Creator's world.* The good life is to be upright—rejecting greed, unjust gain, and bribes. Even if such paths seem lucrative, it is not wise to live that life. The Lord sees all, and has called his image bearers to uprightness. All the same, nonetheless, even if it seems greed, injustice, and bribes might pay off, many people do get caught in the web of their own deceit, and their own corruptions come home to roost. Therefore, it would be wise to resist greed and reject unjust gains and bribes lest this proverb become a byword for your life, even if it should not be read as a guarantee of what will happen every time.

Here is another example to illustrate the point. Proverbs 26:4 says, "Answer not a fool according to his folly, lest you be like him yourself." But the *very next proverb*, 26:5, says, "Answer a fool according to his folly, lest he be wise in his own eyes." Well, which is it!? Which one do I apply? The answer is in remembering the genre; these are proverbs, wise sayings that require wisdom to apply, not do-this and don't-do-that hardened rules or commands from on high. So, if you see a fool and you might be tempted to fall into his folly, then stay away. Apply Proverbs 26:4. But if you think you can help him by saving him from himself, while not placing yourself in the danger of his folly, then by all means apply Proverbs 26:5. It takes wisdom to use wisdom.

Job, Ecclesiastes, and Song of Songs are unique in their own right. But the nature of wisdom and their use of parallelism put these books in the same category.[18] A significant difference that is worth pointing out here is that these works, unlike Proverbs, each display a narratival structure as well. Thus, they are not just sayings but have some of the features we saw above with covenantal history.[19]

---

[18]Will Kynes has a strong point, however, that the grouping of these books together can impede their interpretation ("The 'Wisdom Literature' Category: An Obituary," *JTS* 69 [2018]: 1-24), for there is indeed wisdom in other texts and these books exhibit several characteristics of other genres: history, dialogue, poetry, and lament, to name just a few. The studious interpreter will therefore want to consider such nuance.

[19]This includes Ecclesiastes as well. While it can appear to be a series of disconnected proverbial quips, it too has a flow of thought (almost like an epistle). See John D. Currid, *Ecclesiastes: A Quest for Meaning?*, WCS (Welwyn Garden City: Evangelical Press, 2015).

Finally, it is key to remember that this is covenantal wisdom. I argued in chapter five that the proverbs are the wisdom of the king by which he rules over his people. By Solomon (David's first son) passing this material along to his "son" (subsequent Davidic sons) the idea is conveyed that these are part of the arc of redemptive history, leading to its christotelic climax in the gospel. Thus, these texts embody the wisdom of Christ himself that characterizes his reign as the King of kings. Yet, they are also for us to apply insofar as the King's wisdom is exemplary for us. Christians are *in Christ*, and we have the mind of Christ. Only let us not neglect that first consideration—the christological nature of wisdom—in our haste to make application to ourselves. We should regard these texts as the wisdom of the King, and *then*, after that consideration, reflect on what we learn of such righteousness and wisdom from said King.

Covenantal Prophecy

With prophetic literature we should still remember much of what we learned with poetry because the prophets also employ parallelism and vivid metaphors, often amplifying from line to line. Yet, at other times they also write in the form of historical narrative and so we should remember those dynamics as well.

The prophetic books are Isaiah–Malachi. Where the prophets really stand out compared to the poetry and historical books, though, is their common visions of the future. And here I should emphasize again this is *covenantal* prophecy. I think that the typical first instinct is to understand prophecy as simply future telling, as though any generic projection of the future is "prophecy." But prophecy is like anything else in the Bible: *specifically wrapped into God's purposes of redemption*, particularly vis-à-vis the status of the most recent covenant. Thus, the prophets are not talking about the future generically (in fact they often speak of the past and present too), but as the Lord reveals to them his covenantal purposes pertaining to redemptive history. They can be called, therefore, the watchdogs of the covenant.

This consideration helps us understand why the prophets do, nonetheless, speak of the future so much: at their time the height of God's purposes for redemption were still *future*. So here again we are helped to pause and consider that prophecy *as a literary genre* occupies a unique place in redemptive history. While there certainly are prophetic elements in the New Testament, they are embedded in other predominant genres; there are no books written entirely in the prophetic genre after the coming of Christ. Even Revelation is properly called an "apocalypse," the unique characteristics of which we will explore below. But here in the Old Testament prophetic books we have a special genre of literature, called for uniquely by the historical and redemptive-historical needs of its time. Seeing this is helpful, as so much else, to keep our interpretations firmly contextualized and alert to the prophets' real concerns, those of covenant and redemptive history, not generic "future stuff."

This leads us to remember the near-and-far dynamics of biblical prophecy. When a prophet makes a prediction—or, better, we might say the Lord is making a promise—there is commonly an immediate, though sometimes only partial, fulfillment. In the previous chapter we called this "prophetic telescoping," where a prophet's vision plays out over multiple horizons of time. It is a kind of typology, in fact. As Hans LaRondelle says, the initial fulfillment "reaffirms the promise and intensifies the hope for the future fulfillment."[20] We saw that with the Immanuel prophecy in Isaiah 7:14, where we also noted that it was the state of the Davidic covenant that necessitated the near-and-far prophecy.

Jeremiah's prophecy of seventy years of exile in Jeremiah 25:11-13; 29:10 (discussed briefly in chap. 4) is also a helpful example of this. The people returned and rebuilt after seventy years (Ezra 1; 2 Chron 36:20-23). But Daniel receives a vision that the exile will extend 490 years (9:24)! Thus, while a very real "near" fulfillment of Jeremiah's seventy years happens—addressing the prophet's *historical* concerns—the full glorious restoration of Israel envisioned by many other prophets (including the reenthronement of the house of David and a new creation) must await another redemptive-historical time.

---

[20]Hans LaRondelle, *The Israel of God in Prophecy: Principles of Prophetic Interpretation* (Berrien Springs, MI: Andrews, 1983), 62.

Equally, Ezekiel's prophecy of a new temple at the end of exile (Ezek 40–44) *sort of* happens when the people return. In Haggai 1:14 the people work on the temple, but Haggai 2 envisions a still more glorious house. So genuine, historical temple-rebuilding in Haggai's day is an emblem of the greater temple to come.

Ezekiel also sees a resurrection of all Israel at the end of the exile (Ezek 37) with the house of David reigning over them (37:24-25). But there is no resurrection when Ezra and Nehemiah return. So, the "nearness" of Ezekiel's prophecy is that there is *a release from exile*. But the resurrection will have to wait until the fuller more glorious release from exile *with the coming of the final Son of David*. Thus, Jesus' resurrection is the dawn of that fulfillment,[21] in which Paul sees a still further near-and-far element in that Christ's resurrection guarantees ours as well (1 Cor 15:20, 23).

Joel's locusts, Amos's earthquake, and Habakkuk's armies—to name just a few more—are all read the same way. They are near-and-far predictions that are also bound up within covenant curses and blessings.

A word on flow of thought is in order for the prophets. They seem to wander from point to point and back again, but it is not aimless. Rather, they seem to write in spirals, revisiting some of the same ideas with slightly different nuances. But they are not just running around in circles; the spirals are cumulatively going somewhere. A great example of this is Isaiah 40–55. All the major themes of these chapters are right there in 40:1-11—end of exile, forgiveness, the "way of the LORD," the glory of the Lord, the word of the Lord, all humanity hearing the word and seeing the glory, the "good news," and the reign of God. The subsequent chapters weave all these ideas in and out, over and over again. But it is not just stream-of-consciousness meandering. It is progressing to something final. Why is the reign of God "good news"? *How* will sins be forgiven? Chapters fifty-two and fifty-three tie all this off with the self-sacrifice of the quintessential "servant of the Lord." He will give his life for sins, and usher in the cosmic reign of God. Chapter fifty-four celebrates this, and

---

[21]Daniel M. Gurtner, *The Torn Veil: Matthew's Exposition of the Death of Jesus*, SNTSMS 139 (Cambridge: Cambridge University Press, 2007), 144-52, 160-69.

chapter fifty-five invites all to come. So while much of Isaiah 40–55 traces and retraces the same themes, there is a building to the moment that the "servant" and his work are revealed.

These sorts of dynamics are, of course, difficult to notice sometimes. For that, I again recommend reading and rereading, and particularly rereading ever larger contexts—reading "in and out" as I called it in chapter three.

To summarize, when reading the prophets pay attention to where they write in historical narrative and where they use poetry. All the while, we still need to think in terms of whole book context and discern the flow of thought as they switch from one style to another. Yet, it is the flow of thought that can be so difficult as the prophets often switch between topics and back again. Noticing their spiraling movement and near-and-far elements, therefore, helps keep us within appropriate literary, historical, and christological contexts.

Kingdom Parables

Parables come embedded within narratives. They are employed in Judges, 1 and 2 Samuel, 1 and 2 Kings, Ezekiel, Matthew, Mark, and Luke. As with the rest of the genres, it is important to understand them with a particular bent: they are "kingdom parables." All too often I think we can read the parables as cryptic messages for life's struggles, timeless maxims or riddles for navigating the world. But they are imbued with the language of the kingdom, particularly, and intended to teach something of Jesus and the reign of God through him. That is why so many of them begin, "The kingdom of God is like." They are not acontextual, in other words, and need to be understood, like the genealogies, as wrapped into the larger narratives that are concerned with the covenantal state of affairs. Moreover, parables should be taken as singular images that convey one main point about the kingdom. And commonly enough, other details in the larger narrative explain the parables so readers do not need to guess what they are about. Parables are not isolated truisms, but integrally wrapped into the developing narrative in critical ways. Again, it all goes back to flow of thought. These are not disparate stories, genealogies, and parables heaped together that could just as well be taken in isolation.

For example, in Mark 4:1-9 we have the parable of the sower. Then in Mark 4:13-20 we have the explanation. In dealing with the parable, therefore, we should stick to that interpretation for the larger point, and not try to overanalyze the details. Which soil am I? Are soils two and three people who have lost their salvation? Questions of the sort are distractions. We should let the rest of the text explain the parable.[22]

Missiological Epistles

The aspect of New Testament epistles that is typically neglected is not their theology but the fact that they are written by *Jewish* apostles about the *Jewish* God sending the *Jewish* Messiah in fulfillment of the *Jewish* Scriptures, and addressed to *Gentile* churches! God's redemptive activities are now breaking out of their former primary geographic locations. That should strike us. It is quite significant that the epistles are not a predominant biblical genre until after the resurrection and giving of the Holy Spirit. Only then do God's purposes in redemption go international. These missiological epistles are Romans–Jude.

Flow of thought is always essential, but perhaps no more so than in the epistles. They typically do progress in a linear fashion—line upon line, thought upon thought, each sentence adding to the progression of the argument as a whole. In this case, therefore, the conjunctions are all the more important. They provide the warrant for why an author moves from one idea to another; they pave the path of the flow of thought from beginning to end.

For instance, Romans 3:21 starts with "But now," clearly showing a pivot. Then within Romans 3:21-26 there are all sorts of connecting words like "for" and "because"; they show us logical connections between clauses and sentences. Words like "although," "since," and "whom" do the

---

[22]In this case particularly, see Nicholas Perrin, *The Kingdom of God: A Biblical Theology*, BTL (Grand Rapids, MI: Zondervan, 2019), 88-97.

same. Paying attention here, again, keeps us from atomizing verses, and connects our reading to book-wide literary contexts.

To take a lengthier example, Romans 8:28 is a very popular verse, but if you think for a moment, it is quite perplexing. It reads, "And we know that for those who love God all things work together for good, for those who are the called according to his purpose." Well, how can *all* things be "good"? There are also bad things that happen, even to "those who love God." How can Paul say, "*all things* work together for good"? The key is in the conjunction to the next verse, and therefore the flow of thought. Verse 29 begins with the word "for." Ah! Here comes the *explanation* for why Paul can say such a perplexing thing: "For those whom he foreknew he also predestined to be conformed to the image of his Son." And *that* is the key to why all things could be good. It gives the definition of "good." "Good" is not that all things will turn out pleasantly in my life. But "good" here is to be made *more like Jesus*! Thus, God is working all things (even the clearly recognizably "bad" things in life) to make us more like the perfect man, Jesus Christ. And *that* is good. Yet, the pericope goes on. Verse 30 begins with "and," showing that Paul is taking the line of thought another step: "And those he predestined he also called, and those he called he also justified, and those whom he justified he also glorified." Thus, what seems like a perplexing verse (Rom 8:28) is made clear as we pay attention to the flow of thought, in this case disclosed through the conjunctions. God works all things for these greater purposes of calling, justification, and glorification—all of which make us more like Jesus— and that is *good* even in the difficulties of life. In fact, did you notice that Romans 8:28 itself begins with the word "and"? Well the previous verses speak of fears, sufferings, bondage, groanings, weaknesses—you know, all the bad stuff of the world (vv. 15-27). That is how we know that Paul recognizes that there are certainly bad things in life, but the flow of thought helps us reorient our perspective.

It also helps to recognize the first chapter of epistles will often clue us in to something of the historical context of that church, highlight why the epistle was written, and lay out themes that resurface throughout the rest of the epistle. To demonstrate, Romans 1:1-17 highlights the relationship between Jews and Gentiles. In Galatians 1 Paul emphasizes the need to preach and believe the true gospel. Philippians 1 talks about trials and the need for deliverance. First Timothy 1:3-11 warns against false doctrine. And 1 John 1 echoes the themes of creation. All these, then, become major concerns in the rest of the books, and seeing something of them is another function of attending to the historical context.

One final thought on the epistles: When we see the word "you" we need to bear in mind that that is typically a *plural* you. In some parts of America it would be said "you guys," or "y'all." This is important to remember insofar as these letters were written to congregations predominantly (1 and 2 Timothy and Titus the exceptions). Thus, we should not read them as letters to us directly as individuals, but to local churches. And so we hear them addressing us as *members of* a community. Thus, we should apply the epistles to our churches first, then to us as members of the church. There is application to be gained on the individual level, but we think of that application to individuals as they live in congregational contexts. More on this in the next chapter.

Missiological epistles are likely the easiest for us because, of all the genres in the Bible, it is the one most common to us. Their style of argumentation and flow of thought are the way we often write (like this book!), and they occupy the same place in redemptive history that we do—after the cross and resurrection—so that much of the christological work has already been done by the author. But they can also be difficult because of the depth of thought condensed into tight rhetorical packages, and the historical gap that remains between the first audience and us. Careful attention to openings and conjunctions, therefore, can go a long way in crossing the historical gap and navigating the flow of thought.

Apocalypse

Finally, we come to the apocalyptic genre. No additional adjective is needed here because simply understanding what an apocalypse is enough to challenge us. We typically think of the Book of Revelation when we think of apocalyptic writings. But apocalypses can be found in several books: a part of Isaiah, parts of Ezekiel, a part of Daniel, parts of Zechariah, parts of Matthew, Mark, and Luke, and the book of Revelation. When considering apocalyptic writing, it is crucial to remember that this genre has a historical context. As with all other writings, apocalyptic authors are addressing their contemporary circumstances. And they are doing so with visually charged rhetoric. They describe the theological significance of what is going on in the world *at their time of writing* with imagery that will help the audience see the theological significance of traumatic events around them. Thus, the apocalyptic genre reaches for language from creation and the exodus, two of the most determinative moments in redemptive history. Such imagery gives the audience the opportunity to build strength and confidence when they see that their God is still sovereign over all.

In fact, the Greek word *apokalypsis* means "revelation" or "unveiling." An "apocalypse," therefore, *reveals* what is otherwise hidden. In the case of biblical apocalypses, the people of God are perplexed by what is going on in the world, and so an author uses the genre to interpret such events and reassures them that God is still enthroned. For example, the apocalyptic section of Daniel, chapters ten through twelve (though more of Daniel has apocalyptic elements as well), is designed to help the people of God endure under severe persecution in the exile. The book of Revelation, as well, is less about "future stuff" and more about helping the churches listed in chapters two and three (and all churches everywhere for that matter) theologically frame Rome in redemptive-historical terms. If Jesus is King of kings and Lord of lords, why is the Roman Empire with its Roman Caesar treating Jesus' subjects so poorly (to be mild about it)? The book of Revelation *pulls back the veil*, as it were, to show Christians what is happening in heaven and what is truly happening on earth—the crucified and risen Lamb has all history under his sovereign control. It takes the edge off the scariness of Rome; it is not an all-powerful empire but a beast with a mortal wound destined to fall.

We can therefore define an apocalypse as "a genre of revelatory literature with a narrative framework."[23] It puts forward powerful images (typically redemptive-historical in nature) to provide a competing symbolic universe for those living in a world where events and suffering challenge their faith.[24] But this is not portrayed as just a list of images; apocalypses also tell a story.[25] So once again, we look for a beginning, middle, and end to the whole, and within each pericope.

While these texts do occasionally speak of the future—for that too is an encouragement to beleaguered people in the here and now—the goal is not to give detailed timelines of how it's all going to end. The coming of the Messiah the first time (Daniel) or the second time (Revelation) are certainly predicted with confidence. But to read these books in one hand and the *New York Times* in the other is to completely miss the point. The original historical audiences did not have the *New York Times*. They did not know what credit cards were. They could never have dreamed of a helicopter or the internet—"a text cannot mean what it never meant."[26] To understand the imagery, then, it is key to know something of the historical context under which the authors wrote and the original audiences lived.

Two brief examples will help. In Revelation 12 we have a "woman clothed with the sun, with the moon under her feet, and on her head a crown of twelve stars" (v. 1). She cries out "in birth pains" while a "great red dragon with seven heads and ten horns" tries to devour her child (vv. 2-4). Her son goes on "to rule all the nations with a rod of iron," however, and she escapes into the wilderness (vv. 5-6). Who is this woman, son, and dragon, and what does it all mean? Here our author has painted a rhetorical picture using redemptive-historical brushstrokes, for all these images come from the Old Testament. The woman is surely Eve and

---

[23]John J. Collins, "Introduction: Towards the Morphology of a Genre," *Semeia* 14 (1979): 9.

[24]Richard Bauckham, *The Theology of the Book of Revelation*, NTT (Cambridge: Cambridge University Press, 1993), esp. 17-22, 146-59.

[25]Collins's full definition of an apocalypse is, "a genre of revelatory literature with a narrative framework, in which a revelation is mediated by an otherworldly being to a human recipient, disclosing a transcendent reality which is both temporal, insofar as it envisages eschatological salvation, and spatial, insofar as it involves another, supernatural world" ("Morphology," 14).

[26]Gordon D. Fee and Douglas Stuart, *How to Read the Bible for All Its Worth*, 2nd ed. (Grand Rapids, MI: Zondervan, 1993), 26.

Israel. That is one great thing about these images; they are so elastic. Her "birth pains" echo Genesis 3:16 (Eve) and the sun, moon, and stars she is wearing(!) is an allusion to Genesis 37:9-10, where Israel is described as such. So she is both and that is okay. The point here is that she is the woman who brings the one seed into the world, and in a very real sense Eve and Israel both do that. So while the images are mixed, they are not contradictory. The son, then, is that great one seed of the woman. That he will "rule all the nations with a rod of iron" echoes Psalm 2:8-9 where the Davidic king triumphs over all who oppose him. And we are expressly told that the dragon is "that ancient serpent . . . the deceiver of the whole world" (v. 9). Thus, this is a vivid depiction of all of history using the symbolism of the Old Testament; it is the cosmic battle between the serpent and the seed of the woman. This would have been very encouraging to the persecuted Christians of that day, for their sufferings are not in vain, but "they have conquered him by the blood of the Lamb and by the word of their testimony, for they loved not their lives even unto death" (v. 11). Jesus is the seed and *he* has triumphed by his death and resurrection (1:5-6, 18; 5:9-10; again whole-book context still matters). Thus, even *death* is not defeat to these Christians, because keeping one's testimony unto death is a *triumph* over the serpent, as Jesus was also such a "faithful witness" (1:5).

Do you see how this creates a competing symbolic universe? Death is defeated, and surely Christians were nervous that they were on the wrong side of history, following the so-called "King Jesus" (if *Caesar* actually still dominates). But this is all an outworking of that ancient struggle, and the Lord has always seen his people through. The help of "two wings of the great eagle so that [the woman] might fly from the serpent into the wilderness," is imagery directly from the exodus (Ex 19:4). That kind of sovereign protection will continue for the people of God so long as they "hold to the testimony of Jesus" (v. 17). Thus, there is no need to pin these verses to *particular events*, but to see their redemptive-historical outlines and (with a sane imagination) think on how they would hit the original audience.

Matthew 24–25 is an example where we see prophetic elements, like prophetic telescoping and near-and-far fulfillment, spliced into an apocalyptic discourse. Is Jesus talking about the destruction of the temple in AD 70, or the end of the age? Or is he talking about his own death and resurrection (note the repeated "watch" for the "hour" in 24:42; 25:13 and 26:40, 45)? If it is a combination of these things, then when does he switch from one to the other? It turns out that Jesus is weaving all these things together, and not signaling when he switches from one to the other, even commonly talking about more than one thing at a time. He can talk about multiple things at once because they are theologically aligned in a lot of ways. Thus the near-and-far nature of his speech is really felt, *as several future events are theologically telescoped into one vision*. Apocalyptic discourse creates the space for this and gives readers a redemptive-historically thick set of symbols by which to interpret all those things. Seeing these sorts of dynamics help us feel more at home in a difficult genre.

Conclusion

"When we detach the message from the medium, we muzzle the message itself."[27] Thus, thinking about genre is not just an effort to appreciate the Bible's artistry, but to hear its message more clearly. To think about genre is to think about literary context, historical context, and christological context at the same time. Genre is an author's choice of a *literary style* that *historical events* called for *at particular times in redemptive history*. Navigating the dynamics of how the different genres of the Bible work, therefore, is again a function of good discipleship and "a sine qua non of correct interpretation."[28] If we do not tend to the Bible on its own terms, the only terms left are our own that we force on the Bible. In which case we do not treat the texts *as they are asking to be treated*. That is what genre is: a means by which authors direct readers in interpretation, revealing structure and flow of thought.

---

[27]Peter J. Leithart, *Deep Exegesis: The Mystery of Reading Scripture* (Waco, TX: Baylor University Press, 2009), 34.

[28]Kevin J. Vanhoozer, *Is There a Meaning in This Text?: The Bible, The Reader, and the Morality of Literary Knowledge*, LCS (Grand Rapids, MI: Zondervan, 1998), 3.

Just as misunderstanding which jellyfish is in the water can be deadly, so too a lack of awareness of genre can lead to misinterpretation and have bad consequences. As we discussed in the introduction, all of our theology and ministry are built on the foundation of hermeneutics. We turn now, therefore, in our last chapter to think finally about ministry and application. That, we hope, will be safer than swimming with box jellies.

For Further Study

Fee, Gordon D., and Douglas Stuart. *How to Read the Bible for All Its Worth*. 4th ed. Grand Rapids, MI: Zondervan, 2014. A very popular and helpful book, Fee and Stuart simply go genre by genre.

Ryken, Leland. *How to Read the Bible as Literature*. Grand Rapids, MI: Zondervan, 1984. As the title indicates, this work elucidates the particularly literary features of the Bible, then also its rhetorical devices.

Sandy, D. Brent, and Ronald L. Giese, Jr., eds. *Cracking Old Testament Codes: Interpreting the Literary Genres of the Old Testament*. Nashville: B&H, 1995. Despite the title, this work does not espouse some secretive meaning to the Old Testament; to the contrary the point is that while these genres are far removed from us, they can be negotiated.

For Advanced Study

Bauckham, Richard. *The Theology of the Book of Revelation*. Cambridge: Cambridge University Press, 1993. This work helps readers especially with the nature of the apocalyptic genre.

Blomberg, Craig L. *Interpreting the Parables*. 2nd ed. Downers Grove, IL: InterVarsity Press, 2012. As thorough a work as you will find, Blomberg covers the parables from every critical angle.

LaRondelle, Hans. *The Israel of God in Prophecy: Principles of Prophetic Interpretation*. Berrien Springs, MI: Andrews, 1983. Dated, but still a very helpful work on the way prophecy works. LaRondelle is particularly insightful to encourage us to think of prophecy more as promise than just prediction.

Longman, Tremper, III. *How to Read the Psalms*. Downers Grove, IL: InterVarsity Press, 1988. A lot of helpful books on the Bible's poetry exist. I have found this one helpful because in addition to the technical side of things, Longman also appreciates the Davidic and messianic scope of the Psalter.

Pratt, Richard L. *He Gave Us Stories: The Bible Student's Guide to Interpreting Old Testament Narratives*. Phillipsburg, NJ: P&R, 1990. This is a nearly exhaustive work dealing with hermeneutics in general, then specific focus on the Old Testament's historical books and their application.

Resseguie, James L. *Narrative Criticism of the New Testament: An Introduction.* Grand Rapids, MI: Baker Academic, 2005. With attention to the nature and rhetoric of story, Resseguie helps us appreciate how so much of the New Testament comes to us as a narrative.

Robertson, O. Palmer. *The Christ of Wisdom: A Redemptive-Historical Exploration of the Wisdom Books of the Old Testament.* Phillipsburg, NJ: P&R, 2017. Robertson looks at each book in the wisdom genre, emphasizing that "wisdom manifests itself most fully in connection with kingship" (5).

Schreiner, Thomas R. *Interpreting the Pauline Epistles.* 2nd ed. Grand Rapids, MI: Baker Academic, 2011. This work covers a lot of technical issues and is strong on discerning flow of thought.

8

BE DOERS OF THE WORD

Christological Application

T HE FIRST TIME I SAW A SHARK in the wild I was scuba diving off the coast of Tasmania. My dive partner put his hand up to his head to designate a fin, and then pointed into the kelp off to his left. I peeked around him into the foliage and he must still think it is funny to this day the way my eyes bulged in quiet terror. There it was, just looking right back at me, no more than three feet away. And he looked *huge*! But that was only at first glance. A few breaths and a moment looking him over and I realized he was just a little guy. In my mind I jumped to conclusions because of an uninformed instinct. A little observation then went a long way. But a little more consideration—namely of the context I was in—and I had new things to concern me. Is this a fully grown shark and therefore a species over which I need not fret? Or is this a juvenile wherein other larger sharks of this species are in the area? Is his mother in the area?

Throughout this book I have tried to slow down the rush to application. Why? We *should* apply the word of God to our churches, to ourselves, and to the world. James 1:22 clearly says, "Be doers of the word, and not hearers only" (or "not just readers"). The Bible should awaken in us longings to change ourselves and the world. "We are not interested in knowing more but in becoming more."[1] In fact, it should *challenge* us to these ends, awaken us from our secular slumbers. As Jeannine Brown puts it so well, "If we are routinely experiencing the Bible as 'nonthreatening platitudes' rather than a wake-up call to new ways of thinking, being, and doing, we are probably not reading well."[2] Why, then, have I pumped the brakes on application so much? Because without a legitimate and ethical approach to reading the Scriptures we will make *hasty* application. That can lead to unwise application, or even downright *wrong* application. Had I reacted to the shark based on my first impulse, if I did not observe it closely nor ever think of my context, I would have sped right to the surface, scuffled back onboard and shouted, "I think we need a bigger boat!"

Turns out it was not a great white (though they have been seen in that area before), and we were obviously not eaten. To God be the glory! The point is, for application to be fruitful, it must *wait* so that it can be based on good observations and wise contextual considerations. In other words, we *have* to get our hermeneutics right *first*. Satisfied that we have done that, we can now move on to application.

Three Clarifying Questions Prior to Application

Let us clear some debris first: (1) We need to answer the question, What is the Bible? Then, coming out of that, we need to ask, (2) What kinds of application should we expect from such a book? Finally, we need to ask contextual questions about ourselves: (3) Who are we and where are we in history? Neglecting any of these questions will send us on frustrating

---

[1]Eugene H. Peterson, *Eat This Book: A Conversation in the Art of Spiritual Reading* (Grand Rapids, MI: Eerdmans, 2006), 59.

[2]Jeannine K. Brown, *Scripture as Communication: Introducing Biblical Hermeneutics* (Grand Rapids, MI: Baker Academic, 2007), 125.

errands in search of application that may not be there. But knowing what the Bible is, and therefore what to expect, will prepare us well for sound application in our world.

What is the Bible? First, if we keep in mind what the Bible *is*, then we will be less prone to treat it for what it *is not*. The Bible is *the Spirit-inspired record and interpretation of God's historical acts of redemption that climax in the death and resurrection of Jesus Christ and his ongoing work among the nations.* It is, therefore, a historically embedded revelation about God, and by God, for the glory of God, through the salvation of God's people. It is not an encyclopedia of pithy one-liners or a collection of disparate stories that we can abstract as we please to help us navigate the difficulties of life. It is not a counseling sourcebook or preaching lectionary. It does not aim to distill ten principles of leadership. It is certainly not a recipe book of placebos to distract us from reality. To be clear, it does help us navigate life, provide counseling wisdom, and give us material to preach. But that is not *what* it is. It is a historical record of God's saving acts. Understanding that first will guide us in what legitimate and ethical application looks like. First, we deal ethically and legitimately with the Bible in interpretation, then our application will also be ethical and legitimate. Then we can think carefully about things like counseling or preaching or leadership, and so on, as long as we have gone through these necessary hermeneutical considerations in line with what the Bible is. If we skip that step, then we shortcut our interpretations and reduce the Bible to less than what it is. When we skip straight to application in any arena we always get less out of the Bible and make less helpful application (and more times than not less accurate application).

What can we expect from the Bible? Second, application is sometimes difficult because we have unrealistic expectations. We think, How does *that* verse affect *me* at *this* moment? It is unrealistic because it is asking the Bible to do what it was never designed to do: to take its parts and give advice to individuals living in twenty-first century cultures. Its goal is not to give handy advice or life verses, but to declare God's cosmic saving activities. So we can expect that it has big-picture, redemptive-historical concerns primarily in view.

Now I should be clear: the Bible does have clear and concise teachings on a variety of issues, even in single verses. It can be applied to individuals. And it certainly speaks powerfully into our twenty-first century world. But to race to these considerations without the appropriate reflection on what the Bible is and what its aims are is like eating the Jell-O before it has set. A little work and a little patience first.

What is my context? Third and finally, we must bear in mind that application is also shaped by contexts as much as interpretation is. But the question above—How does *that* verse affect *me* at *this* moment?—is contextless. It focuses on:

▶ A single verse out of context, or a single pericope detached from its whole-book setting

▶ A single person unreflective of how they live as part of the universal church, and particularly a local church

▶ A single moment in time without regard to discipleship as a lifelong commitment

Instead, our leading question should be, What does this pericope tell me about God, humanity, salvation in Christ, the mission of the church, the role of local churches, and my place in my local church? Yes, that is a lot. But look at what it does: it puts application in a series of contexts. It does eventually get to me as an individual right now in my life, but only after passing through several layers of application context that orient the final individual application. More on this shortly.

Unrealistic and contextless efforts in application result in frustration when the Bible does not deliver as we expected, though it never promised to do so in the first place. Then, we also miss what application is truly available! So I would propose here a handful of considerations that will help free us from unrealistic contextless expectations and equally position us to gather what riches the Bible truly does have for application.

Four Helpful Reflections on What Application Is

In addition to answering these questions with clarity, here are four considerations worth bearing in mind.

First, we must resist the temptation to make all application *individual*. Application is first of all to the church universal. In our time it is so natural to think about our own individual discipleship. As we should! But that instinct can be so strong in the West that it is easy to forget that the Bible is not written to me as an individual. Rather, it is written to all the people of God and often has application for the whole thereof. This is *corporate* application. Closely related to this are the spatially and temporally bound manifestations of the people of God called "local churches." Local churches are the most tangible place where corporate application is lived out. It is where the rubber of theology hits the road of life, where love has to actually show up amid hardships in the lives of others. Thus, *their* discipleship is of equal interest as my own. It is worth observing that twenty-two of the twenty-seven New Testament books are written directly to local churches, or to individuals then told what to do in a church setting. The other five also show signs of being written to *communities*. And excepting some psalms and proverbs, the entire Old Testament was written to corporate Israel.

Second, we need to appreciate that right knowledge *is* application. To correct our thinking is a beautiful thing, and a necessary first step toward any other application. When we stop thinking error, and start thinking truth, application *is* happening. Insofar as our Lord called us to love him with all our *minds* (Mt 22:37), the natural question becomes, How do I do *that*? Insofar as we are judged by our thoughts as much as our actions (Jer 17:10; Heb 4:12-13), the question also becomes, How can I please God in my *thought* life too? The answer to both questions is, Keep learning what the Scriptures teach and you will think his thoughts after him. Paul straight out says it in Philippians 4:8: "Whatever is true, whatever is noble, whatever is just, whatever is pure, whatever is lovely, whatever is commendable, if there is any excellence, and if there is anything worthy of praise, *think* about these things" (emphasis added). The next verse also says, "What you have learned and received and heard and seen in me—practice these things, and the God of peace will be with you." So Paul seems to have two kinds of application in Philippians: thinking rightly, then taking what is learned and doing rightly. We need both. But notice the order between the two: first we learn, then we do.

Third, and very closely related to the previous consideration, we have to accept that application may be delayed. It does not have to be right here and now. But a steady diet of Bible-intake shapes our worldview and character in ways to prepare us for future application. In Matthew 7 Jesus gives this brilliant teaching:

> Therefore whoever hears these sayings of mine, and does them, I will liken him to a wise man who built his house on the rock: and the rain descended, the floods came, and the winds blew and beat on that house; and it did not fall, for it was founded on the rock. But everyone who hears these sayings of Mine, and does not do them, will be like a foolish man who built his house on the sand: and the rain descended, the floods came, and the winds blew and beat on that house; and it fell. And great was its fall. (vv. 24-27 NKJV)

These two houses are different because one is founded on Jesus' teaching and one is not. They are also different because one stands and one does not. Yet where they are the *same* is very interesting. They are the same in that natural disasters threaten both. Neither is immune. But when does one build such a house? Surely not while the rain is falling, the floods are rising, and the winds are beating. I have never seen anyone fixing their foundation *during* the storm. Rather, the house has to be prepared long in advance. So too, regular attention to Jesus' teaching (which, as we have seen, equates to the entire Bible) fortifies the house for when the disasters hit. Therefore, we should expect the Bible to work application into us slowly, even at times and in ways we are not aware, so that we have a rock to stand on when we need to.[3] When asked, "Why do you preach so

---

[3]To be sure, Jesus' teaching here has an application to the universal church first (as mentioned above) on the biblical-theological axis pertaining to wise Solomon, the original builder of God's house on the rock (Michael Patrick Barber, "Jesus as the Davidic Temple Builder and Peter's Priestly Role in Matthew 16:16-19," *JBL* 132 [2013]: 939-42).

much on suffering?" one pastor answered, "Because my people *are going* to suffer." He understood that much preaching—and we can say here, much reading—forms a certain kind of person little by little for *big* application that will be needed down the road. So I say let Bible study be patient and have its long-term impact.

Fourth, we should revel in that the Bible gives us *wisdom*! Some decisions in life do not have "chapter and verse," but require sound thinking to draw together serval biblical teachings and relate them to several factors in life. This is related to the two previous points. "Christians do not simply learn or study or use Scripture; we assimilate it, take it into our lives in such a way that it gets metabolized into acts of love, cups of cold water, missions into all the world, healing and evangelism and justice in Jesus' name, hands raised in adoration of the Father."[4] Filling out our minds with Bible, and being patient with the Spirit's work on us digs a reservoir of wisdom from which complex life-situations can draw fresh water.

With all these considerations, I am trying to guard against the assumption that everything in my life is addressed directly somewhere in the Bible, or that everything in the Bible has something to do directly with the details of my day. But the Bible is not a collection of pithy one-liners to help us navigate the challenges of postmodern life.[5] It is about God, the general human condition, and the former's saving activities in response to the latter. In our day to day, however, there will be all sorts of issues for which the Bible does not have precise application. Equally, there are some pericopes and passages that do not immediately apply to where we are in life at the time of study. That is fine. Keep walking down the narrow road of discipleship and you will experience the Bible's relevance more and more. This goes back to having realistic expectations for application in light of what the Bible *is* (and is not). It is not a self-help recipe book, but the historically revealed, saving activities of God.

---

[4]Eugene H. Peterson, "Eat This Book: The Holy Community at Table with the Holy Scripture," *Theology Today* 56 (1999): 6.

[5]Or again Peterson: "We do not form our personal spiritual lives from a random assemblage of favorite texts in combination with individual circumstances" ("Eat this Book," 5).

Application, therefore, that is corporate, intelligent, patient, and wisdom-filled will have more staying power in one's life than to-do lists coming out of every verse.[6]

In sum, recognizing what the Bible *is* and what to rightly expect in our current context of local church membership after the resurrection of Christ will provide us with *christological* application; that is "gospel-logical" application. Christians believe in Jesus Christ. Christians want to be like Jesus Christ. We are not interested in generically religious abstractions, but solidly Christian application. With that in mind, we turn now to consider some ethical and legitimate steps in moving toward such application. Then we will look at some examples.

Christological Application Has a Gospel-Logic

Occasionally it is argued that to make application we should take any passage, understand the theology of the text, then apply the theology in contemporary terms. This approach, however, lifts theology out of the unfolding biblical metadrama. But no theology should make an end-run around the gospel. There must be another path to application that remains consistent with the shape of the Bible, following the flow and terrain of any text *to and through the gospel*. Since it is the gospel that binds all together, it can never be ignored. Therefore, the gospel always becomes the application in some way.

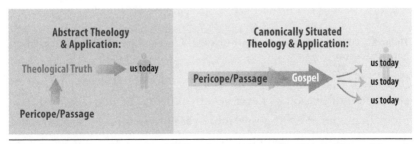

Figure 8.1. Biblical application should follow the trend lines of the Bible itself, to and through the gospel.

---

[6]See particularly Graeme Goldsworthy, *Gospel-Centered Hermeneutics: Foundations and Principles of Evangelical Biblical Interpretation* (Downers Grove, IL: IVP Academic, 2006), 251-57.

This is an appropriation of what I am calling the "climactic meaning" of any text. Does this flatten out the Bible, because everything is about the gospel? No, it highlights the beautiful diversity of the different ways to look at the gospel. And from there, we make application. We make application *from the gospel*. As we see the various ways biblical texts flow into the gospel, we will also see various ways to apply the gospel. Every text flows into it; application therefore flows out of it.

Imagine a prism. Depending on how intense and at what angle you shine a light on the prism will determine how the light comes out on the other side. The gospel is that prism into which all the biblical texts are shining their light. Depending on how that light shines into the gospel (how the terrain of texts flow to the gospel) it refracts a slightly different light out the other side of application. This prevents application from just being the "same ol' thing" every time; the point is not just to believe the gospel. But every pericope provides a different path to the gospel and reveals some different aspect of the gospel.

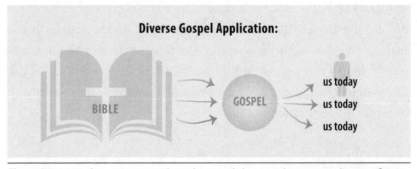

Figure 8.2. Just as there are many paths to the gospel, there are also many applications flowing out of the gospel.

Thus, applying the gospel can never wear out. But to be clear, it is also an application of *the gospel*, never generic religious advice. To make application that skips over the gospel is to treat a text in theological abstraction from the totality of redemptive history.

Let us remind ourselves what the gospel is before we go any further. I am using the term gospel here to mean the full panorama of biblical material that elucidates the pith of it all: who Jesus Christ is and what he has done to create the universal church. The Father sends the Son in fulfillment of Old Testament expectations. The Son lives a perfectly righteous life, dies for sinners and is raised to life. The Spirit is sent by Father and Son to regenerate individuals and build up the people of God. In all this, forgiveness of sins and the gift of eternal life are brought to Adam's children. I have tried to argue throughout this book that this is the overall christologic of the Bible, and an understanding of that informs our hermeneutic. Now, if the *Bible itself* is running toward the gospel, then our application should follow the same trek.

I have called this a christology focused on person and *work*—the work of Jesus through his death and resurrection to create the universal church, the people of God across all places and times. The universal church, then, manifests itself at specific places and at particular times in local churches, which are of course made up of individuals (some living in family units but not all). Thus our application should think along these same lines. With each pericope, after employing our legitimate and ethical hermeneutic, we can move toward application by asking questions in this order:

▶ What does this passage tell me about what we should believe about God?

▶ What does this passage reveal about some aspect of the gospel?[7]

▶ How should the universal church look and behave based on who God is and the particular aspect of the gospel revealed here?

▶ How can our local congregation participate in that calling in the time and place God has us?

▶ How can I as an individual Christian contribute to these efforts of my local church?

▶ How can I as an individual Christian take these applications into my home, neighborhood, work, and so on?

Anywhere and throughout this process, we can equally ask:

▶ What message to unbelievers emerges out of all this?

---

[7]These first two are what Bryan Chapell calls the "Fallen Condition Focus" (*Christ-Centered Preaching: Redeeming that Expository Sermon*, 2nd ed. [Grand Rapids, MI: Baker Academic, 2005], 48-57). It leads the way because of how prevalent the sin-judgment-grace theme is throughout the Bible.

The order of questions is important because of what the Bible *is*, a revelation of God's glory through his acts of cosmic redemption, not a how-to guide for individuals. The result is that we have contextualized *ourselves too* within the larger redemptive-historical drama before we start thinking about that individual application.

If we see the entire Bible is christological, then our biblical application must have a gospel-logic to it as well. "No revealed truth drops by the wayside in the course of God's redemption and revelation. All truths come to their realization in relation to Christ."[8]

Christological Application Attends to Redemptive-Historical Locations

In addition to following the biblical-theological contours of any text to the gospel, we also need to recognize *where in redemptive history* is the text located. Are we studying a book of Moses? Are we studying a psalm or prophetic book? Are we studying a Gospel or New Testament epistle? These are not just redemptive-historical questions affecting our hermeneutic, but they also bear on *how* we make application to our lives today. Consider this diagram again.

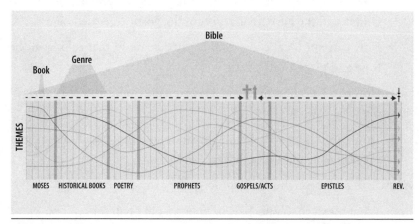

Figure 8.3. Biblical application is also affected by the stratum of redemptive history in which any text is found, and therefore its relation to the unfolding christodrama.

---

[8]Edmund P. Clowney, *Preaching Christ in All of Scripture* (Wheaton, IL: Crossway, 2003), 32.

If we are reading the Old Testament, we need to remember its forward-leaning orientation, relating events in anticipation of the coming of Christ. The seed of the woman has not yet come, so theology is written in types and prophecies. Now that we have the full canon, we can take this into consideration and appreciate *how* application reaches us. In such cases, the application of anything before Christ would need to run along the thematic lines, or through whole-book contexts, before reaching us today. More on this below.

In the Gospels and Acts we have the unique days of fulfillment. Those books mark the redemptive-historical zenith of God's purposes—entirely unique narratives that rarely find one to one correspondences for application today. In other words, I do not believe that we should turn water into wine, walk on water, miraculously reproduce bread, or heal with our shadows. Those were unique salvific moments in history intended to demonstrate who Christ is and his apostles' authority, and to bring Old Testament expectations to realization. Where Jesus says, "Do this in remembrance of me" is clear enough. We should do that in remembrance of him. And where Jesus teaches on ethics, we should of course obey. Thus, we looked at Matthew 7:24-27 above. But much of these books are narratives describing the unique redemptive-historical epoch of Jesus and the apostles. In such cases, consider above how application must first run through the gospel, then to us. More on this when we look at a Gospel text below as well.

As for Romans onward, we have a church living "between the times." The authors and first audiences of Romans–Revelation are living after the resurrection, ascension, giving of the Spirit, and awaiting the return of Christ. This consideration makes a large impact on how we interpret, as I have argued, and equally on how we apply. Let us recall this image one more time.

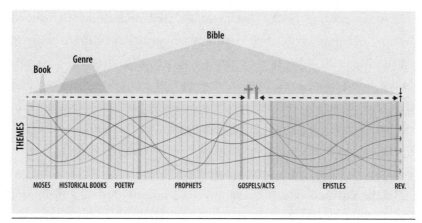

Figure 8.4. As with the authors of the NT epistles we too live between Christ's first and second advent, making application from these texts more immediate than those in other redemptive historical strata.

It is important to notice here that *redemptive-historically thinking* we live in this shaded area. Yes, *culturally and geographically* we live far away from the entire Bible and that needs to be reckoned, as we thought about in chapter four. But in terms of God's purposes for redemption, we live in the same era in which Paul lived: between Christ's resurrection, ascension, giving of the Spirit, and awaiting his return. This means that application from these books is *more direct*. It is a lot easier to apply teachings from Romans–Revelation because we occupy the same redemptive-historical moment that they do. Moreover, as commented above, those books are all written either to churches or to individuals leading churches. Thus, their life situation is equivalent to ours. In the Old Testament we have the premonarchic period, the monarchic period, and the time of exile. But none of those are our redemptive-historical moment. Rather we live under the authority of the risen Christ who has called together an *international worshiping and witnessing community* that knows no borders (for Christ is the Lord of all). We are not wandering the wilderness in search of a typological Eden. We are not the army of God's justice through Joshua or the judges. We do not live within the localized dynastic boundaries of David and Solomon or their successors. We do not live in exile waiting to be restored to the presence of God. *We live in the age of fulfillment wherein the seed of the woman has struck the mortal wound to the serpent, the resurrection of the dead has begun, the Spirit continues to be poured out on every tongue, tribe, and nation, and the church is being built of Jews and Gentiles into a holy temple for the Lord the world over!* And *that* is the context of the New Testament epistles. When reading the Old Testament, and even the Gospels and Acts, we need to think along the Bible's redemptive-historical terrain to understand those texts and apply them. But with the New Testament epistles, that work has already been done for us! Paul and the others are writing with the climactically redemptive events behind them, and able to write and apply to churches the fully developed message of God. Therefore, application is that much closer at hand with the New Testament epistles.

I am not making a canon within the canon, though. I am not claiming the New Testament epistles carry greater authority. No, we need it all. But in the *process of application* the New Testament epistles are a bit more accessible to us. "All Scripture is given by inspiration of God, and is profitable for doctrine, for reproof, for correction, for instruction in righteousness, that the man of God may be complete, thoroughly equipped for every good work" (2 Tim 3:16-17 NKJV). Amen! Only in some it is easier to see that reproof, correction, and instruction. And in some we need to work harder at it to get it right.

In short, *we* are in a context as well: the redemptive-historical context of the New Testament epistles. That consideration influences our application of all texts from the various parts of the Bible.

Examples of Christological Application

Let us pull all this together with some examples from the pericopes we have already considered. We looked at 1 Samuel 3 a couple of times. What is the application to us of Samuel's first hearing God's voice? It is *not* that we should also listen for audible voices from God or be on the lookout for signs because God might be calling us to ministry. Application is rarely simply to do what we see biblical characters doing.[9] We are told of these events in biblical characters' lives because they are wrapped up in God's works of redemption leading to Christ. So in thinking about 1 Samuel 3 in its literary and christological contexts we see that Samuel is a *type* of Christ, as a momentary manifestation of the Deuteronomy 18 prophet. In Deuteronomy 18:15-22 we are told to "listen to him." And there is the application. When *the* prophet comes, of whom Samuel was a type, we are to listen to him. Therefore, the application to take away from 1 Samuel 3 is the urgency to listen to the Son of God, and to hear, believe, and, yes, apply, the things *he* teaches. And there you go, we have arrived at the gospel, for the pinnacle of Jesus' message is the meaning of his death and resurrection. We must hear, believe, and apply that. Specific application to the universal church would be to sharpen our understanding of *where and how* Jesus, the great high prophet, speaks: through his Spirit-inspired apostles who wrote the New Testament, as well as the Old Testament writers who of course are also prophetic types of Christ along the way. Application to local churches would be to think about how urgent it is to be a Bible-reading, Bible-believing people and to put systems in place where that can happen. I commonly hear church leaders speak of their high view of the Scriptures, but do not have much of a teaching ministry, or at least it is not emphasized. Well, the whole dynamic with Eli's sons, Samuel, Deuteronomy 18, and so on should drive down into our minds how *urgent* a Bible-hearing, Bible-reading, Bible-believing church culture should be. Application to the individual and

---

[9]For sure, there are exemplary characters in the Bible. Joseph and Daniel come immediately to mind. Equally, Jonah seems to be a foil, and there are plenty of negative examples. Application, therefore, should be made along these lines *when it is clear in the text* that such is the goal. We need to guard, however, against importing our own moralist ideas (like of courage or attributes of leadership) into these stories where such characteristics are not highlighted by the text. An example would be Daniel 1. There, Daniel *is* commended for his wisdom. This is clearly a teaching (at least in part; there is more to Daniel 1) on what godly wisdom looks like in a hostile climate. There is a lot to take away from that. But we get in danger when we import into the story teenagers' feelings and fears *today*. Therein, again, lies the value of studying historical contexts: we can make application from the lives of the saints when it is clearly a goal of the text and seems likely that the original audience would have done the same. That would be faithfulness to the text.

home would sound much the same. The point here is that ethical and legitimate application of 1 Samuel 3 means doing our good hermeneutics with attention to literary, historical, and christological contexts and *then* making application to the people of God universally, locally, and then individually, following the pattern of Scripture itself.

Moving to another genre, we commonly puzzle over the capital punishment laws in the Old Testament. We are pretty sure we should not execute transgressors, but we are also not quite sure, then, why the Old Testament would have these laws. So how do we apply these texts? If we remember that Deuteronomy is descriptive law, then we are on our way. Deuteronomy is applying the Ten Commandments to Israel's life in the land. So when someone would violate certain laws they had to be removed from the covenant community so that the influence of the sin would not spread to others. Thus, Deuteronomy 17:7 concludes, "So you shall purge the evil from your midst." It was a way of protecting the larger covenant community.[10] It is interesting, therefore, that Paul quotes that very verse in 1 Corinthians 5:13 in conclusion to his teaching on *excommunication*. Paul is concerned that the sin of one will spread to the rest of the church, so he uses the same rationale to apply to the church.[11] He does not use the same law (no one is killed), but he uses the same logic: the unrepentant has to be removed to protect the purity and witness of the rest.[12] Thus, insofar as God's people are always called to holiness, the principle remains today, as the epistles provide us with *our* descriptive law in light of the coming of Christ and international spread of the gospel.

We looked at a lot of psalms in the previous chapters as well. Given particularly what we saw of the psalms' place in redemptive history (chap. 5), we should also apply these first to Jesus, then we can apply

---

[10]It is also typological, for the wages of sin is still death (Rom 6:23). Even if the church is in no way called to carry out the judgment, it remains that God "has fixed a day on which he will judge the world in righteousness by a man [Jesus Christ] whom he has appointed" (Acts 17:31).

[11]DeRouchie has several examples on this nice three-step process: (1) original revealed application; (2) how fulfillment in Christ of entire Old Testament impacts the application; (3) lasting significance for the church and world today (*How to Understand and Apply the Old Testament: Twelve Steps from Exegesis to Theology* [Phillipsburg, NJ: P&R, 2017], 439-59).

[12]The hope is also, of course, that this man will repent and, therefore, still be saved (v. 5).

them to his people, then to ourselves as one of his people. Often, however, I think we appropriate the psalms directly to our individual selves without any regard for their place in redemptive history or their meaning for and through Christ. Thus, the psalms are reduced to a kind of religious self-help book, with nothing distinctly Christian about them. For example, we looked at the structure of Psalm 42 in the last chapter. There are some beautiful phrases in this psalm that can easily be drawn into our own emotions and prayers: "As a deer pants for flowing streams, so pants my soul for you, O God" (v. 1); "My soul thirsts for the living God" (v. 2); "Why are you cast down, O my soul?" (vv. 5, 11); people mocking saying "Where is your God?" (vv. 3, 10); "Hope in God!" (vv. 5, 11); "I shall again praise him!" (v. 11). We should slow down, however, lest we turn this into self-talk psychobabble for whatever ails us. This psalm is likely expressed by someone outside the land of promise who actually used to be a leader of the temple worship (vv. 2, 4, 6). It is therefore about being away from God's presence, even oppressed by enemies (v. 9), and longing to return to worship in the temple. Perhaps it was written in exile. If so, the psalmist does not just miss the temple worship because he is away from it, but *the temple has been destroyed* and *all* God's people are denied God's saving presence. With that we have a little more of the psalmist's context, and already rebuked for layering our own lives over the text, forcing it to shape up the way we want it to. At any rate, it is very interesting that Jesus echoes verse 6 in Mark 14:34 and Matthew 26:38, when he knows he is about to be betrayed and face the cross.[13] He says, "My soul is very sorrowful." He is thereby invoking the entire ethos of the psalm. In this we see that Jesus is the true temple of God about to be destroyed. But the resurrection marks the beginning of answering the psalmist's plea, "When shall I come and appear before God?" (that is, reenter his presence; v. 2). Jesus' death and resurrection is the permanent rebuilding of the temple-presence of God. Jesus, therefore, is the true mourner who is rejected from the presence of God

---

[13]Joel Marcus, *Mark 8–16: A New Translation with Introduction and Commentary*, AB (New Haven/London: Yale University Press, 2009), 983-84.

on the cross and restored in the resurrection.[14] Then, *through him* do we enter into the presence of God and quench our thirsty souls. Thus, the language of the psalm *can and should* be appropriated by us, but first with this sort of christological shape. To suggest that thirsts are quenched, or the presence of God is enjoyed *without Jesus* is not only redemptive-historically ignorant, it is simply non-Christian. The psalmist is expressing the despair of all humanity alienated from God, and Christ alone brings us back. Application of Psalm 42 for the universal church, therefore, is (ironically) to rejoice! The true sufferer has borne our iniquity and endured the judging expulsion from the presence of God, to then re-present himself before God as the great high priest who takes us there with him (Heb 9:24-28). Our local churches, and individuals therein, are encouraged to remind themselves of these wonderful gospel truths when we do feel distant from God. When we have that sting of a guilty conscience from something we have done or left undone, we must remember that Christ has carried our iniquity for us and restored us to God as forgiven people. When we are mocked ("Where is your God?"), the answer is "He is out of the grave and pleading our case before the mercy seat." This application puts staying power on verses 5 and 11, which say, "Hope in God, for I shall again praise him!" Well, *why* should we hope in God? What makes me so confident I will praise him again? The psalm does not tell us. Yet the final horizon of interpretation in the gospel—the climactic meaning—*gives us a reason* to hope in God again. Our application, in turn, is not just generically religious God-talk, but a gospel-anchored rationale for *why* we could possibly hope in God! This psalm—like everything else in the Old Testament—is on the upward slope to the gospel. Following the terrain through this particular psalm highlights a particular aspect of the gospel that then becomes unique application flowing out of the gospel. There should be no fear that gospel-application would ever become stale. Rather, every text flows *in*

---

[14]On the relationship between Jesus' death and resurrection and the destruction and rebuilding of the temple see Nicholas G. Piotrowski, "'Whatever You Ask' for the Missionary Purposes of the Eschatological Temple: Quotation and Typology in Mark 11–12," *SBJT* 21 (2017): 97-121.

unique ways to the gospel, and application comes out just as unique on the other side.[15]

We also looked at Jeremiah 29:11 in chapter four. Often this verse is used to tell young people that God has a plan for their lives, "plans to prosper you." In America that is too easily interpreted as "a beautiful spouse, career success, bodily health, and economic security." But as we saw when we attended to the historical context of this statement, it was first uttered to people about to live seventy years in exile. Most of the people would *never come home*. Jeremiah told them, in essence, "Most of you will die in captivity, but God has a great plan for your future!" How can he say this? Well "*your* future" means *all of the people's* future. Jeremiah is speaking to them as a corporate whole, not individuals. He is saying God has plans for *Israel*. While you yourselves have to live the rest of your days far from home, this is not the end of God's redemptive purposes. The people of God *as a whole* will continue and God's creation-reclamation project will continue. Now, I do believe God has plans for each of his people; we will see that when we look at Romans 8 again below. I am simply saying that the application is greatly misleading when we simply say to people, "God has plans to prosper you," and just leave it at that because the "you" is heard as individual "me," and "prosper" is heard in terms of Western worldly comforts. Rather, God has plans to prosper *the universal church* in terms of ongoing blessings from God even in the face of great trials and tribulations. And since local churches, of which individuals are participants, are part of the universal church, we can take great confidence in that whatever we are facing—even when it seems as terrible as Israel's experience of exile—God will bring his people en masse through his full plan of salvation. We *will* reach the New Creation, come what may, guaranteed by the historic cross and resurrection (1 Cor 15:20-23). Even if we die along the way, God will raise us to eternal life. Now that is a plan for *eternal* prospering. The broad perspective of

---

[15]For another, and particularly helpful example of this kind of application to Jesus—*and therefore to us*— that is neither simplistic nor contrived, see Dane C. Ortlund, "Reflections on Handling the Old Testament as Jesus Would Have Us: Psalm 15 as a Case Study," *Themelios* 42 (2017): 74-88.

God's redemption gives us a large world-and-life view, an intellectual framework, to think gospel-logically about all matters. We do not need chapter and verse for everything we think and feel and do. But we do need the *whole Bible* to have its impact on us and shape everything we think and feel and do.

We looked at Mark 4–5 many times throughout this book. It should be obvious that I will argue against the application that "God will calm all the storms of your life." This passage is just not about the "storms" of postmodernity. Away with such allegory! Remember, the parable of the mustard seed is about *the kingdom of God*. The experience of the disciples in the boat and the demoniac on the other side of the Sea of Galilee are still about the kingdom of God. And the echoes of and allusions to the Old Testament (see chap. 6) should create a greater confidence in Jesus' words about the kingdom of God. And that is the application of it all. We should have faith—as Jesus himself asked, "Have you still no faith?" But it is not faith in faith, as though with enough belief (somehow existentially defined) Jesus will change your life circumstances. To the contrary, the historical context reveals Mark's church was very small and quite beleaguered. The application is that we should not let such worldly challenges to the kingdom frighten us, but have faith that the sovereign creator God will grow and sustain the kingdom. The application for local churches and individuals is the great value of lifting up our eyes out of our individual problems—as very real and relevant as they certainly are— to the wider horizon of what God is doing the cosmos over. It helps put our own daily struggles into the larger context of the sweep of history and God's plans for the ages. When the church seems small (small like a mustard seed) or tossed about (tossed like a small boat in a great storm) or attacked (attacked as though by thousands of demons) have the kind of faith and confidence that Jesus has in the certain growth of his small, tossed, and attacked kingdom. That larger context to life can reach down into our individual life problems far better and have more staying power than allegorical placebos.

To Romans 8:28 now. It certainly does teach that God has a plan for each Christian's life. But similarly to Jeremiah 29:11, we have to be careful about what it means that God works everything together for our "good." I have heard applications of that which basically amounted to "God will work out your situation." Water in the basement? Hang in there, you'll see, when you go to sell your house your newly updated basement will be a great selling point. Trouble at work? Trust in God. You'll see how it was all good when you leave and get a higher-paying job. Relationship difficulties? You'll see it was actually good when you're both bigger people next year. That is just some facile application. As we saw in the last chapter, the good in this verse is to be remade into *the image of Christ*. Water in your basement? God is teaching you not to value your earthly belongings so much and to think more gospel-logically in this still-fallen world, because that is Christ-like. Thieves, moths, and rust (and water) will abide; put your treasures in heaven. Trouble at work? God is putting you into situations so you can learn honesty, patience, and peacemaking because that is Christ-like. *That* is good. Relationship difficulties? It is good to learn how to have empathy, how to forgive, how to turn the other cheek and walk the extra mile, because that is Christ-like. Or maybe you need to realize some (all?) of the fault lies with you. Humility, repentance, and receiving forgiveness are also good. These are all trials for growth in Christlikeness, the sine qua non of all application.[16]

Finally, an example from Revelation will help as well. As we saw in the previous chapter, Revelation is not a spiritual decoder for watching the news. It is a historically embedded apocalypse for publicizing the lordship of Christ and the end of God's purposes in history, in the already-not-yet new creation. How do we apply such things today?

Revelation is difficult to apply in the West because it is written for a persecuted people (as is common for the apocalyptic genre). It is, therefore, a work that particularly invites us to that first level of application: to the universal church. Whether we think of the church

---

[16]Dennis E. Johnson, *Walking with Jesus Through His Word: Discovering Christ in All the Scriptures* (Phillipsburg, NJ: P&R, 2015), 266-69.

historically or *globally* today, the Messiah's people are a suffering people. Revelation teaches us, therefore, to envision the world through a montage of redemptive-historical symbols for endurance and faithfulness, and not through the propaganda of rival kingdoms. And therein lies some application indeed for Western churches and individuals. One of the great challenges to discipleship anywhere in this fallen world is the cultural trappings that would sway us to (mis)trust in those rival kingdoms. In America, for example, just think of the messianic hopes we attach to our political candidates. Think of the sort of security we seek in money (indeed one of the churches addressed in Revelation was rich; 3:17). We even call it the *Almighty* Dollar.[17] Think of all the advertisements, everywhere we seem to turn, constantly orienting us to look at (obsess over) ourselves, generating unbiblical mirages of the good life, the problem with humanity, and the "gospel" solutions in every new purchasing fad, ready for new disciples at only $39.95. As we navigate this culture it is impossible to escape the influence of such institutions. Thus, they can actually reshape our hearts in their image and compel us to adopt their values in leading our church ministries.[18] A passage like Revelation 12, therefore, is helpful "to purge and to refurbish the Christian imagination" by giving us "discernment of the contemporary situation by prophetic insight into God's nature and purpose."[19] Behind every rival kingdom is the dragon, and "those who keep the commandments of God and hold to the testimony of Jesus" (12:17) neither fear him nor give their allegiance to him, but deeply feel their solidarity with those oppressed by him.

A lot of the bogus applications above have two things in common: they are very *individualistic* and they have a bit of a *health-wealth-prosperity* tinge to them. While most evangelicals would quickly reject the

---

[17]Daniel M. Doriani, *Getting the Message: A Plan for Interpreting and Applying the Bible* (Phillipsburg, NJ: P&R, 1996), 117-18.

[18]James K. A. Smith, *You Are What You Love: The Spiritual Power of Habit* (Grand Rapids, MI: Brazos, 2016), 27-55.

[19]Richard Bauckham, *The Theology of the Book of Revelation*, NTT (Cambridge: Cambridge University Press, 1993), 159, 148.

health-wealth-prosperity pseudo-gospel in its most crass articulations, I do think more subtle forms of it show up in our churches through applications like the ones I just contradicted. On a subconscious level the thinking goes like this: I want to be secure (which in itself is an appropriate desire), but there are ways that I am not; when the Bible speaks of hope, and goodness, and so on those must be the verses that can be applied to my longing for security. In other words, if we think back to the first chapter called "The Text as a Mirror," the prevalence of our creature comforts in the West have created an expectation that things should always come up roses. Therefore, we naturally assume the Bible must be speaking to such comforts, ease, and security in life. So when we see verses like Jeremiah 29:11 or Romans 8:28 or the stilling of the storm we are preconditioned to start thinking right away in terms of individualistic creature comforts and believe those verses must promise something like that. This kind of impulse deep down in our bones, coupled with audiences' expectations, puts pressure on preachers to deliver sermons that basically amount to "God can get you through the week."

Now, *in the new creation* we will be healthy and secure and blessed forevermore because the kingdom will be eternal and the glory of God will be all in all. Amen! We will return to the "rest" of Eden. But in this world, we need to understand that the scope of the fall is unremitting, and we will all experience hardships. We will all die. And it is this blood-honest realization that makes the gospel—the *true* gospel—so sweet. The gospel provides a huge overarching umbrella for the meaning of life, the universe and everything, and gives a powerful response to the pressing reality of death (Heb 2:14-15).[20] Thus, application that runs *through the gospel first* is true, and can bear the great weight our brief lives need to put on it. And that new outlook on God, self, world, history, sin, salvation then creates a powerful world-and-life view that prepares a person (or better, a whole community) to think gospel thoughts and make gospel application every day.

---

[20]A very sober and reflective work on this is Matthew McCullough, *Remember Death: The Surprising Path to Living Hope* (Wheaton, IL: Crossway, 2018).

Thinking *gospel-logically* will prove itself in application without fail. Sermons, in turn, will be about whatever the pericope is about. They will not have the goal of "meeting the people where they are." They will have the goal to "bring the people to where God is." They will be worshipful, mind- and heart-exulting. They will make us *look up*, not at ourselves.

Conclusion

Application is a must. But we also must slow down. Recognizing first what the Bible *is* and, therefore, what to realistically expect from it goes a long way toward legitimate and ethical application that is communal, thoughtful, patient, wise, and above all contextual and gospel-logical (=christological), just like the shape of the Bible itself. When I saw that shark it was in a context, *but so was I*. My first instinct was to flee, but better hermeneutics applied to both the shark and my own surroundings resulted in a longer dive for both myself and my dive partner. Likewise, christological hermeneutics that result in christological application blesses both the reader and anyone in their circle of influence.

For Further Study

Bartholomew, Craig G., and Michael W. Goheen. *The Drama of Scripture: Finding Our Place in the Biblical Story*. 2nd ed. Grand Rapids, MI: Baker Academic, 2014. As the title indicates, this work focuses on application that takes seriously the grand narrative of the Bible. I particularly appreciate its application on the worldview level.

Goldsworthy, Graeme. *Preaching the Whole Bible as Christian Scripture: The Application of Biblical Theology to Expository Preaching*. Grand Rapids, MI: Eerdmans, 2000. Goldsworthy considers the nature of the Bible as a whole before providing helpful guidance on preaching from every genre.

Lawrence, Michael. *Biblical Theology in the Life of the Church: A Guide for Ministry*. Wheaton, IL: Crossway, 2010. Lawrence contends that one's working understanding to what the Bible is (not just a *right* understanding) will shape their ministry. In this work, therefore, Lawrence argues for a hermeneutically wise and biblical-theologically founded systematic theology that results in practical application in local church settings.

Piper, John. *Think: The Life of the Mind and the Love of God*. Wheaton, IL: Crossway, 2010. This is a very helpful and accessible book that emphasizes the life of the mind in ways that result in love of God and not arrogance.

For Advanced Study

Greidanus, Sidney. *Preaching Christ from the Old Testament: A Contemporary Hermeneutical Method*. Grand Rapids, MI: Eerdmans, 1999. I put this work in the advanced section merely because of its size, not its complexity; it is actually an easy read. Greidanus distinguishes well between allegory and typology, and provides steps toward christological sermons that deal well with the literary and historical contexts of the Old Testament.

Vanhoozer, Kevin J., and Daniel J. Treier. *Theology and the Mirror of Scripture: A Mere Evangelical Account*. Studies in Christian Doctrine and Scripture. Downers Grove, IL: IVP Academic, 2015. This work makes application to larger cultural, and even global, considerations for evangelical unity, particularly in light of our commitment to the authority of Scripture and its central teachings: the Trinity and the gospel.

CONCLUSION

From Him and Through Him and to Him Are All Things

†

HAVE YOU EVER NOTICED how much the Bible trades in ecological imagery? It is all over the place. Of course, it is in Genesis 1–2. Then the Lord says he "bore [Israel] on eagles' wings" (Ex 19:4). The tabernacle is decorated with pomegranates and tree-like features (Ex 39:24-26, 33, 37). Israel is a "vine" the Lord "plants" in the land (Ps 80:8; Jer 32:41). The exile is described as a kind of uncreation (Is 24). The return from exile will be a time when "the mountains and the hills . . . break forth into singing, and all the trees of the field shall clap their hands" (Is 55:12). Then, of course, Jesus performs a host of nature miracles (Mt 8:23–9:8; Jn 2:1-11). And Paul says, "if anyone is in Christ, he is a new creation" (2 Cor 5:17). Finally, the eternal state is full of rivers, trees, leaves, fruit, light, earth, and sky (Rev 21–22). This kind of imagery seems to naturally percolate from the Creator's continual insistence to reclaim what he originally made, and so the language is used throughout his self-revelation. The Creator is also the speaker.

Throughout this book I have tried to use nature images as metaphors for the tenets of hermeneutics. It seems only fitting given the arboreal imagery of the Bible. The additional advantage, though, has been the opportunity to talk again and again about *contexts*, for all ecosystems intermarry diverse contextual realities and, as we have seen, so does hermeneutics. So allow me one more such illustration, the biggest one yet. The largest ecological system is our solar system. All environments on Earth are directly related to the relationship of the Earth to the sun. Because the Earth tilts on a 23.5 degree axis and orbits approximately 92 million miles from the sun, life on Earth is what it is. These constants exist because the sun exerts a gravitational force on the Earth to keep it in orbit. If the sun were to lose its gravity, shrink in size, or simply disappear, the Earth would jettison off in a straight line into the cold uninhabitable universe. The same is equally true with all the other planets. The sun, therefore, keeps everything else in its proper location, and planets do not get lost nor do they bump into each other. And therein lies the connection with hermeneutics. Hermeneutics, as a discipline, is like the sun in the middle of a ministerial solar system. It is the gravitational loadstar that orients all other ministry practices. One's hermeneutic directly influences their interpretation of passages, and therefore their systematic theology, and therefore what they perceive in church history, and therefore how they assess their cultural moment, and finally therefore how they execute preaching, discipleship, counseling, evangelism and so forth. These other disciplines and practices are like the planets. The nature of the hermeneutical sun at the center will line up such ideas and ministries in a determinative pattern. The danger, then, is that an illegitimate or unethical hermeneutic will, over time, send our minds and ministries along equally illegitimate and unethical trajectories. Or, not to have a conscious and deliberate hermeneutic will result in a disorganized theology and chaotic ministry. Pull the sun from the solar system and the planets all spin off in disparate directions.

But this is really only the *second* reason why hermeneutics are so important. The *first* reason is far more basic. Our approach to Scripture will greatly influence whether the text points us to God or serves as a mirror of ourselves. A legitimate and ethical hermeneutic guards us, therefore, against creating God in our own image. Reading is hard, and there are a lot of personal and cultural crosscurrents that can sway us in our interpretation in ways we are not even aware. Thus we become unwitting servants to "the tyranny of hidden presuppositions." We see what we are predisposed to see, and we do not see what we are not ready to see. If, therefore, the Bible is the locus where the risen Lord speaks, then we need methods to clearly hear the voice of the Good Shepherd through such personal and cultural static.

For guidance in all this we look, as would be expected, to the Bible itself, and notice how biblical authors both wrote and read each other in *literary* context, *historical* context, and *redemptive-historical/christological* context. They attended to large literary units, thought historically, and saw all of God's purposes coalescing around Jesus' person and work. In turn, "their stance and method as interpreters are normative for us; we are their apprentices in the art of reading Scripture, learning from them how to understand Christ (and all things) in the light of Scripture and Scripture (and all things) in the light of Christ."[1] In short, "a Christian hermeneutic is grammatical-historical-biblical-theological."[2]

Literary context involves understanding the flow of thought through *an entire book* as the parts interact with the whole to give one coherent metatheology. Each book holds itself together and aims to drive home one main point to which all subpoints are angled. Attention to these dynamics helps us avoid atomizing verses or pericopes and gives us confidence that our interpretations of the verses and pericopes are nonetheless appropriately oriented to the rest of the book.

Attending to a book's historical contexts is critical because the books of the Bible were always written in response to historical events. Knowing

---

[1]David I. Starling, *Hermeneutics as Apprenticeship: How the Bible Shapes Our Interpretive Habits and Practices* (Grand Rapids, MI: Baker Academic, 2016), 19.

[2]Dane C. Ortlund, "Reflections on Handling the Old Testament as Jesus Would Have Us: Psalm 15 as a Case Study," *Themelios* 42 (2017): 78.

something of the latter, therefore, is indispensable to understanding the former, lest we read these books as though their first level of engagement were our own world and our own problems. To ignore historical dynamics and read the Bible for "what it says to me" is not the pious devotion of engagement with God, but the beginning of eisegesis. Additionally, authors and audiences have a tacit shared knowledge that makes communication efficient. If we do not join in that cognitive environment then it is easy to miss the point on the one hand, and simply misconstrue the point on the other. Moreover, a historic mindedness is simply core to the Christian worldview. It is, therefore, unnatural (and not slightly un-Christian) to think and read ahistorically.

Christological contexts attune us to the way the Old Testament anticipates a time when the developments of redemptive history would culminate in its intended goal; its expectations would be realized and its hopes consummated. The New Testament writers saw this historical climax in Jesus' life, death, resurrection, outpouring of the Holy Spirit, creation of the church, and the international preaching of the gospel. Thus, "Jesus is the prism by which the OT promises are beautifully refracted in the Church."[3] The biblical currency for this is quotations, literary echoes and allusions, prophecy, typology, major recurring themes, and the canonical role of whole-book contexts. With such considerations we conclude that the Old Testament is christo*telic*, the New Testament is christo*centric*, and the entire Bible is christo*logical*.

Yet, there is a danger in *underinterpreting* the Old Testament in our zeal to "get to Jesus." In aiming for an ethical and legitimate hermeneutic, we need a way of understanding the christological context of any verse, pericope, and passage that runs in tandem with literary and historical contexts as well. We do not want to bully over the Old Testament or to flatten out the beautiful landscape of the Old Testament; we want to see the big picture *and* the intricate details. The Old Testament's many tributaries empty confluently into the New Testament sea of christological

---

[3] David Schrock, "From Beelines to Plotlines: Typology That Follows the Covenantal Topography of Scripture," *SBJT* 21 (2017): 46.

fulfillment; only we also want to observe all the nuanced terrain through the Old Testament riverscape on the way. When we do, we actually appreciate *more* of Christ as we let the various genres and literary techniques of the Old Testament dictate at what *pace* we "get to Jesus," and what it is specifically about Jesus we will see when we get there. Some paths will be direct and quick. Others will be subtle and require our patience. And it will be that *careful attention to literary and historical contexts that provide the controls so as not to run off into allegory.*

In attending to these three layers of context we will have more *coherent* interpretations. Books themselves, and the Bible as a whole, have an innate integrity. Interpretations, therefore, that cohere well with a text's literary parts, historical and cultural milieu under which it was written, and its gospel-logic will be legitimate, and therefore also ethical. What makes one interpretation better than another? The answer is, *demonstrated coherency with literary, historical, and christological contexts.*

As these three come together, we have genre. Genre is a literary consideration, but also a historical reality as we see various redemptive-historical epochs call for their diversity. When navigating the attributes of different genres, therefore, it is crucial to keep in mind the development of the canon on *covenantal* axes. Remembering this will help us appreciate better what these genres are trying to accomplish and what we can expect from them.

When we take account of all this, we can then finally turn our attention to application. If these hermeneutical issues drive the train, application *naturally* also becomes literary, historical, and christological. Again, we must remember that we too live in contexts: the contexts of the universal church, our local church, our family, neighborhood, work, and so on. Application that runs through these channels helps guard us against treating the Bible as a collection of pithy one-lines meant to help us navigate our difficult postmodern lives, placebos for getting through the week. But instead, the Bible becomes our worldview-redirecting metadrama that we ourselves inhabit to the end of being conformed into the image of the true man and image-bearer, Jesus Christ. For "the history of salvation [provides] the identity of the worshiper and the reason for worship."[4]

Would you not agree with me that the Bible is simply beautiful!? The way its parts work together to form the whole, the diversity that coheres in unity, and above all the subject and object of the Bible, the Lord Jesus Christ, are all just breathtaking! God is glorious, and all his works are perfect. So we are not surprised that the book that reveals him would bear the same characteristics. Chapter five of the *Westminster Confession of Faith* states,

> the heavenliness of the matter, the efficacy of the doctrine, the majesty of the style, the consent of all the parts, the scope of the whole (which is, to give all glory to God), the full discovery it makes of the only way of man's salvation, the many other incomparable excellencies, and the entire perfection thereof, are arguments whereby it doth abundantly evidence itself to be the Word of God.

Amen! Reading the Word of God *ethically and legitimately*, therefore, glorifies our Creator and Savior, edifies the church, and results in a plausible worldview to fuel our worship and witness. No wonder, after Paul reflects on redemptive history and its climax in the gospel for eleven chapters in Romans, quoting, echoing, and alluding to much of Scripture along the way, he concludes:

> Oh, the depth of the riches and wisdom and knowledge of God!
>   How unsearchable are his judgments and how inscrutable his ways!
> "For who has known the mind of the Lord,
>   or who has been his counselor?"
> "Or who has given a gift to him that he might be repaid?"
> For from him and through him and to him are all things.
>   To him be glory forever. Amen.

---

[4]Graeme Goldsworthy, *Christ-Centered Biblical Theology: Hermeneutical Foundations and Principles* (Downers Grove, IL: IVP Academic, 2012), 66.

GLOSSARY OF
HERMENEUTICAL TERMS

a priori—describing beliefs held before observation and experience

accretion—a layer of material that slowly grows on a surface; used by the Reformers to speak of extrabiblical doctrines that developed in the Middle Ages

Alexandria/Alexandrians—famous Egyptian city at the mouth of the Nile; known for its learning, philosophy, and "Great Library"; its most influential biblical interpreters had an appreciation for Greek philosophy and used it to demonstrate that Christianity was not a philosophically regressive system; resulted in the (sometimes excessive) use of allegory

allegory—an interpretive method that digs under the straightforward literary and historical sense of the text to find a hidden, mystical meaning, usually in concert with the immediate philosophical and ethical concerns of the reader; the hermeneutical antithesis to typology

Antioch/Antiochenes—early major city of Christian influence; its interpreters were known for emphasizing the historical locatedness of biblical texts, and found meaning inherently bound to the actual events they describe; more prone to use typology than allegory

antitype—the corresponding element of Christ's person and work that provides the climactic meaning of a type or several types

apocalypse—a genre of biblical literature that provides a theological interpretation of historical events in Old Testament symbols to emphasize the Messiah's sovereignty

background—a book that explains the customs, worldview, and recent major events at the time a biblical text was written

biblical theology—a term used for several methodological approaches to biblical studies; in this book the term biblical theology is primarily used to describe the discipline of study that understands the Scriptures as the record of the history of salvation, or redemptive history, as the coherent witness to God's actions in history for the salvation and redemption of humanity, culminating in the person and work of Jesus Christ canon—the sixty-six books of the Old and New Testament which the early church recognized as inspired by God

ceremonial law—a subgenre of biblical literature that provides instructions for priests as they minister in the tabernacle or temple in typological preparation for the great high priestly ministry of Jesus Christ

chiasm—a type of inclusio that incorporates an organized middle section with mirroring components; the effect is to highlight the very middle within the context or frame of the outer components

christocentric—describing ideas or interpretations that conceptually revolve around the person and work of Christ; used to describe the way the New Testament ideologically centers on Jesus

christological—pertaining to the person and work of Christ as a unifying rationale; used as an umbrella term to describe the way the gospel brings coherency to the Bible in its entirety

christotelic—an overall orientation and goal toward the person and work of Christ; used to describe the nature in which the Old Testament progressively leads to Jesus

climactic meaning—an interpretation in full light of the person and work of Christ

close reading—giving careful attention to intricate and big-picture details so as to appreciate the literary artistry of a text

coherency—the attribute of a book wherein its various parts fit together, or relate to and depend on each other; the attribute of an interpretation that can demonstrate such relationship between a book's parts thereby commending that interpretation's legitimacy

commentary—a style of book that discusses the details of a biblical book by way of verse-by-verse consideration; usually emphasizing either an interpretive tradition, helps for devotional reading, sermon preparation, theological reflection, or the historical milieu of the biblical author and/or first audience

covenantal genealogy—a subgenre of biblical literature that lists names in a way that supplements narratives and provides a theological angle on historical events

covenantal history—a genre of biblical literature that narrates redemptive-historical events vis-à-vis the most recent covenant

covenantal law—a genre of biblical literature that stipulates prescriptive, descriptive, and ceremonial laws for God's people vis-à-vis their place in redemptive history

covenantal poetry—a genre of biblical literature that particularly employs parallelism and vivid imagery in an expression of Israel's kingdom and eschatological hopes

covenantal prophecy—a diverse genre of biblical literature that particularly employs near-and-far visions in an expression of Israel's kingdom and eschatological hopes

covenantal wisdom—a poetic genre of biblical literature that expresses the wisdom by which David's sons are to lead the people of God

deconstructionism—a philosophical approach to reading that searches for ways to move the center of interpretation away from traditional and historically common emphases, and giving voice to the characters and ideas at the margins deism/deists—the belief that God created but is not involved in the world in any ongoing way

demythologization—an interpretive approach to the Bible that reinterprets miraculous and dogmatic elements in terms of modern and postmodern sensibilities; coined by Rudolf Bultmann

descriptive law—a subgenre of biblical literature that describes how God's prescriptive law should be applied at a particular moment in redemptive history

discourse analysis—the study of grammatical and syntactical details of a pericope or passage that work developmentally within the overall flow of thought from beginning to end of an entire book

eisegesis—the process of reading foreign ideas into the biblical text; the opposite of exegesis

empiricism—the philosophical commitment to the idea that only that which can be discerned through the human senses can provide certainty of truth

Enlightenment—the period of history (roughly the eighteenth and nineteenth centuries) in the West marked by confidence in autonomous human cognitive abilities

epistemology—the study of how we know, how we learn, synthesize knowledge, remember, etc.

eschatology—the study of matters pertaining to accomplishing God's last purposes or goals in redemption

ethical interpretation—a reading that respects the will of the author as discerned in the text, and leads audiences to an appropriate application of the text

exegesis—the process of drawing the meaning out of the biblical text; the opposite of eisegesis

existentialism—the Western philosophical reaction to nihilism, driven by the human need to create one's own identity in postmodernity's atheistic vacuum of meaning; necessitates a high view of free will and human autonomy

first level meaning—a pericope's meaning vis-à-vis its literary context only

flow of thought—the main idea running through a passage, pericope, or book; discerned through discourse analysis

frames—cues and major ideas in a text that guide readers in an overall system of interpretation; these can be literary, cultural or historical

general inquiry—an investigation into basic questions of geography, history, culture, etc.; typically accomplished with a strong study Bible

Hellenism—the historical and philosophical designation for Greek culture in the time of Jesus and the apostles

hermeneutical spiral—the cognitive process by which the Bible interrupts and corrects our presuppositions; typically accomplished through self-awareness and constant Bible reading

hermeneutics—the theoretical study of the science and art of how to legitimately and ethically interpret texts

higher criticism—the academic practice of attempting to recreate the historical events that lay behind the testimony of a text; typically done with a philosophical precommitment to the impossibility of miracles; sometimes called the "historical critical method" hinge verse/pericope—those parts of a text where the flow of thought significantly takes a new direction

historical critical method—see higher criticism

history of salvation—see redemptive history

hypermodernism/hypermodernity—an alternative term for postmodernism; preferred by some for its emphasis that the current Western philosophical climate is marked less by something after modernity, but rather the fruits or results of modernity

incarnation—the historical event in which the second person of the Trinity added the full human nature (without sin) to his divine nature

inclusio—a set of repeated terms or ideas at the beginning and end of a pericope, passage, or book that create a context or frame for the material in between

inspiration—the sovereign act of the Holy Spirit whereby he guided the authors of Scripture to write God's Word

integrity—the attribute of a book wherein its parts hold themselves together, providing everything necessary for the book's interpretation

introduction—a book that explores the historical background and other critical or interpretive issues surrounding individual books of the Bible

kingdom parable—a subgenre of biblical literature that compares elements of the kingdom to typical life scenarios in a way that supplement narratives

large-scale biblical literacy—a familiarity not only with the stories and teachings of the Bible, but also how they all come together into a coherent whole

legitimate interpretation—a reading that commends itself by its respect of a book's integrity and ability to express the book's coherency

liquid modernity—an alternative term for postmodernism; preferred by some for its emphasis on the elasticity and transiency of Western cultures

loadbearing verse—those parts of a text that provide particular interpretive insight into the rest of the text; commonly a climax to developing ideas in the flow of thought

metanarrative—an all-encompassing and totalizing story (or worldview principally expressed in a story) that provides an interpretation and judgment on other stories; the rejection of such being a hallmark of postmodernity

metatheology—a book's overall message to which its finer theological teachings contribute

missiological epistle—a genre of biblical literature that extends the gospel to distant lands, with argumentation in mostly lineal flows of thought

modernism/modernity—the philosophical school of thought and cultural experience, throughout and following the Enlightenment of the eighteenth and nineteenth centuries; marked by confidence in autonomous human cognitive abilities, giving ascendency to rationalism, empiricism, and naturalism

naturalism—the philosophical commitment to the idea that only matter exists, and all phenomena can be explained in terms of observable and predictable chains of cause and effect near-and-far prophecy—a description of the way several successive events that share a theologically conceptual alignment are described in one oracle

nihilism—the Western philosophical consequence of naturalism, emphasizing the lack of meaning in history, ethics, and the human experience

parallelism—a poetic literary device where multiple lines repeat similar ideas with different emphases, usually to heighten the intensity of the previous statement, or to reverse the viewpoint of the previous statement

passage—several pericopes functioning together to make up a discrete larger section of a book

pericope—a discrete, self-contained story or teaching with a discernable beginning, middle, and end (the plural is pericopae or pericopes)

person of Christ—an umbrella term to speak of who Jesus is with particular focus on his human and divine natures, as well as the particular roles he fulfills in the scope of Israel's eschatological expectations (prophet, priest, king, and sage, for example)

Platonism—the ancient belief that all objects and events in this world reflect ideal forms outside of time and space

postmodernism/postmodernity—a descriptive term for the Western philosophical and cultural experience after modernity; seen by some as a reaction to or consequence of modernity, and seen by others as more of a result or development of modernity; marked by a disappointment in the unfulfilled promises of the Enlightenment, "an incredulity toward metanarratives," and the philosophical commitment to the idea that truth is relative to the community in which one participates

prescriptive law—a subgenre of biblical literature that lists the moral behavior expected of God's image bearers, grounded in creation and the exodus; the Ten Commandments

presuppositional repair—the process by which unbiblical preconceptions are challenged through self-awareness and constant Bible reading to draw the reader's worldview into closer alignment with that of the Scriptures

presuppositions—assumptions, precommitments, and expectations a reader has before engaging a text; a belief one supposes by which they filter observations and experiences; commonly held, though not always, a priori

progressive revelation—the process by which the Scriptures were inspired over time, each subsequent part reacting to and developing the prior

prophetic telescoping—see near-and-far prophecy

Quadriga, the—a medieval development of Origen's multiple levels of interpretation into four senses: the literal, the allegorical, the moral, and the anagogic (the nature of future hope)

rationalism—the philosophical commitment to the elevation of human reason as the arbiter for judging that which can be considered true

reader-response—an approach to interpretation wherein meaning is located in the experience of reading; bringing one's presuppositions and precommitments to bear in interpretation reading in and out—a process for discerning the influence of the literary context by reading increasingly larger passages around a pericope

redemptive history—the sum of historical events, as well as the recording and interpretation thereof, that testify to God's redeeming acts in the course of time and space; sometimes called the "history of salvation," "salvation history," or *heilsgeschichte*

Reformation, the—the northern European reaction to Roman Catholic dogmas seen as unbiblical in the sixteenth century, marked by a commitment to *sola Scriptura* and its doctrinal consequences; commonly called the "Protestant Reformation"

relativism—the philosophical commitment to the idea that there are no objective standards for what is good, true, or beautiful, but that such matters are adjudicated by individuals or communities for themselves

resurrection—the historical event by which the man Jesus Christ was raised bodily and gloriously from the dead, forming the Christian hope that all his followers will share in the same such experience at his return

revelation—the miraculous communication of God to humanity through signs, wonders, visions, theophanies, inspiration, etc., most clearly and consummately in the person and work of Jesus Christ; now codified in the sixty-six books of the Bible

sane imagination—the ability of the reader to appreciate how a text would have resonated with its original readers; constructed by a responsible study of history

second level meaning—a pericope's meaning vis-à-vis its literary and historical contexts together

sola Scriptura—the theological commitment that the Bible is the highest (and thus ultimately the only) authority that can bind consciences and adjudicate between differing doctrinal perspectives; coined as a term in the Reformation but a commitment that long predates that

study Bible—a translation of the Bible that includes editorial notes that help readers in interpretation

text-driven inquiry—an investigation into questions of interpretation raised by the text (an entire testament, book, passage, pericope, or verse); typically accomplished with the use of backgrounds, introductions, and commentaries

textual controls—literary details that limit the possible range of legitimate interpretations

textual markers—cues in a text that signal a transition to a new idea or pericope, a conclusion to a running idea, or a change in the flow of thought; often technical literary devices or simple transitional phrases

topic-driven inquiry—an investigation into questions of interpretation raised by the reader's interest in broad biblical and historical themes; typically accomplished with the use of Bible dictionaries, encyclopedias, and atlases

type—a redemptive-historical person, institution, or event that prefigures the person and work of Christ; often seen in recurring patterns in several theologically aligned persons, institutions, and events typology—a hermeneutical conviction that God has sovereignly organized history and revelation such that Old Testament persons, institutions, and events prefigure the person and work of Christ in concert with literary genre and history; the hermeneutical antithesis to allegory

West, the—a broad term used to describe the culture, history, and lands most influenced by the European Enlightenment and subsequent philosophical movements

whole-book context—a consideration of how the scope and content of an entire book come to bear on understanding a single verse or pericope

work of Christ—an umbrella term that summarizes what Jesus has accomplished (and is still accomplishing) in his ministry, principally in relation to his teaching, miracles, death on the cross, resurrection, ascension and current session, the giving of the Spirit, and the creation and upbuilding of the church

worldview—a synthesis of beliefs concerning major metaphysical issues (origins, ethics, knowledge, fundamental problem with humanity, the meaning of history, etc.) that provides interpretive orientation for understanding and navigating life

Zeitgeist—the collection of pervasive and dominant philosophical ideals at any given cultural moment; also called "the spirit of the age"

BIBLIOGRAPHY

Albright, W. F., and C. S. Mann. *Matthew: A New Translation with Introduction and Commentary.* Anchor Bible 26. New York: Doubleday, 1971.

Alexander, T. Desmond. "From Adam to Judah: The Significance of the Family Tree in Genesis." *Evangelical Quarterly* 61 (1989): 5-19.

———. *From Eden to the New Jerusalem: An Introduction to Biblical Theology.* Grand Rapids, MI: Kregel Academic, 2008.

———. "Genealogies, Seed and Compositional Unity of Genesis." *Tyndale Bulletin* 44 (1993): 255-70.

———. "Messianic Ideology in the Book of Genesis." In *The Lord's Anointed: Interpretation of Old Testament Messianic Texts*, edited by Philip E. Satterthwaite, Richard S. Hess, and Gordon J. Wenham, 19-39. Carlisle, UK: Paternoster. Reprint, Grand Rapids, MI: Baker Books, 1995.

Alexander, T. Desmond, Brian S. Rosner, D. A. Carson, and Graeme Goldsworthy. *New Dictionary of Biblical Theology: Exploring the Unity and Diversity of Scripture.* IVP Reference Collection. Downers Grove, IL: IVP Academic, 2000.

Alkier, Stefan. "Intertextuality and the Semiotics of Biblical Texts." In *Reading the Bible Intertextually*, edited by Richard B. Hays, Stefan Alkier, and Leroy A. Huizenga, 3-22. Waco, TX: Baylor University Press, 2009.

Alter, Robert. *The Art of Biblical Narrative.* Upd. and rev. ed.; New York: Basic Books, 1981.

Ansberry, Christopher B. *Be Wise, My Son, and Make My Heart Glad: An Exploration of the Courtly Nature of the Book of Proverbs.* Beihefte zur Zeitschrift für die alttestamentliche Wissenschaft 422. Berlin: de Gruyter, 2011.

Arnold, Bill T., and Brent A. Strawn. *The World around the Old Testament: The People and Places of the Ancient Near East.* Grand Rapids, MI: Baker Academic, 2016.

Arnold, Bill T., and Bryan E. Beyer, eds. *Readings from the Ancient Near East: Primary Sources for Old Testament Study.* Grand Rapids, MI: Baker Academic, 2002.

August, Jared M. "The Messianic Hope of Genesis: The *Protoevangelium* and Patriarchal Promises." *Themelios* 42 (2017): 46-62.

Augustine. *On Christian Doctrine.* Edited by Philip Schaff. *The Nicene and Post-Nicene Fathers*, Series 1. 1886–1889. 14 vols. Reprint, Peabody, MA: Hendrickson, 1994.

Barber, Michael Patrick. "Jesus as the Davidic Temple Builder and Peter's Priestly Role in Matthew 16:16-19." *Journal of Biblical Literature* 132 (2013): 935-53.

Barrett, C. K. ed. *The New Testament Background: Writings from Ancient Greece and the Roman Empire That Illuminate Christian Origins.* San Francisco: HarperOne, 1989.

Bartholomew, Craig G., and Michael W. Goheen. *The Drama of Scripture: Finding Our Place in the Biblical Story.* 2nd ed. Grand Rapids, MI: Baker Academic, 2014.

Bauckham, Richard. *The Theology of the Book of Revelation.* Cambridge: Cambridge University Press, 1993.

Beale, G. K. "The Eschatological Conception of New Testament Theology." In *Eschatology in Bible & Theology: Evangelical Essays at the Dawn of a New Millennium,* edited by Kent E. Brower and Mark W. Elliott, 11-52. Downers Grove, IL: InterVarsity Press, 1997.

———. *Handbook on the New Testament Use of the Old Testament: Exegesis and Interpretation.* Grand Rapids, MI: Baker Academic, 2012.

———. *A New Testament Biblical Theology: The Unfolding of the Old Testament in the New.* Grand Rapids, MI: Baker Academic, 2011.

———, ed. *The Right Doctrine from the Wrong Text?: Essays on the Use of the Old Testament in the New.* Grand Rapids, MI: Baker Academic, 1994.

Beale, G. K., and D. A. Carson, eds. *Commentary on the New Testament Use of the Old Testament.* Grand Rapids, MI: Baker Academic, 2007.

Blomberg, Craig L. *Interpreting the Parables.* 2nd ed. Downers Grove, IL: InterVarsity Press, 2012.

Boersma, Hans. *Scripture as Real Presence: Sacramental Exegesis in the Early Church.* Grand Rapids, MI: Baker Academic, 2017.

Bray, Gerald. *Biblical Interpretation: Past & Present.* Downers Grove, IL: InterVarsity Press, 1996.

Brendsel, Daniel J. "Plots, Themes, and Responsibilities: The Search for a Center of Biblical Theology Reexamined." *Themelios* 35 (2010): 400-412.

Brown, Jeannine K. "Creation's Renewal in the Gospel of John." *Catholic Biblical Quarterly* 72 (2010): 275-90.

———. *Scripture as Communication: Introducing Biblical Hermeneutics.* Grand Rapids, MI: Baker Academic, 2007.

Bryan, Christopher. *Listening to the Bible: The Art of Faithful Biblical Interpretation.* Oxford: Oxford University Press, 2014.

Bultmann, Rudolf. *New Testament and Mythology, and Other Basic Writings.* Edited and translated by Schubert M. Ogden. Philadelphia: Fortress, 1984.

Caird, G. B. *New Testament Theology.* Completed and edited by L. D. Hurst. Oxford: Oxford University Press, 1994.

Calvin, John. *Commentaries on the Four Last Books of Moses: Arranged in the Form of a Harmony.* Translated by Charles William Bingham. 2 vols. Edinburgh: Calvin Translation Society, 1845-1846. Reprint. Grand Rapids, MI: Baker Books, 1979.

———. *Commentary on a Harmony of the Evangelists, Matthew, Mark, and Luke.* Translated by William Pringle. 3 vol. Edinburgh: Calvin Translation Society, 1845–1846. Reprint, Grand Rapids, MI: Baker Books, 1981.

———. *The Institutes of the Christian Religion.* Edited by John T. McNeill. Translated by Ford Lewis Battles. 2 vols. Philadelphia: Westminster, 1960.

Carson, D. A., and Douglas J. Moo. *An Introduction to the New Testament.* 2nd ed. Grand Rapids, MI: Zondervan, 2005.

Carson, D. A., and H. G. M. Williamson. *It Is Written: Scripture Citing Scripture: Essays in Honour of Barnabas Lindars.* Cambridge: Cambridge University Press, 1988.

Chalmers, Aaron. *Interpreting the Prophets: Reading, Understanding and Preaching from the Worlds of the Prophets.* Downers Grove, IL: InterVarsity Press, 2015.

Chapell, Bryan. *Christ-Centered Preaching: Redeeming that Expository Sermon.* 2nd ed. Grand Rapids, MI: Baker Academic, 2005.

Charlesworth, James H., ed. *The Old Testament Pseudepigrapha.* 2 vols. Anchor Bible Reference Library. New York: Doubleday, 1983–1985.

Childs, Brevard S. *Biblical Theology of the Old and New Testaments: Theological Reflections on the Christian Bible.* Philadelphia: Fortress, 1993.

Clement of Alexandria. *Exhortation to the Heathen.* Edited by Alexander Roberts, and James Donaldson. *The Ante-Nicene Fathers.* 1885–1887. 10 vols. Reprint, Peabody, MA: Hendrickson, 1994.

Clowney, Edmund P. *Preaching Christ in All of Scripture.* Wheaton, IL: Crossway, 2003.

———. *The Unfolding Mystery: Discovering Christ in the Old Testament.* Phillipsburg, NJ: P&R, 1988.

Collins, John J. "Introduction: Towards the Morphology of a Genre." *Semeia* 14 (1979): 1-20.

Collins, John J., and Daniel C. Harlow, eds. *The Eerdmans Dictionary of Early Judaism.* Grand Rapids, MI: Eerdmans, 2010.

Collins, Jon, and Tim Mackie. "The Bible Project." www.thebibleproject.com.

Coogan, Michael, D., Marc Z. Brettler, Carol A. Newsom, and Pheme Perkins, eds. *The New Oxford Annotated Apocrypha.* 5th ed. Oxford: Oxford University Press, 2018.

Crouch, Andy. *Culture Making: Recovering Our Creative Calling.* Downers Grove, IL: InterVarsity Press, 2008.

Crowe, Brandon D. *The Last Adam: A Theology of the Obedient Life of Jesus in the Gospels.* Grand Rapids, MI: Baker Academic, 2017.

Currid, John D. *Against the Gods: The Polemical Theology of the Old Testament.* Wheaton, IL: Crossway, 2013.

———. *Ecclesiastes: A Quest for Meaning?* Welwyn Commentary Series. Welwyn Garden City: Evangelical Press, 2015.

———. *A Study Commentary on Exodus.* 2 vols. Darlington: Evangelical Press, 2000–2001.

———. *A Study Commentary on Genesis.* 2 vols. Darlington: Evangelical Press, 2003–2004.

Currid, John D., and David P. Barrett, eds. *Crossway ESV Bible Atlas.* Wheaton, IL: Crossway, 2010.

Daniélou, Jean. *From Shadows to Reality.* Translated by Wulstan Hibberd. Studies in the Biblical Theology of the Fathers. Westminster, MD: Newman, 1960.

————. *The Lord of History: Reflections on the Inner Meaning of History.* Translated by Nigel Abercrombie. London: Longmans, 1958.

Davis, Dale Ralph. *2 Kings: The Power and the Fury.* Focus on the Bible. Fearn, Ross-Shire: Christian Focus, 2005.

DeClaissé-Walford, Nancy, Rolf A. Jacobson, and Beth LaNeel Tanner. *The Book of Psalms.* New International Commentary on the Old Testament. Grand Rapids, MI: Eerdmans, 2014.

Dempster, Stephen G. *Dominion and Dynasty: A Theology of the Hebrew Bible.* New Studies in Biblical Theology 15. Downers Grove, IL: InterVarsity Press, 2003.

————. "From Slight Peg to Cornerstone to Capstone: The Resurrection of Christ on 'The Third Day' According to the Scriptures." *Westminster Theological Journal* 76 (2014): 371-409.

DeRouchie, Jason S. *How to Understand and Apply the Old Testament: Twelve Steps from Exegesis to Theology.* Phillipsburg, NJ: P&R, 2017.

Dockery, David S. "New Testament Interpretation: A Historical Survey." In *Interpreting the New Testament: Essays on Methods and Issues,* edited by David Alan Black and Davis S. Dockery, 41-71. Nashville: B&H, 2001.

Dodd, C. H. *According to the Scriptures: The Sub-Structure of New Testament Theology.* London: Nisbet, 1952.

Doriani, Daniel M. *Getting the Message: A Plan for Interpreting and Applying the Bible.* Phillipsburg, NJ: P&R, 1996.

Dorsey, David A. *The Literary Structure of the Old Testament: A Commentary on Genesis–Malachi.* Grand Rapids, MI: Baker Academic, 1999.

Dumbrell, William J. *The End of the Beginning: Revelation 21–22 and the Old Testament.* The Moore Theological College Lectures 1983. Grand Rapids, MI: Baker Academic, 1985. Reprint, Eugene, OR: Wipf & Stock, 2001.

————. *The Search for Order: Biblical Eschatology in Focus.* Eugene, OR: Wipf & Stock, 1994.

Dyrness, William A., and Veli-Matti Kärkkäinen, eds. *Global Dictionary of Theology.* Downers Grove, IL: IVP Academic, 2008.

Eco, Umberto. *The Role of the Reader: Explorations in the Semiotics of Texts.* Advances in Semiotics. Bloomington: Indiana University Press, 1979.

Elliott, Mark W. "Allegory and Allegorical Interpretation." In *The Oxford Encyclopedia of Biblical Interpretation,* edited by Steven L. McKenzie, 1:17-27. 2 vols. Oxford: Oxford University Press, 2013.

Elwell, Walter A., and Robert W. Yarbrough, eds. *Readings from the First-Century World: Primary Sources for New Testament Study*. Encountering Biblical Studies. Grand Rapids, MI: Baker Academic, 1998.

Enns, Peter. *Inspiration and Incarnation: Evangelicals and the Problem of the Old Testament*. Grand Rapids, MI: Baker Academic, 2005.

Eswine, Zack. *Preaching to a Post-Everything World: Crafting Biblical Sermons That Connect with Our Culture*. Grand Rapids, MI: Baker Books, 2008.

Evans, John F. *A Guide to Biblical Commentaries and Reference Works*. 10th ed. Grand Rapids, MI: Zondervan Academic, 2016.

Fee, Gordon D., and Douglas Stuart. *How to Read the Bible Book by Book: A Guided Tour*. Grand Rapids, MI: Zondervan, 2002.

———. *How to Read the Bible for All Its Worth*. 2nd ed. Grand Rapids, MI: Zondervan, 1993.

———. *How to Read the Bible for All Its Worth*. 4th ed. Grand Rapids, MI: Zondervan, 2014.

Ferguson, Everett. *Backgrounds of Early Christianity*. 3rd ed. Grand Rapids, MI: Eerdmans, 2003.

Foulkes, Francis. "The Acts of God: A Study of the Basis of Typology in the Old Testament." In *The Right Doctrine from the Wrong Text?: Essays on the Use of the Old Testament in the New*, edited by G. K. Beale, 342-71. Grand Rapids, MI: Baker Academic, 1994. Reprint, from *The Acts of God: A Study of the Basis of Typology in the Old Testament*. Tyndale Old Testament Lectures 1955. London: Tyndale, 1958.

Froehlich, Karlfried, trans. and ed. *Biblical Interpretation in the Early Church*. Sources of Early Christian Thought. Philadelphia: Fortress, 1984.

———. "Thomas Aquinas." In *Dictionary of Major Biblical Interpreters*, edited by Donald K. McKim, 979-85. Downers Grove, IL: InterVarsity Press, 2007.

Gadamer, Hans-Georg. *Truth and Method*. Translation revised by Joel Weinsheimer and Donald G. Marshall. 2nd rev. ed. London/New York: Bloomsbury Academic, 2004.

Gage, Warren Austin, with Leah Grace Gage. *Milestones to Emmaus: The Third Day Resurrection in the Old Testament*. Fort Lauderdale, FL: St. Andrews House, 2015.

Gentry Peter J., and Stephen J. Wellum. *Kingdom through Covenant: A Biblical-Theological Understanding of the Covenants*. 2nd ed. Wheaton, IL: Crossway, 2018.

George, Timothy. *Reading Scripture with the Reformers*. Downers Grove, IL: IVP Academic, 2011.

———. *Theology of the Reformers*. Nashville: B&H, 1988.

Gladd, Benjamin L. *From Adam and Israel to the Church: A Biblical Theology of the People of God*. Essential Studies in Biblical Theology. Downers Grove, IL: InterVarsity Press, 2019.

Gladwell, Malcom. *David and Goliath: Underdogs, Misfits, and the Art of Battling Giants*. New York: Back Bay Books, 2015.

Goldingay, John. *Do We Need the New Testament?: Letting the Old Testament Speak for Itself*. Downers Grove, IL: IVP Academic, 2015.

Goldsworthy, Graeme. *According to Plan: The Unfolding Revelation of God in the Bible.* Downers Grove, IL: InterVarsity Press, 1991.

———. *Christ-Centered Biblical Theology: Hermeneutical Foundations and Principles.* Downers Grove, IL: IVP Academic, 2012.

———. *Gospel and Kingdom.* Carlisle: Paternoster, 1981.

———. *Gospel-Centered Hermeneutics: Foundations and Principles of Evangelical Biblical Interpretation.* Downers Grove, IL: IVP Academic, 2006.

———. *Preaching the Whole Bible as Christian Scripture: The Application of Biblical Theology to Expository Preaching.* Grand Rapids, MI: Eerdmans, 2000.

González, Justo L. *The Story of Christianity, Volume 1: The Early Church to the Dawn of the Reformation.* New York: HaperCollins, 1984.

Goppelt, Leonhard. *Typos: The Typological Interpretation of the Old Testament and the New.* Translated by Donald H. Madvig. Grand Rapids, MI: Eerdmans, 1982.

Gowan, Donald E. *Theology of the Prophetic Books: The Death & Resurrection of Israel.* Louisville: Westminster John Knox, 1998.

Graves, Michael, ed. *Biblical Interpretation in the Early Church.* Ad Fontes Early Christian Sources. Minneapolis: Fortress, 2017.

Green, Joel B., gen. ed. The New International Commentary on the New Testament. 21 vols. Grand Rapids, MI: Eerdmans, 1974–2020.

Green, Joel B., and Lee Martin McDonald, eds. *The World of the New Testament: Cultural, Social, and Historical Contexts.* Grand Rapids, MI: Baker Academic, 2013.

Gregory the Great. *Forty Gospel Homilies.* Translated by David Hurst. Kalamazoo, MI: Cistercian, 1990.

Greidanus, Sidney. *Preaching Christ from the Old Testament: A Contemporary Hermeneutical Method.* Grand Rapids, MI: Eerdmans, 1999.

Gundry, Robert H. *The Use of the Old Testament in St. Matthew's Gospel, With Special Reference to the Messianic Hope.* Supplements to Novum Testamentum 18. Leiden: Brill, 1967.

Gurtner, Daniel M. *The Torn Veil: Matthew's Exposition of the Death of Jesus.* Society for New Testament Studies Monograph Series 139. Cambridge: Cambridge University Press, 2007.

Guthrie, Donald. *New Testament Introduction.* 4th ed. Downers Grove, IL: IVP Academic, 1989.

Hall, Christopher A. *Reading Scripture with the Church Fathers.* Downers Grove, IL: InterVarsity Press, 1998.

Hamilton, James M., Jr. *God's Glory in Salvation through Judgment: A Biblical Theology.* Wheaton, IL: Crossway, 2010.

———. "The Skull Crushing Seed of the Woman: Inner-Biblical Interpretation of Genesis 3:15." *Southern Baptist Journal of Theology* 10.2 (2006): 30-54.

Harris, R. Laird, Gleason L. Archer, Jr., and Bruce K. Waltke, eds. *Theological Wordbook of the Old Testament.* 2 vols. Chicago: Moody, 1980.

Hasel, Gerhard. "Biblical Theology: Then, Now and Tomorrow." *Horizons in Biblical Theology* 4 (1982): 61-93.

——. "Proposals for a Canonical Biblical Theology." *Andrews University Seminary Studies* 34 (1996): 23-33.

Hays, Richard B. *The Conversion of the Imagination: Paul as Interpreter of Israel's Scripture.* Grand Rapids, MI: Eerdmans, 2005.

——. *Echoes of Scripture in the Gospels.* Waco, TX: Baylor University Press, 2016.

——. *Reading Backwards: Figural Christology and the Fourfold Gospel Witness.* Waco, TX: Baylor University Press, 2014.

Helm, David. *Expositional Preaching: How We Speak God's Word Today.* 9Marks Building Healthy Churches Series. Wheaton, IL: Crossway, 2014.

Hoffmeier, James K. *The Archaeology of the Bible.* Oxford: Lion Scholar, 2008.

Hoffmeier, James K. and Dennis R. Magary, eds. *Do Historical Matters Matter to Faith?: A Critical Appraisal of Modern and Postmodern Approaches to Scripture.* Wheaton, IL: Crossway, 2012.

Holland, Tom. *Contours of Pauline Theology: A Radical New Survey of the Influences on Paul's Biblical Writings.* Fearn, Ross-Shire: Mentor, 2004.

Holmes, Michael W., ed., *The Apostolic Fathers: Greek Texts and English Translations.* 3rd ed. Grand Rapids, MI: Baker Academic, 2007.

Hood, Jared C. "The Decalogue of Genesis 1-3." *Reformed Theological Review* 75 (2016): 35-59.

Hubbard, Robert L., Jr., and Bill T. Arnold, gen. eds. *The New International Commentary on the Old Testament.* 27 vols. Grand Rapids, MI: Eerdmans, 1976–2020.

Hunter, Trent, and Stephen Wellum. *Christ from Beginning to End: How the Full Story of Scripture Reveals the Full Glory of Christ.* Grand Rapids, MI: Zondervan, 2018.

Irenaeus. *Against Heresies.* Edited by Alexander Roberts and James Donaldson. *The Ante-Nicene Fathers.* 1885–1887. 10 vols. Reprint, Peabody, MA: Hendrickson, 1994.

The IVP Bible Dictionary Series. 8 vols. Downers Grove, IL: IVP Academic, 1993–2013.

Johnson, Dennis E. *The Message of Acts in the History of Redemption.* Phillipsburg, NJ: P&R, 1997.

——. *Walking with Jesus through His Word: Discovering Christ in All the Scriptures.* Phillipsburg, NJ: P&R, 2015.

Josephus. *The Works of Josephus: Complete and Unabridged.* Upd. ed. Translated by William Whiston. Peabody, MA: Hendrickson, 1987.

Kaiser, Walter C. *The Uses of the Old Testament in the New.* Chicago: Moody, 1985. Reprint, Eugene, OR: Wipf & Stock, 2001.

Keener, Craig S. *The IVP Bible Background Commentary: New Testament.* 2nd ed. Downers Grove, IL: InterVarsity Press, 2014.

Klink, Edward W. III, and Darian R. Lockett. *Understanding Biblical Theology: A Comparison of Theory and Practice.* Grand Rapids, MI: Zondervan, 2012.

Kraus, Hans-Joachim. "Calvin's Exegetical Principles." Translated by Keith Crim. *Interpretation* 31 (1977): 8-18.

Kruger, Michael J. *Canon Revisited: Establishing the Origins and Authority of the New Testament Books*. Wheaton, IL: Crossway, 2012.

Kynes, Will. "The 'Wisdom Literature' Category: An Obituary." *The Journal of Theological Studies* 69 (2018): 1-24.

Ladd, George Eldon. *A Theology of the New Testament*. Edited by Donald A. Hagner. Rev. ed. Grand Rapids, MI: Eerdmans, 1993.

———. *The Gospel of the Kingdom: Scriptural Studies in the Kingdom of God*. Grand Rapids, MI: Eerdmans, 1959.

Lawrence, Michael. *Biblical Theology in the Life of the Church: A Guide for Ministry*. Wheaton, IL: Crossway, 2010.

Leithart, Peter J. *Deep Exegesis: The Mystery of Reading Scripture*. Waco, TX: Baylor University Press, 2009.

———. "The Quadriga or Something Like It: A Biblical and Pastoral Defense." In *Ancient Faith for the Church's Future*, edited by Mark Husbands and Jeffrey P. Greenman, 110-25. Downers Grove, IL: IVP Academic, 2008.

Lints, Richard. *The Fabric of Theology: A Prolegomenon to Evangelical Theology*. Grand Rapids, MI: Eerdmans, 1993.

Litwak, Kenneth Duncan. *Echoes of Scripture in Luke-Acts: Telling the History of God's People Intertextually*. Journal for the Study of the New Testament Supplement Series 282. London: T&T Clark, 2005.

Longenecker, Richard N. *Biblical Exegesis in the Apostolic Period*. 2nd ed. Grand Rapids, MI: Eerdmans, 1999.

Longman, Tremper, III. *How to Read the Psalms*. Downers Grove, IL: InterVarsity Press, 1988.

Longman, Tremper, III, and Raymond Dillard, eds. *An Introduction to the Old Testament*. 2nd ed. Grand Rapids, MI: Zondervan Academic, 2006.

Louw, J. P. "Discourse Analysis and the Greek New Testament." *The Bible Translator* 24 (1973): 101-18.

Marcus, Joel. *Mark 8–16: A New Translation with Introduction and Commentary*. Anchor Yale Bible Commentaries. New Haven/London: Yale University Press, 2009.

McCartney, Dan, and Charles Clayton. *Let the Reader Understand: A Guide to Interpreting and Applying the Bible*. 2nd ed. Phillipsburg, NJ: P&R, 2002.

McCullough, Matthew. *Remember Death: The Surprising Path to Living Hope*. Wheaton, IL: Crossway, 2018.

McGrath, Alister E. *Reformation Thought: An Introduction*. 3rd ed. Oxford: Blackwell, 1999.

McKim, Donald K., ed. *Dictionary of Major Biblical Interpreters*. Downers Grove, IL: IVP Academic, 2007.

Melito of Sardis. *The Catena on Genesis*. Edited by Alexander Roberts, and James Donaldson. The Ante-Nicene Fathers. 1885–1887. 10 vols. Reprint, Peabody, MA: Hendrickson, 1994.

———. *On Pascha.* Translated by Alistair Stewart-Sykes. *On Pascha: With the Fragments of Melito and Other Material Related to the Quartodecimans.* Popular Patristics Series. Crestwood, NY: St. Vladimir's Seminary Press, 2001.

Merrill, Eugene H., Mark F. Rooker, and Michael A. Grisanti. *The World and the Word: An Introduction to the Old Testament.* Nashville: B&H Academic, 2011.

Mitchell, David C. *The Message of the Psalter: An Eschatological Programme in the Book of Psalms.* Journal for the Study of the Old Testament Supplement Series 252. Sheffield: Sheffield Academic, 1997.

Motyer, Alec. *Look to the Rock: An Old Testament Background to Our Understanding of Christ.* Grand Rapids, MI: Kregel, 1996.

Naselli, Andrew David. *How to Understand and Apply the New Testament: Twelve Steps from Exegesis to Theology.* Phillipsburg, NJ: P&R, 2017.

Origen. *On First Principles.* Translated by G. W. Butterworth. London: SPCK, 1936. Reprint, Notre Dame: Ave Maria, 1966, 1973.

Ortlund, Dane C. "Reflections on Handling the Old Testament as Jesus Would Have Us: Psalm 15 as a Case Study." *Themelios* 42 (2017): 74-88.

———. "What Does It Mean to Fall Short of the Glory of God?: Romans 3:23 in Biblical-Theological Perspective." *Westminster Theological Journal* 80 (2018): 121-40.

Osborne, Grant R. *The Hermeneutical Spiral: A Comprehensive Introduction to Biblical Interpretation.* Rev. ed. Downers Grove, IL: IVP Academic, 2006.

Packer, J. I. *Knowing God.* 2nd ed. Downers Grove, IL: InterVarsity Press, 1993.

Pao, David W. *Acts and the Isaianic New Exodus.* Biblical Studies Library. Grand Rapids, MI: Baker Academic, 2002. Reprint, Wissenshaftliche Untersuchungen zum Neuen Testament. Second Series 130. Tübingen: Mohr Siebeck, 2000.

Patton, Matthew H. *Hope for a Tender Sprig: Jehoiachin in Biblical Theology.* Bulletin for Biblical Research Supplement 16. Winona Lake, IN: Eisenbrauns, 2017.

Perrin, Nicholas. *The Kingdom of God: A Biblical Theology.* Biblical Theology for Life. Grand Rapids, MI: Zondervan, 2019.

Peterson, Eugene H. *Eat this Book: A Conversation in the Art of Spiritual Reading.* Grand Rapids, MI: Eerdmans, 2006.

———. "Eat this Book: The Holy Community at Table with the Holy Scripture." *Theology Today* 56 (1999): 7-17.

Piotrowski, Nicholas G. "'After the Deportation': Observations in Matthew's Apocalyptic Genealogy." *Bulletin for Biblical Research* 25 (2015): 189-203.

———. "'Discern the Word and Understand the Vision': Ongoing Exile in Second Temple Judaism and its Relevance for Biblical Theology." *Criswell Theological Review* 16 (2018): 21-42.

———. *Matthew's New David at the End of Exile: A Socio-Rhetorical Study of Scriptural Quotations.* Supplements to Novum Testamentum 170. Leiden: Brill, 2016.

———. "Nazarene." In *Dictionary of Jesus and the Gospels*, edited Joel B. Green, et al, 624-25. 2nd ed. Downers Grove, IL: IVP Academic, 2013.

———. "Saul Is Esau: Themes from Genesis 3 and Deuteronomy 18 in 1 Samuel." *Westminster Theological Journal* 81 (2019): 205-29.

———. "'Whatever You Ask' for the Missionary Purposes of the Eschatological Temple: Quotation and Typology in Mark 11–12," *Southern Baptist Journal of Theology* 21 (2017): 97-121.

Piper, John. *Reading the Bible Supernaturally: Seeing and Savoring the Glory of God in Scripture.* Wheaton, IL: Crossway, 2017.

———. *Think: The Life of the Mind and the Love of God.* Wheaton, IL: Crossway, 2010.

Powell, Mark Allen, gen. ed. *Harper Collins Bible Dictionary.* Rev. and upd. ed. San Francisco: HarperOne, 2001.

Poythress, Vern S. *Reading the Word of God in the Presence of God: A Handbook for Biblical Interpretation.* Wheaton, IL: Crossway, 2016.

Pratt, Richard L. *He Gave Us Stories: The Bible Student's Guide to Interpreting Old Testament Narratives.* Phillipsburg, NJ: P&R, 1990.

Provan, Iain. *The Reformation and the Right Reading of Scripture.* Waco, TX: Baylor University Press, 2017.

Resseguie, James L. *Narrative Criticism of the New Testament: An Introduction.* Grand Rapids, MI: Baker Academic, 2005.

Ridderbos, Herman N. *Redemptive History and the New Testament Scriptures.* Revised by Richard B. Gaffin, Jr. Translated by H. De Jonge. 2nd rev. ed. Phillipsburg, NJ: P&R, 1988.

Roberts, Alastair J., and Andrew Wilson. *Echoes of Exodus: Tracing Themes of Redemption through Scripture.* Wheaton, IL: Crossway, 2018.

Roberts, Alexander, and James Donaldson, eds. *The Ante-Nicene Fathers.* 1885–1887. 10 vols. Reprint, Peabody, MA: Hendrickson, 1994.

Roberts, Vaughn. *God's Big Picture: Tracing the Storyline of the Bible.* Downers Grove, IL: InterVarsity Press, 2002.

Robertson, O. Palmer. *The Christ of the Covenants.* Phillipsburg, NJ: P&R, 1980.

———. *The Christ of the Prophets.* Phillipsburg, NJ: P&R, 2004.

———. *The Christ of Wisdom: A Redemptive-Historical Exploration of the Wisdom Books of the Old Testament.* Phillipsburg, NJ: P&R, 2017.

———. *The Flow of the Psalms: Discovering Their Structure and Theology.* Phillipsburg, NJ: P&R, 2015.

Ryken, Leland. *How to Read the Bible as Literature.* Grand Rapids, MI: Zondervan, 1984.

Ryken, Leland, James C. Wilhoit, and Tremper Longman III, eds. *Dictionary of Biblical Imagery.* Downers Grove, IL: IVP Academic, 1998.

Sandy, D. Brent, and Ronald L. Giese, Jr., eds. *Cracking Old Testament Codes: Interpreting the Literary Genres of the Old Testament.* Nashville: B&H, 1995.

Schreiner, Thomas R. *Interpreting the Pauline Epistles.* 2nd ed. Grand Rapids, MI: Baker Academic, 2011.

Schrock, David S. "From Beelines to Plotlines: Typology That Follows the Covenantal Topography of Scripture." *Southern Baptist Journal of Theology* 21.1 (2017): 35-56.

———. *The Royal Priesthood and the Glory of God*. Short Studies in Biblical Theology. Wheaton, IL: Crossway, 2022.

———. "What Designates a Valid Type?: A Christotelic, Covenantal Proposal." *Southeastern Theological Review* 5 (2014): 3-26.

Sim, Margaret G. *A Relevant Way to Read: A New Approach to Exegesis and Communication*. Eugene, OR: Pickwick, 2016.

Sire, James. *The Universe Next Door: A Basic Worldview Catalog*. 6th ed. Downers Grove, IL: IVP Academic, 2020.

Sloan, David B. "Interpreting Scripture with Satan?: The Devil's Use of Scripture in Luke's Temptation Narrative." *Tyndale Bulletin* 66 (2015): 231-50.

Smith, James K. A. *You Are What You Love: The Spiritual Power of Habit*. Grand Rapids, MI: Brazos, 2016.

Starling, David I. *Hermeneutics as Apprenticeship: How the Bible Shapes Our Interpretive Habits and Practices*. Grand Rapids, MI: Baker Academic, 2016.

Stott, John R. W. *Between Two Worlds: The Challenge of Preaching Today*. Grand Rapids, MI: Eerdmans, 1982.

Tamfu, Dieudonné. "The Songs of the Messiah: Seeing and Savoring Jesus in the Psalms." Series of lectures at the Indianapolis Theological Seminary Symposium on the Psalms, Indianapolis, IN, September 2017.

Tenney, Merrill C., and Moisés Silva, eds. *The Zondervan Encyclopedia of the Bible*. 5 vols. Rev. ed. Grand Rapids, MI: Zondervan Academic, 2010.

Theodoret of Cyrus, "Commentary on Psalm 30." In *A Commentary on the Psalms: Psalms 1–72*, translated by Robert C. Hill, 187-191. Vol. 101 of *The Fathers of the Church: A New Translation*. Washington, DC: Catholic University of America Press, 2000.

Thiselton, Anthony C. *Hermeneutics: An Introduction*. Grand Rapids, MI: Eerdmans, 2009.

Treier, Daniel J. *Introducing Theological Interpretation of Scripture: Recovering a Christian Practice*. Grand Rapids, MI: Baker Academic, 2008.

Vanhoozer, Kevin J. *Is There a Meaning in This Text?: The Bible, The Reader, and the Morality of Literary Knowledge*. Landmarks in Christian Scholarship. Grand Rapids, MI: Zondervan, 1998.

Vanhoozer, Kevin J., and Daniel J. Treier. *Theology and the Mirror of Scripture: A Mere Evangelical Account*. Studies in Christian Doctrine and Scripture. Downers Grove, IL: IVP Academic, 2015.

Walton, John H. *Ancient Near Eastern Thought and the Old Testament: Introducing the Conceptual World of the Hebrew Bible*. 2nd ed. Grand Rapids, MI: Baker Academic, 2018.

———. *Old Testament Theology for Christians: From Ancient Context to Enduring Belief*. Downers Grove, IL: IVP Academic, 2017.

Walton, John H., Victor H. Matthews, and Mark W. Chavalas, eds. *The IVP Bible Background Commentary: Old Testament.* Downers Grove, IL: InterVarsity Press, 2000.

Watts, Rikki E. *Isaiah's New Exodus in Mark.* Biblical Studies Library. Grand Rapids: Baker Academic, 2000. Reprint, Wissenschaftliche Untersuchungen zum Neuen Testament. Second Series 88. Tübingen: Mohr Siebeck, 1997.

Wenham, John. *Christ and the Bible.* 3rd ed. Grand Rapids, MI: Baker, 1994.

Westerholm, Stephen, and Martin Westerholm. *Reading Sacred Scripture: Voices from the History of Biblical Interpretation.* Grand Rapids, MI: Eerdmans, 2016.

Wilson, Gerald H. "Psalms and Psalter: Paradigm for Biblical Theology." In *Biblical Theology: Retrospect & Prospect,* edited by Scott J. Hafemann, 100-110. Downers Grove, IL: IVP Academic, 2002.

———. "The Shape of the Book of Psalms." *Interpretation* 46 (1992): 129-42.

———. "The Use of Royal Psalms at the 'Seams' of the Hebrew Psalter." *Journal for the Study of the Old Testament* 35 (1986): 85-94.

Wise, Michael, Martin Abegg Jr., and Edward Cook, eds. *The Dead Sea Scrolls: A New Translation.* San Francisco: HarperOne, 1996, 2005.

Wood, A. S. *Luther's Principles of Biblical Interpretation.* London: Tyndale, 1960.

Yarchin, William. *History of Biblical Interpretation: A Reader.* Grand Rapids, MI: Baker Academic, 2004.

Young, Frances. "Typology." In *Crossing the Boundaries: Essays in Biblical Interpretation in Honour of Michael D. Goulder.* Edited by Stanley E. Porter, Paul Joyce, and David E. Orton, 29-48. Biblical Interpretation Series 8. Leiden: Brill, 1994.

Zacharias, H. Daniel. *Matthew's Presentation of the Son of David.* T&T Clark Biblical Studies. London: Bloomsbury T&T Clark, 2017.

FIGURE CREDITS

Figure 1.1   Alexandria & Antioch Map / Photo 18263899 © Pancaketom | Dreamstime.com

Figure 1.2. Jerome & Gregory the Great / Photo 70688555 © Jozef Sedmak | Dreamstime.com

Figure 1.3. Thomas Aquinas / Photo 141206757 © Zvonimir Atletić | Dreamstime.com

Figure 1.4. John Calvin / Photo 20383497 © Nicku | Dreamstime.com

Figure 1.5. David Hume / Photo 84595150 © Prakich Treetasayuth | Dreamstime.com

Figure 1.6. Friedrich Schleiermacher / Photo 189349655 © Matthias Zabanski | Dreamstime.com

Figure 1.7. Friedrich Nietzsche / Illustration 188445932 © Ivona17 | Dreamstime.com

Figure 3.1. Global Currents / Illustration 73409160 © Rainer Lesniewski | Dreamstime.com

Figure 4.1. Tree Rings / Photo 109519901 © Ievgenii Tryfonov | Dreamstime.com

Figure 5.1. Kelp Forest / Photo 102363011 © Erin Donalson | Dreamstime.com

Figure 5.2. Maria Island / Photo 88507082 © Julian Peters | Dreamstime.com

Figure 5.3. The Painted Cliffs / Photo 94438389 © Michael Rodway | Dreamstime.com

Figure 5.4. Maria Island Terrain / Photo 130070708 © Martin Pelanek | Dreamstime.com

Figure 6.1. Road Map / Illustration 106895607 © Rainer Lesniewski | Dreamstime.com

Figure 6.2. Topographical Map / Illustration 101077403 © Igor Korets | Dreamstime.com

Figure 6.4. Typology / Illustration 68472264 © Cornelius20 | Dreamstime.com

Figure 7.1. Moon Jellyfish / Photo 141493306 © Silkstocking2014 | Dreamstime.com

Figure 7.2. Box Jellyfish / Photo 53669502 © R. Gino Santa Maria / Shutterfree, Llc | Dreamstime.com

SCRIPTURE INDEX

Finding the Textbook You Need

The IVP Academic Textbook Selector
is an online tool for instantly finding the IVP books
suitable for over 250 courses across 24 disciplines.

---

ivpacademic.com
